Neighbour Disputes:
A Concise Guide to the Law and Practice

CALLOW PUBLISHING

Neighbour Disputes: A Concise Guide to the Law and Practice

by Donald Agnew
and
Amanda Morris

London
Callow Publishing
2006

ISBN 1 898899 81 9

First published 2006

Published by Callow Publishing Limited,
4 Shillingford Street, London N1 2DP
www.callowpublishing.com
Printed and bound in Great Britain by MPG Books Ltd, Bodmin, Cornwall.

Preface

In this book, the authors have sought to provide an overview of the law relating to the problems which most commonly arise between neighbours. Disputes among groups of people living in close proximity – whether in a hamlet of a few cottages or an urban metropolis – are increasingly common. The unfettered exercise of rights by one person may infringe the rights of neighbours. Over the centuries, the civil law has developed a comprehensive set of mechanisms to regulate the rights and responsibilities of people living side by side. Initially, the common law covered these matters; in recent times, statute law has supplemented the common law.

Neighbour Disputes: A Concise Guide to the Law and Practice ranges across many aspects of the law – from the torts of nuisance and negligence, the statutory provisions on party walls, rights of light and high hedges – through boundaries, trees and hedges, weeds and pests – to water, waste and drainage. A chapter on resolving disputes is also included. The book is not a comprehensive treatise and does not deal with every aspect of this wide topic, but it is hoped that it will enable the practitioner to give at least preliminary advice. If the matter requires more detailed research, reference to specialist works may well be needed.

This book adopts a practical approach and is primarily intended for the busy legal practitioner, as a first port of call when a client telephones, perhaps in distress, to relate some terrible act or course of conduct being perpetrated by a neighbour, and asks what can be done about it.

The authors were invited to write this book after their firm was involved in the case of *McMeekin v Long*, which features in Chapter 1. Having specialised in property litigation for a number of years, they felt that there is a need for a book dealing with common problems faced by house and flat owners, and upon which the authors are regularly asked to advise. Although written by solicitors for the assistance of fellow solicitors, it is hoped that this book is sufficiently readable and jargon-free to enable the interested non-lawyer to derive some benefit from it.

The grateful thanks of the authors are due to Catherine Paget, a senior solicitor with the authors' firm, for contributing the chapter on party walls, and to David Higham, visiting Professor at Nottingham Law School, whose theories on, and patient explanation of, decision trees (as expounded in his article, *Decision Trees*, Solicitors Journal 21 January 2005) form part of Chapter 12.

Finally, thanks are also due to barristers Nicholas Taggart and Charlotte Woodhead of Landmark Chambers who kindly read the draft and offered their suggestions and corrections to the text, most of which have been adopted. If any errors do remain the authors take sole responsibility.

The law is stated as at November 2005.

Contents

Table of Cases

Table of Legislation

Chapter 1

Misrepresentations About Neighbours

1. Introduction

The purchase of a house or flat is likely to be one of the most important investments that the average person ever makes. It is therefore curious how little time is usually taken, before the purchase, to ensure that the money is well spent. Sometimes a house is bought after only one or two brief visits; indeed the opportunities to have a really good look at the property may be rare, particularly if the sellers are still in residence. A buyer is almost certainly not able to assess, for example, what the neighbours are like, and yet how the neighbours behave can be a major factor in whether the purchase proves a success or a failure in the long run. It is not surprising, therefore, that some people discover, shortly after moving into a new home, that certain aspects are not as they expected.

As part of the conveyancing process, the buyer's solicitor sends to the seller's solicitor a questionnaire, the Seller's Property Information Form ("SPIF"), in which the buyer and his solicitor seek information from the seller. The form is in plain, straightforward language and makes clear that the buyer will be relying on the answers given. A seller who fails to answer the questions truthfully may be liable to a claim by the buyer for damages for misrepresentation.

2. A Case in Point

This is what occurred in the case of *McMeekin v Long* [2003] 2 EGLR 81 (QBD), which seems to have been the first reported case of misrepresentation concerning answers on the SPIF. The case does not change the law on misrepresentation, but does bring home to sellers that there may be serious consequences if the answers given are not truthful.

The facts of *McMeekin v Long* are as follows. In 1999, Mr and Mrs McMeekin were interested in purchasing a four-bedroomed detached house in Waterlooville, Hampshire. It was one of three houses, the access to which was along a small gravel lane. They asked the sellers, Mr and Mrs Long, about the neighbours and were told that they were friendly. Their solicitor, on the SPIF, asked: "Do you know of any disputes about this or any neighbouring property?" and "Have you received any complaints about anything you have or have not done as owners?". The answer in each case was "no". The form included the usual "Important note to sellers". The note explained that it was important that the answers to the questions on the form were correct, because the buyer would be relying on them, and any incorrect information could mean that the buyer could claim compensation or refuse to complete.

The McMeekins completed their purchase, paying £124,000 for the house. For eleven months all was well, although they did learn from neighbours that there had been arguments with the owners of the gravel road (who lived in the house opposite), over which the McMeekins had a right of way. Trouble started when the McMeekins ordered groceries to be delivered by van from a local supermarket and this sparked off a dispute with the neighbour who owned the road. It turned out that there had been what the judge later described as "a running sore of constant disputes and antagonism" between the sellers and those neighbours.

Mr and Mrs McMeekin sued their sellers, alleging negligent and/or fraudulent misrepresentation by saying in the SPIF that there had been no disputes. They succeeded. Astill J said in his judgment:

> "The lives of the claimants . . . are now devalued by a continuation of a running dispute . . . about the use of motor vehicles and the parking of motor vehicles on the access road, which is a continuation of the problem that was suffered by the occupants when the defendants were there. That is precisely the kind of information which must be disclosed to a potential purchaser for them to be able to make up their minds whether they wish to buy a property with the running sore of constant disputes and antagonism existing between the owners of the access road and those who have rights of way over it."

3. Liability in Misrepresentation and Deceit

McMeekin v Long was a case in the tort of misrepresentation, but this is not the only tort which may be relevant in these situations. A person commits the related tort of deceit if he makes a fraudulent representation either:

(a) knowing that his representation is false or not believing that it is true; or

(b) being reckless as to whether it is true or false (*Derry v Peek* (1889) 14 App Cas 337, HL), but intending that the claimant should act on that representation, and the claimant does so.

This is to be contrasted with negligent misrepresentation, which occurs where a representation is made carelessly or without reasonable grounds for believing it to be true. The Misrepresentation Act 1967 creates a cause of action where a person has been induced to enter into a contract by virtue of a negligent representation. Section 2(1) provides:

"Where a person has entered into a contract after a misrepresentation has been made to him by another party thereto and as a result thereof he has suffered loss, then, if the person making the representation would be liable to damages in respect thereof had the misrepresentation been made fraudulently, that person shall be so liable notwithstanding that the representation was not made fraudulently, unless he proves that he had reasonable grounds to believe and did believe up to the time the contract was made that the facts represented were true."

Section 2(1) of the Misrepresentation Act 1967 makes clear that, once it has been proved that a negligent statement inducing a party to enter a contract has been made, the burden of proof then shifts to the person making the representation; if that person is to escape liability, he must prove "that he had reasonable grounds to believe and did believe up to the time the contract was made that the facts represented were true". The person making the representation must believe his statement to be true and have reasonable grounds for so believing right up to the time when the contract is entered into, which in some cases is a significant period of time. It is therefore incumbent upon a seller to notify a potential purchaser if he discovers, before exchange of contracts, that a reply previously given in a SPIF form is incorrect, or has become incorrect, even if it was originally correct.

In cases of both fraudulent and negligent misrepresentation, the representation must have induced the recipient to enter into the contract. The representation does not need to be the *only* reason for entering into the contract, however: it need only be one of the factors inducing the contract: *Geest plc v Fyffes plc* [1999] 1 All ER (Comm) 672. In cases of fraudulent misrepresentation, there is a presumption that if the misrepresentation had not been made the buyer would not have entered into the contract: *Esso Petroleum Ltd v Mardon* [1976] QB 801, [1976] 2 WLR 583, [1976] 2 All ER 5 (CA). It will be recalled that in *McMeekin v Long*, the SPIF specifically stated that the buyer would be relying on the answers given to the questions asked, thereby making it difficult for the seller to argue to the contrary.

4. Calculating Damages

In *McMeekin v Long* the sellers were found liable for fraudulent misrepresentation. The case was then adjourned for damages to be assessed, but the parties agreed the amount of damages and costs without going back to court. Damages were agreed at £67,000. In addition, Mr and Mrs Long had to pay a substantial sum in costs. It was therefore a very expensive mistake on their part to have concealed the truth in their answers on the SPIF. Since the case did not return to court for the assessment of damages, we do not have the benefit of a judgment setting out the principles to be applied by the court when fixing damages for untruthful answers on the SPIF form. However, in the analogous 1997 House of Lords case of *Smith New Court Securities Ltd v Scrimgeour Vickers (Asset Management) Ltd* [1997] AC 254, [1996] 3 WLR 1051, [1996] 4 All ER 769 (HL), it was decided that where a claimant had been induced by a fraudulent misrepresentation to purchase property, the defendant is bound to make reparation for all the damage flowing directly from the transaction. The claimant is entitled to recover by way of damages the full price paid by him, but must give credit for any benefits received as a result of the transaction. As a general rule the benefits received include the market value of the property as at the date of its purchase, but the general rule is not to be inflexibly applied. The general rule does not apply where the effect of the misrepresentation continues after the acquisition of the property, or if the claimant is, by reason of the fraud, locked into the property.

Applying these principles to the case of *McMeekin v Long*, had the parties not settled the damages by agreement, it could be argued that the amount of damages should not have been limited to the difference between the purchase price and the value of the property as at the date of the contract. This would not fully compensate the McMeekins because they were effectively still locked into the property and disputes were continuing. It is arguable that the McMeekins could have claimed damages on the basis of the difference between the market value the house would have had but for the disputes, and the market value it would have commanded with the disputes disclosed as at the date of the assessment of damages. If the McMeekins had sold the property at a loss, before the case had come to trial or before the assessment of the damages, the court could, alternatively, use the date of sale as the valuation date. The court is entitled to choose whichever of the possible dates is the most appropriate in the particular case in order properly to compensate the claimant.

5. Disclosing a Dispute

The basis of the sellers' defence in *McMeekin v Long* was that there had been "areas of doubt" about the rights of the owners of the three houses served by the access road, about which they had obtained legal advice which was favourable to the owner of the road, and that that was an end to the matter. They did not consider that there was a "dispute". While the judge found that the true situation was more serious than the sellers were admitting, their defence does raise the question of what constitutes a "dispute". Does the assertion of a right by one party which is immediately accepted by the other who changes his or her position accordingly amount to a "dispute" that should be disclosed on the SPIF? In the light of *McMeekin v Long* the advice to the seller in such a position must be to disclose the matter, including the extent of the disagreement. It is then for the buyer to decide whether or not to proceed with the purchase in the circumstances.

What of the situation where a neighbour wishes, for some malicious reason, to frustrate the sale of a property, and manufactures a dispute, which must then be disclosed to all prospective purchasers? The advantage of a requirement for disclosure in these circumstances is that it may save someone from buying into a neighbourhood where there is such a difficult individual. The converse is that those unfortunate people who have neighbours whose bizarre, irrational or unreasonable behaviour causes trouble for others can find themselves trapped, unable to sell and move away until the awkward neighbour himself moves or alters his behaviour. The innocent party who wishes to move may have to reduce the sale price and suffer a considerable loss in order to achieve a sale, without any obvious or easy recourse against the difficult neighbour.

There are signs that the obligation to disclose a dispute, and the difficulties of defining a "dispute", are leading people to refrain from complaining about their neighbours' conduct for fear of themselves creating a "dispute" which they would have to disclose to a prospective purchaser. The result is that people are tempted to sell up and move away from a problem with a neighbour, rather than confronting it and seeking a solution. The buyers in these circumstances are completely without a remedy when they discover what their neighbours are like.

6. Other Questions

It is not only disputes with neighbours that the SPIF is designed to reveal to the intended purchaser of a property. The purchaser is not restricted to asking the standard questions printed on the form, and it is in the purchaser's interests to cover as wide an area of enquiry as possible.

One useful line of questioning concerns any applications for planning permission for development of neighbouring properties of which notice has been given to the vendor. This is helpful because a local search (enquiries of the local authority) discloses only applications for planning permission in respect of the vendor's own property, and not the surrounding land. A purchaser would be well advised to make his own enquiries of the planning department of the local authority, or instruct his solicitor to make those enquiries on his behalf. Most purchasers do not do this, however, largely because of the inconvenience or cost. An enquiry of the vendor, by way of an additional question on the SPIF, should disclose any notices of applications in respect of neighbouring properties which have been served on the vendor, and may reveal, for example, that the next-door neighbour intends to build a large extension that would overlook the garden of the property being purchased.

If the vendor fails to disclose any such notices, the purchaser would be able to sue him for any diminution in the value of the property suffered as a result of the development. While the purchaser may well receive compensation in such circumstances, this is far less satisfactory to the purchaser than having the opportunity to avoid the purchase in the first place by ascertaining the situation before contracts are exchanged. Compensation in monetary terms may not truly compensate the purchaser for the detriment suffered, but it is the best remedy that the law can devise.

7. Liability for the SPIF

There is one further practical drawback to relying on the right to sue the vendor for damages for misrepresentation, and that is that the vendor may not be good for the amount of damages awarded. His assets may be insufficient even to justify contemplating proceedings against him, in which case there is probably no remedy for the aggrieved purchaser. SPIFs are usually signed by the vendor personally; most solicitors ensure that it is the client, and not they on the client's behalf, who signs. As long as the vendor signs personally, the solicitor has no liability for any misrepresentation by the client.

If, on the other hand, a solicitor signs a SPIF as agent for the vendor, answering the questions in accordance with the client's instructions, the vendor is liable as principal for his agent's misrepresentations. If the client's representations are false, and the solicitor knows that they are false, the solicitor is liable jointly with the client. In those circumstances, there is a right of action against the solicitor as well as the vendor, although it may be difficult to prove knowledge on the part of the solicitor. If, however, the solicitor acted for the vendor in his dispute with the neighbour, or wrote on behalf of his client to object to a planning application, for example, then the necessary evidence of the solicitor's knowledge is likely to be available. The solicitor may or may not be good for the damages in his own right, but should be insured. If he has been fraudulent, however, his indemnity policy is likely to be avoided by the insurer and a claimant would have to have recourse instead to the compensation fund administered by The Law Society. If the guilty solicitor is an employee of a firm of solicitors, the firm would be vicariously liable for the solicitor's acts carried out within the scope of his employment; the partners in the firm would be entitled to be indemnified by the insurers, as would the innocent partners in the firm if the fraudulent solicitor is himself a partner.

8. Other Preliminary Enquiries

Misrepresentation may occur not only in the answers given on the SPIF. This form has largely replaced the old form of preliminary enquiries, or enquiries before contract, in residential conveyancing, but misrepresentations in response to a preliminary enquiries form can equally lead to liability.

The practice grew of answering the questions raised in the preliminary enquiries form using a formula which, in effect, amounted to avoiding the question. For example, a question such as "has the property suffered from dry rot?" was likely to be answered, "not as far as the vendor is aware". As a result of the case of *Clinicare Limited v Orchard Homes and Developments Limited* [2004] EWHC 1694 (QB), a vendor is less likely to escape liability by giving such a reply if it turns out that the property was in fact suffering from dry rot at the time. The Court of Appeal has ruled that this reply imported two representations; first, that the property was not suffering from dry rot; and secondly, the implied representation that the vendor had taken reasonable steps to ascertain the situation. In that case, dry rot had in the past been discovered and the vendor thought that it had been dealt with and no longer existed. In fact, it had been attended to in only one area and not another. The representation contributed to the purchaser's decision not to have a survey carried out, which was likely to have revealed the problem. In those circumstances the purchaser succeeded against the vendor. It might have been a different outcome, however, if the property had never suffered from dry rot to the vendor's knowledge and he had no reason to suspect that it was suffering from the problem. In such cases that most basic of rules of English property law, *caveat emptor* (let the buyer beware), is likely still to apply.

9. Estate Agents

Misrepresentations which induce a purchaser to enter into a contract to buy may be made by persons other than the vendor or the vendor's solicitor. The estate agent is the most likely person to fall into this category. To establish liability under the Misrepresentation Act 1967, the person making the representation relied upon must be either the other party to the contract or his agent. The estate agent is the vendor's agent. The misrepresentation need not necessarily be in writing, although it is much easier to prove if it is. The false or inaccurate statement may be contained in the estate agent's particulars of the property, although these particulars are also likely to contain a disclaimer from liability in respect of the accuracy of the facts stated in them.

Although the agent cannot disclaim liability for a dishonest representation made with the intention that it should be acted upon (*Commercial Banking of Sydney v R H Brown & Co* [1972] 2 Lloyd's Rep 360, High Court of Australia), a disclaimer may be effective to avoid liability in respect of a negligent misstatement (*Hedley Byrne & Co Ltd v Heller and Partners Ltd* [1964] AC 465, [1963] 3 WLR 101, [1963] 2 All ER 575 (HL)).

In the case of *McCullagh v Lane Fox and Partners Ltd* [1996] PNLR 205, [1996] 1 EGLR 35 (CA), it was stated in estate agents' particulars that "all statements contained in these particulars are made without responsibility". It was held that the existence of a disclaimer was one of the facts relevant to determining whether the estate agents had assumed responsibility to the claimant purchaser. In that case, the disclaimer was effective to absolve the estate agent from liability not only for statements in the written particulars, but also for oral statements which repeated the false statements in the particulars when the agent was showing the purchaser around the property.

An estate agent may commit a criminal offence under the Property Misdescriptions Act 1991 if he makes a false or misleading statement about certain matters relating to land. It is a defence for the estate agent to show that he took all reasonable steps and exercised all due diligence to avoid committing the offence. While an aggrieved purchaser may have the satisfaction of seeing a recalcitrant estate agent punished in this way, a prosecution under this Act does not itself afford the purchaser any redress, section 1(4) of the Act specifically providing that:

"No contract shall be void or unenforceable, and no right of action in civil proceedings in respect of any loss shall arise, by reason only of the commission of an offence under this section."

10. Checklist

1. Check the questions asked of the vendor in the SPIF.
2. If there was a question directly on the point complained of, examine the reply.
3. If the reply was false, consider whether the vendor knew it was false, or was reckless whether it was true or false. Look for evidence to suggest that the vendor had knowledge.
4. Ascertain whether the purchaser knows of anything that might have led the vendor to have reasonable grounds to believe that the reply given was true.
5. Estimate the value of the loss resulting from the misrepresentation. Expert evidence of value may well be needed.
6. Consider whether or not the vendor would be good for the amount claimed.
7. If anyone other than the vendor made the representation, consider whether that person knew the representation was false, or was reckless. Seek evidence to suggest knowledge; if none, it may be possible to show negligence.
8. Consider whether, if potentially liable, an agent would be good for damages.
9. Ascertain the insurance situation.

For a specimen statement of claim based on misrepresentation in relying to questions in the SPIF, see page 195.

Chapter 2

Boundaries

1. Introduction

"To hear the words 'a boundary dispute' is to fill a judge, even of the most stalwart and amiable disposition, with a deep foreboding since disputes with neighbours tend always to compel . . . some unreasonable and extravagant display of unneighbourly behaviour which profits no one but the lawyers."

So said Lord Justice Ward in *Alan Wibberley Building v Insley* [1998] 1 WLR 881, [1998] 2 All ER 82 (CA). On the other hand, it is often just such an unreasonable and extravagant display that compels a landowner to take legal proceedings to protect his land from what may be an unjustified incursion by his neighbour.

Indeed, the most common reason for neighbours to come into conflict with one another is a dispute over a boundary. This can arise in a number of ways and is usually precipitated by an event of some kind, often a change of ownership. Occurrences that may prompt a property owner to seek advice include:

(a) the construction of an extension to a building that encroaches on another's land;

(b) the desire to build a house at the end of a narrow lane that requires the lane to be reconfigured, or the boundary of the lane to be more accurately defined, in order to comply with building or planning regulations;

(c) the need for additional land to accommodate a structure, a car park, or storage space;

(d) the replacement of fences, or the removal or planting of hedges.

2. The General Boundaries Rule

The term "boundary" means nothing more nor less than the dividing line (which may or may not be visible) between one legal title and another, and has no special meaning in law. There is, however, an important distinction between the "legal" boundary and the "physical" boundary and it is often the failure to recognise this distinction which creates conflict. The physical boundary – that is, a fence, wall or hedge, may or may not be the same as the legal boundary. Further, the fact that a boundary feature exists does not necessarily mean that it is consistent with the legal boundary. It may follow the line of the legal boundary, but more often than not lies inside or beyond it, or crosses it in places.

In seeking to determine where a boundary lies, the starting point is the deeds, although these are not always conclusive. With respect to registered titles, the title plan is based on the Ordnance Survey, which shows features that may or may not be legal boundaries. Section 60 of the Land Registration Act 2002 (formerly rule 278 of the Land Registration Rules 1925), which is commonly known as the "general boundaries rule", provides that the filed plan indicates "general boundaries" only, and cannot therefore generally be relied upon for its accuracy: it indicates only the general line of the boundary. Rule 278 stated:

> "the exact line of the boundary will be left undetermined – as, for instance, whether it includes a hedge or wall and ditch, or runs along the centre of a wall or fence, or its inner or outer face, or how far it runs within or beyond it; or whether or not the land registered includes the whole or any proportion of any adjoining road or stream."

In other words, the effect of the rule is to make most of the Land Registry's plans avowedly inaccurate.

In its report which led to the 2002 Act, the Law Commission commented:

> "Although there is power to fix boundaries, it has hitherto hardly ever been used for two main reasons. The first is the expense of so doing . . . The second is that the process of fixing of a boundary is all too likely to create a boundary dispute where none had existed . . .". (*Land Registration for the 21st Century:* Law Commission Report No 271 (2001) at paragraph 9.10).

As an example of the general boundaries rule, two properties may be divided by a feature such as a hedge, the Ordnance Survey map showing as the boundary a line representing the middle line of the hedge. This does not necessarily mean that the owner of each property owns the land up to the middle of the hedge; the hedge may be wholly on the land of one or the other of the neighbours.

Under rule 118 of the Land Registration Rules 2003 (SI 2003 No. 1417), the proprietor of a registered estate may now apply to the registrar for the exact line of a boundary to be determined. The application must be made in the prescribed form. It must be accompanied by a plan, or a plan and a verbal description, identifying the exact line of the boundary claimed, and showing sufficient surrounding physical features to allow the general position of the boundary to be drawn on the Ordnance Survey, together with evidence to establish the exact line of the boundary. The procedure is set out in rule 119 of the Land Registration Rules 2003. If the registrar is satisfied that the plan, or plan and verbal description, identifies the exact line of the boundary, that the applicant has shown an arguable case and that there is no objection from the adjoining owner(s) (to whom notice of the application must be given), the registrar must make an entry in the applicant's title and that of any other title affected. The entry would state that the exact line of the boundary is determined under section 60 of the Land Registration Act 2002, with particulars of the exact line of the boundary, with or without reference to a plan. In reality, however, things are rarely that simple.

3.   The Deeds

Even if measurements are scaled up from the title plan, the scaling up exercise itself can produce results that are widely different from measurements taken on site. Wherever possible, it is advisable to go back to the oldest conveyance, which is the primary source of evidence of where a true legal boundary lies. Conveyance plans can be extremely useful, particularly where they include measurements. It goes without saying that originals should, if possible, be consulted rather than photocopies which can distort size, particularly where they have been coloured by hand.

If the land is unregistered, then the oldest conveyance should be with the deeds, which should be in the custody of either the owner or a mortgagee. If the land is registered, then the owner may have kept the pre-registration deeds, or the solicitor who acted on the registration may have retained them. The Land Registry does keep some pre-registration deeds, copies of which can be obtained on application. The applicant has to show, however, that he has a proprietary interest in the land. Rule 204 of the Land Registration Rules 2003 provides that a person may, for a period of five years from 13 October 2003 (the date the Land Registration Act 2002 came into force), request the return of any document delivered to the registrar. If, in a particular dispute, the opponent owns the land, it is necessary to ask the opponent for sight of the conveyance – a document that must be disclosed in any legal proceedings. If such a request is refused, and the exact line of the boundary is of real importance, it may be worth considering making an application for pre-action disclosure under Rule 25.1(i) of the Civil Procedure Rules 1998 (SI 1998 No 3132 as amended) if the conveyance in question is or has been in the opponent's possession, custody or power.

The text of a conveyance usually refers to a plan, but the wording dictates the importance to be attached to the plan. If the property is described in the text as "more particularly delineated on the plan attached", then the plan is important because it shows the true extent of the land being conveyed. If, on the other hand, the property conveyed is described as "shown on the plan attached for identification only", then the plan cannot be relied upon wholly, as it simply shows the general location of the land being conveyed. In such a case the plan can be used as an aid to construction (*Wigginton & Milner Ltd v Winster Engineering Ltd* [1978] 1 WLR 1462 at 1473). Occasionally, older conveyances describe land as "more particularly delineated and shown on the plan for identification only" so that it is not clear how much weight can be attached to the plan. In any case, it is usual for further evidence to be required to determine the true boundary, particularly where the scale of the plan is small and the lines marking the boundaries are thick.

If the text of the conveyance or transfer describes the extent of the land, then the wording must be read in conjunction with any plan. If there is a conflict between the words and the plan, then the words referring to the plan must be looked at carefully to see whether there is an express limitation, such as "for the purposes of identification only". If there is, then the words take precedence. If there are no such words, then the conflict must be resolved. If there is no obvious reason to prefer the words to the plan (such as a lack of clarity in measurements), it is likely that extrinsic evidence will be necessary.

4. "T" Marks

Conveyance plans often include "T-marks", sometimes also called "tau-marks". The direction in which the "T" is pointing is indicative of who owns a particular boundary feature. In *Seeckts v Derwent* [2004] EWCA Civ 393, Mr Derwent destroyed a length of laurel hedge which divided his property from that of Mr Seeckts; the ownership of the hedge turned on the construction of a conveyance and its plan. The defendant appealed against a decision that Mr Seeckts was the owner and argued that the dimensions on the plan should prevail over the T-marks as the determinative features. The Court of Appeal held that the dimensions were intended to provide a general indication of the boundary, but not to detract from the natural implication of the T-marks that the hedge belonged to Mr Seeckts. Thus the T-marks took priority over the dimensions on the plan.

5. Planning Permission

A common misconception among litigants is that a grant of planning permission is conclusive as to the location of the boundary. A planning authority is concerned only with issues of planning law and policy. It has no duty to investigate the boundaries of any land in respect of which it grants permission and, if a dispute over a boundary arises during the planning process, it has no jurisdiction to determine that dispute. Accordingly it is quite possible for a planning authority to grant permission over land the ownership of which is in dispute, or indeed grant permission to someone who is not the owner of the site to which the application relates. A person objecting has no right of action against the planning authority; the proper recourse is to obtain an interim injunction against the person to whom the permission has been granted, to prevent any building works being commenced pending resolution of the dispute. (Injunctions are discussed at page 23).

6. Expert Evidence

Having identified the most reliable plan(s) it is often advisable to employ an expert land surveyor, preferably one who specialises in boundaries. Many solicitors have a bank of experts they can call upon; otherwise the Royal Institution of Chartered Surveyors can recommend a surveyor with the appropriate qualifications and experience. The expert should be able to take measurements on site using electronic plotting equipment and then compare the results with the deed plan(s). Sometimes this is conclusive, but more often than not there are discrepancies. For example, the surveyor may find that a building lies on what appears to be the legal boundary line so that it is not possible to reinstate the legal boundary. In those circumstances, a surveyor may produce a line of "best fit" that is, the line that most closely follows the legal boundary.

It is sometimes necessary to obtain the surveyor's written opinion as to the true location of the boundary in addition to his plan, as his results may require explanation and interpretation. The surveyor should be provided with the original deeds and as much other physical evidence as it is possible to muster, including photographic evidence, if available. Old photographs showing the original line of the boundary can be useful, provided that reliable evidence as to their provenance can be adduced. Aerial photographs can also be particularly useful, and an archive of stereoscopic photographs is kept by Ordnance Survey, although specialist equipment is needed to interpret them. If the matter proceeds, photographs at worst provide useful background and enable the judge to visualise the site; at best they are invaluable in corroborating a witness's memory. If boundary features are to be moved, or are being moved, altered or removed, it is wise to keep a photographic record for future reference.

A surveyor considers all physical features, but even these may not be conclusive, and the role of the lawyer, and ultimately the court, is to use the surveyor's opinion, in conjunction with legal principle, to determine the line of the boundary.

7.   The Hedge and Ditch Presumption

There are certain presumptions that may be drawn upon to assist in fixing the line of the boundary, the best known being the "hedge and ditch" presumption. Hedge and ditch features are common in the British countryside. A ditch is dug to mark the boundary. The soil that is dug out is piled up behind the ditch (on the land of the person digging it, since he cannot trespass onto his neighbour's land) to form a bank, and a hedge planted on top of the bank. In this instance, the boundary is presumed to be the edge of the ditch that lies on the far side of the hedge.

This presumption can, however, be rebutted by evidence. For example, the ditch may have been in existence before the boundary was drawn, or it may be a stream, or a ditch may have been dug next to a pre-existing hedge.

A very good example of the hedge and ditch presumption and attempts to displace it is the case of *Alan Wibberley Building Limited v Insley* [1999] 1 WLR 894, [1999] 2 All ER 897 (HL). Mr Insley, relying on the presumption, grubbed up the hedge along his section of the boundary and erected in its place a post and wire fence along the far side of the ditch. Wibberley claimed that the true boundary ran along the middle of the hedge and issued proceedings in the county court to recover possession of the strip of land. Wibberley was successful at first instance and the judgment was upheld by the Court of Appeal. Mr Insley went to the House of Lords, which found that there had for many years been a hedge and ditch on the boundary and that there was no evidence to displace the presumption that the boundary between the two farms was drawn before the ditch was dug. Accordingly, Mr Insley won his appeal.

A competent surveyor should therefore examine all available evidence to ascertain, for example, whether the hedge and ditch presumption can be displaced. On instructing the surveyor, the lawyer should draw to the surveyor's attention the presumption, and the ways in which it can be rebutted.

8.   Costs and Tactics

If the plans and other evidence suggest that there has been an encroachment, then the owner needs to consider whether he wants to prepare for the issue of legal proceedings, and one of the determining issues is costs. Employing a surveyor can be expensive, particularly in view of the fact that, if proceedings are issued, the court may in any event order the appointment of a joint expert (see below). However, without expert evidence at the outset, it is not always possible to plead the case effectively. An expert surveyor should be able to locate all relevant physical features and explain their importance. For example, the discovery of an old fence post buried beneath vegetation may transpire to be extremely important, or even conclusive, evidence that may justify an application for summary judgment early in the case, thus saving costs. The combination of the litigant's memory and a surveyor's expert opinion can be very persuasive. Conversely, if the expert's opinion is unfavourable, the litigant may decide not to embark on what is likely to be expensive and risky litigation, in which case the investment in a surveyor's report will have been worthwhile.

If a report is obtained before proceedings are issued, and relied on in those proceedings, it is likely that the opponent will argue that he should not have to pay the costs of that report. This argument would be on the basis that the case is one in which the use of a single joint expert is appropriate, and therefore a report obtained unilaterally by one party only is a luxury that should be paid for by the party who commissioned it, even if that party is ultimately successful in the proceedings. A useful response is that the report is intrinsic to the pleaded case, and that the report was necessary in order fully and properly to state the case. Accordingly, the party who commissions it should, if successful, be entitled to recover the costs from the losing party.

9. Joint Experts

If the client is confident about the outcome of a surveyor's report, or if he simply wants certainty, a useful tactic is to ask the opponent to appoint a joint surveyor to determine the position of the boundary, on the basis that both parties will share the costs and be bound by the result. This can sometimes solve the dispute and save all concerned a good deal of money and anxiety. It also makes the property a good deal easier to sell. A buyer is much more likely to purchase in a case where a dispute has been resolved quickly and relatively painlessly than where he discovers a lengthy dispute with the parties at loggerheads, because the latter is likely to be taken as an indication of a difficult neighbour. Finally, if the neighbour refuses to comply and proceedings are issued, the letter suggesting a joint expert can be shown to the court, which immediately raises the question why the neighbour refused to appoint a surveyor. There may be costs consequences for the recalcitrant neighbour if he is found to have acted unreasonably and the judge finds that the dispute could have been resolved at an early stage by this mechanism.

A surveyor's report must comply with part 35 of the Civil Procedure Rules and the Practice Direction (see below). Many surveyors who are used to court procedures are well aware of this, but it is good practice to refer to it in the instructions to the surveyor. The instructions should give a clear and concise summary of the background to the dispute and precise instructions on what the expert is being asked to do. If the expert is being asked to express an opinion as to the line of the legal boundary, he should be asked to prepare a detailed plan, with dimensions, representing the line, onto which can be overlaid the conveyance plan or plans. If one party has already obtained an expert report, the court may be persuaded to allow the opposing party to obtain his own report, particularly if the first report is an intrinsic part of the pleaded case.

However, the court always considers the appointment of a single joint expert, particularly in low value cases, whether or not one or other party has already obtained expert evidence. The advantage of a single joint expert is that both parties contribute equally to his fees, so it is a more cost-effective way of proceeding. Secondly, both parties are entitled to instruct him either by way of a jointly agreed instruction or, more commonly, by sole instructions that are exchanged with the opponent. Rule 35.8 of the Civil Procedure Rules provides that when a party gives instructions to a single joint expert, that party must at the same time send a copy of the instructions to the other party.

If the use of a single joint expert is agreed or ordered by the court, the court's direction should:

    (a) state clearly what the expert is to be instructed to do;

    (b) state the date by which he is to report;

    (c) make provision for questions to be put to the expert by either party following his report;

    (d) make provision for his responses; and

    (e) provide that his costs be borne jointly by the parties.

Rule 35.8(5) provides that, unless the court otherwise directs, the instructing parties are jointly and severally liable to pay the expert's fees and expenses.

The parties should try to agree on who is to be appointed as single joint expert. It is usual for both parties to put forward a number of nominations. Often litigants insist on an expert who has no connection with either the opposing party or the opposing party's solicitors. This can make it difficult to find an appropriate expert, as solicitors' firms often have relationships with local surveyors; further, the case may demand local knowledge, making the appointment of a surveyor from outside the area undesirable. If it proves impossible to agree on an expert, the usual course is for the parties to ask the Royal Institution of Chartered Surveyors to make the appointment. RICS charges a fee for this service, which is borne jointly by the parties and is payable at the time the request is made.

When instructing the agreed or nominated expert, care should be taken to ensure that he has all the relevant documentation and that he understands precisely what he is being asked to do. Litigants should avoid bias and must not refer to any "without prejudice" correspondence. Sometimes an expert surveyor wishes to visit the site, and more often than not, the litigants themselves would like the chance to speak to him. This should be avoided, since the expert's instructions are contained in the letter(s) he receives from the parties' solicitors rather than in oral representations made by the parties themselves. If, despite that, one or other party insists, then the same courtesy must be extended to both, and it is usually advisable for the expert to visit them one at a time before he undertakes his inspection, rather than for them to be present as he conducts it.

10. Procedure in Relation to Expert Reports

Part 35.10 of the Civil Procedure Rules and the accompanying Practice Direction set out what must be included in the expert's report. In particular, the report must include a statement that the expert understands his duty to the court and that he has complied with that duty. The purpose of this is to remind the expert that his duty to assist the court overrides any obligation he may owe to the person(s) who instructed him or who is responsible for paying his fee. This duty applies as much to experts instructed by one party alone as it applies to single joint experts.

Once the expert has reported, the directions given by the court may provide for both parties to raise written questions. In any event, rule 35.6 of the Civil Procedure Rules provides that a party may put written questions to an expert instructed by another party, or to a single joint expert, within twenty-eight days of service of the report. Questions may be put once only and must be for the sole purpose of clarifying the report. The expert's answers are then treated as part of the report.

11. Avoiding Litigation

At the outset of any dispute, the lawyers acting for the parties should immediately be thinking about possible settlement. First, a solicitor should check that his client has not already agreed something with his opponent. It is possible for litigants to enter into informal boundary agreements which are binding between them, even if that agreement is not recorded in writing. In *Joyce v Rigolli* [2004] EWCA Civ 79, [2004] 1 P&CR DG 55, the Court of Appeal found that section 2 of the Law of Property (Miscellaneous Provisions) Act 1989, which requires all dispositions of land to be in writing, did not apply to trivial dispositions of land consciously made pursuant to an informal boundary agreement of the demarcating kind. Solicitors should therefore ascertain at the outset whether any such agreement has been entered into.

Agreement
If agreement has not already been reached, a solicitor should discuss settlement opportunities with the client. When a boundary dispute begins, people often feel extremely strongly about it, want their day in court and resist suggestions that they should try and reach a settlement. There are, however, two good reasons why a settlement proposal should be put forward at an early stage. The first is to protect the party as far as possible against the risk of costs. If a realistic offer, made openly or under part 36 of the Civil Procedure Rules (see page 184) is made before proceedings are issued, then this can be shown to the judge at the end of the case when he is determining who should pay whose costs. If a litigant loses, but is able to show the judge that he made an offer at the outset which is substantially the same or better than what the winner has achieved, then the winner may not be awarded his costs, and may even have to pay the loser's costs. The second reason is that an offer made at the outset may be very similar to what is achieved at the end of court proceedings, the only difference being the price tag; judges often opt for a middle way and make no order for costs, resulting in an unsatisfactory outcome and a large legal bill to boot.

An offer can be boosted by service of the surveyor's report. Although it is privileged and there is no requirement to disclose it, a litigant is entitled to waive that privilege. A well-worded letter explaining how the report supports a litigant's case often goes a long way to resolving the dispute and lays the groundwork for the claim (or counterclaim) should attempts at settlement fail.

Mediation

If this strategy does not bear fruit, and the litigant's position on costs has been protected as far as possible by judicious offers, then another option that should be explored is mediation. In the current judicial climate, parties ignore or refuse reasonable requests to mediate at their peril. Chapter 12 contains a discussion of the mediation process and how to prepare for it, together with a consideration of the possible adverse costs consequences of unreasonably refusing to mediate. The adverse costs risk is alone sufficient to make it an attractive option, but in boundary disputes in particular, there are good practical reasons why mediation should be considered. As the trial judge in *Reed Executive plc v Reed Business Information Ltd* [2004] EWCA (Civ) 887 commented, "A good and tough mediator can bring about a sense of commercial reality to both sides which their own lawyers, however good, may not be able to convey."

The longer a dispute, particularly a boundary dispute, is allowed to drag on, and the higher the stakes become, the more litigants are at risk of finding themselves in a situation where the primary concern is no longer the boundary, but the need to recover the substantial costs which have been incurred in fighting the case. If the reality of this can be instilled into litigants at an early stage in the proceedings, they are much more likely to be amenable to mediation or to other forms of alternative dispute resolution.

Litigants also have to recognise that they have to continue as neighbours, and the more acrimonious and drawn-out the dispute, the lower the likelihood that neighbourly relations will be restored. A solution reached through discussion and agreement is far more likely to achieve that (as well as ensure that the agreement is adhered to), than a resolution imposed by a court, particularly if one party is clearly the loser. Further, if a case proceeds to litigation, the prospect of selling the property becomes more remote, as buyers would be put off by the fact that their potential neighbours have been involved in litigation with the seller. A seller may, therefore, have to discount the purchase price heavily, or recognise that he may have to live next door to his adversary for a very long time. Despite all that, if one party refuses to engage in mediation, reasonably or unreasonably, or if mediation fails, the parties may have no choice but to proceed to litigation.

12. Remedies

A claim in the case of a boundary dispute usually includes a claim for a declaration as to the position of the boundary, but damages for trespass may also be sought. A claimant may seek an injunction restraining trespass, including an order preventing the erection of a structure, or the removal of a structure, possibly even a building. For a specimen form of particulars of claim, see page 198.

Where there is no actual damage to the property, damages for trespass are based on a reasonable charge for the use of the land over which the trespass is perpetrated (*Strand Electric & Engineering Co v Brisford Entertainments* [1952] 2 QB 246, [1952] 1 All ER 796 (CA)). If the land is not capable of being let, then the measure of damage is usually taken as the value of the benefit of the occupation to the trespasser (*Ministry of Defence v Thompson* [1993] 2 EGLR 107, [1993] EG 148 (CA)).

If a structure or building encroaches over a boundary, the court grants an injunction only where damages would not be an adequate remedy. Therefore, before proceedings are issued, careful thought should be given to whether a claim for an injunction is likely to succeed. If, for example, a building is found to have encroached but has been in position for some time before the issue of the claim, the court is unlikely to be persuaded that it should be removed. An injunction is likely to be appropriate where a neighbour has obtained planning permission to build, and there is a concern that the building will encroach over a boundary. In such a case, an interim injunction may be necessary to restrain the building work pending the resolution of the dispute. The litigant must be advised that the court will require an undertaking from him to pay his opponent any damages that arise if it is ultimately found that the injunction ought not to have been granted.

For more on remedies, see Chapter 12.

13. Adverse Possession

In many cases, there are arguments not only about where the legal boundary is situated, but also about whether a party's right to claim land on his side of a boundary has been defeated by limitation. Although the Land Registration Act 2002 has changed the law on adverse possession in relation to registered land, the law on limitations still applies to unregistered land and to registered land where adverse possession has already been established at the time a claim is brought. A full discussion of the law on limitation and adverse possession is included in Chapter 4.

14. Evidence

Witness Statements

In a classic boundary case, the expert evidence is likely to be of the greatest assistance to the court. Oral evidence may also be important. A statement should be taken from the litigant and all relevant witnesses at the earliest possible stage. It can be refined and updated before it is actually served, but, at the outset of the case, a draft statement performs three useful functions. First, it ensures that the litigant recalls everything he can remember before his memory starts to fade. A boundary dispute may take a year or more to come to trial and with every month that goes by, recollection becomes less reliable. Secondly, a statement provides the solicitor with an easy reference document detailing the background to the dispute. Thirdly, a detailed explanation of the evidence assists the solicitor in determining the strength of the case.

As the case progresses it is, of course, necessary to add to the statement as issues may arise during the course of the proceedings that were not apparent at the start of it. The statement(s) should address every issue in the case in a clear and concise manner, but giving as much relevant detail as possible, and should provide cross-references to any documents mentioned in it.

Documents

Any such documents, including photographs and video evidence, are disclosed upon exchange of documents. Great care needs to be taken with video evidence. Litigants may be tempted to install security cameras with a view to catching their neighbours in the process of some act such as digging up a fence. While such evidence is undoubtedly useful, a vast quantity of footage, or footage that is visually unclear or inconclusive, may be counter-productive, not least because it would increase costs (because the lawyers would have to watch and analyse it in full), but also because it would be likely to cause impatience if it has to be viewed at a hearing. One clear piece of video evidence can be compelling; three hours of inconclusive clips are likely to be far less helpful and may result in an adverse costs order. Video recordings made without the knowledge of the person being filmed are also vulnerable to a challenge under the Human Rights Act 1998 – see, for example, *Jones v University of Warwick* [2003] EWCA Civ 151, [2003] 1 WLR 954, [2003] 3 All ER 760 (CA).

Site visit
Once all the evidence has been exchanged, and assuming no settlement has been reached, the matter proceeds to trial. It is increasingly common for the judge to visit the site. If this is anticipated, the directions should provide for it, and lawyers should consider, when agreeing a trial timetable, whether a site visit would be desirable. Usually, the site visit takes place on the first day, before the trial starts, or, possibly, after the opening argument.

A site visit is often a vital step; lawyers advising in a boundary dispute should try to visit the site, even if the costs are high; there is rarely any substitute for seeing the disputed land itself. Moreover, the judge may want a site visit. In *Gillon v Baxter & Another* [2003] EWCA Civ 1591, the plan referred to in a transfer had been reduced to such a small scale, and the red-edging marking the land being transferred had been applied with such a thick pen, that the judge found that it was not definitive of where the boundaries lay. The judge made a site visit and held that the parties had intended each and every boundary to be marked by a physical feature. On the evidence from the site visit, that feature was, in respect of the disputed boundary, a gate dating from the time of the transfer. The Court of Appeal held that if a conveyance or transfer described land by reference to a plan of very small scale, the effect of that plan had to be judged in the light of the circumstances or physical features of the land; the judge had done exactly what was required of him as set out in *Alan Wibberley*

Building Limited v Insley (see page 17), in which Lord Hoffman held that the precise boundary must, if the deed plan is not conclusive, be established by topographical or other evidence.

If a claim for adverse possession (see Chapter 4) is to be pleaded, the evidence in support must be as full and unequivocal as possible. The litigants themselves may be able to give direct evidence of their use of the land over the requisite period, but they may have to seek help from neighbours or other third parties who can give evidence about the use of the land before they acquired it. Again, photographic evidence, and particularly aerial photographs, can be useful, particularly if the physical boundary has strayed from the line of the legal boundary but has been established for a long period of time.

15. Settling a Claim

Civil trials are often settled at the door of the court and boundary disputes are no exception. Solicitors must take care when recording the terms of the settlement, particularly where there are time pressures. The most common way of bringing such a dispute to an end is by the parties entering into a "Tomlin agreement". The proceedings are stayed pending compliance with the terms of the agreement reached between the parties. These terms are recorded in a schedule attached to an order and the parties have permission to apply to the court to enforce the terms of the schedule in the event of any failure to comply. The schedule may require the parties to execute further documents, for example a deed of compromise, particularly if it is intended to fix legal boundaries or transfer parcels of land. For a specimen form of order, see page 201.

Attempts to fix legal boundaries can be problematic, particularly if the effect of the settlement is to alter the title. The parties may record their agreement in a deed incorporating a plan which differs from the title plan, and then attempt to register it. The Land Registry notes it on the register but does not alter the title plan. This may cause problems in the future when the property comes to be sold. The more certain method is to execute transfers of the appropriate parcels of land and then register the transfers. The titles and title plans are then amended to reflect the change, which should satisfy the conveyancers.

16. Checklist

Evidence
1. Locate the oldest conveyance.
2. Use original conveyance plans wherever possible.
3. Read the parcels clause, looking closely at the deed plan and reading any text.
4. Check for any T-marks.
5. Obtain detailed witness statements at an early stage.
6. Ensure any expert to be appointed is suitably qualified.
7. Ensure the expert has all the relevant information and documents and precise instructions as to what he is expected to do; and that he complies with Practice Direction 35.
8. Adduce video evidence only if it is compelling and conclusive.
9. When using photographic evidence, it must be possible to prove when and by whom it was taken.
10. Check that the parties have not already entered into an informal boundary agreement.

Practical steps
1. Offer to share the cost of appointing a joint surveyor to determine the boundary.
2. Offer mediation.
3. Use part 36 offers and open offers.
4. Apply for an injunction only where damages would not be an adequate remedy or where an injunction is necessary to prevent a trespass.
5. Arrange a judicial site visit.
6. If any settlement affects the title, ensure that the title is rectified to reflect the change.

Chapter 3

Party Walls

1. Introduction

Certain types of boundary dispute concern party walls or other party structures. A homeowner may wish to demolish the fence that marks the boundary between his garden and that of his neighbour, replacing it by a brick wall, and entering his neighbour's land to construct the wall. Another example may be where a homeowner wishes to build a garage close to his neighbour's house. In situations such as these, the Party Wall etc Act 1996 comes into play.

2. Definitions

The 1996 Act recognises two main types of party wall, and a "party structure". A "party wall":
-   (a) forms part of a building and stands astride the boundary of land belonging to two or more different owners; or
-   (b) separates two buildings, and either stands astride the boundary of land belonging to two or more different owners, or stands wholly on one owner's land but is used by two or more owners to separate their buildings.

Where one neighbour built the wall in the first place and another constructed a building up against it without building his own wall, only the part of the wall that effects the separation is a "party wall". Sections above or on either side are not.

A "party fence wall" is a wall which is not part of a building, that stands astride the boundary line between land of different owners and is used to separate those lands; for example, a garden wall.

The Act also uses the term "party structure". This could be a party wall or floor partition, or other structure separating buildings or parts of buildings approached by separate staircases or entrances. So, for example, floors separating three flats in a building are party structures.

The 1996 Act refers to the neighbour who wishes to carry out work covered by the Act as the "building owner". An "adjoining owner" is anyone with an interest greater than a tenancy from year-to-year in the adjoining property.

3. Scope of the Party Wall etc Act

The essence of the Act is that a building owner has a duty to notify the adjoining owner, or all of them if more than one, before commencing works to which the Act applies. An adjoining owner can then agree or disagree with what is proposed. Where there is a disagreement, the Act provides for the resolution of disputes.

The scope of the works covered by the Act is as follows:

  (a) work to be carried out directly to an existing party wall or structure;
  (b) new building at, or astride, the boundary line between properties;
  (c) excavation within three or six metres (depending on the depth of the hole or foundations – see page 39) of a neighbouring building or structure.

The Act provides a framework for preventing and resolving disputes in relation to party walls, boundary walls and excavations near to neighbouring buildings. If a person intends to carry out work of a kind described in the 1996 Act, he must give the adjoining owner(s) notice of his intention. If the adjoining property is occupied by a long term tenant or leaseholder, the landlord must also be notified. Notice must be given even if the work will not extend beyond the centre line of a party wall.

The 1996 Act provides a building owner, who wishes to carry out certain types of work to an existing party wall, with rights to do so which go beyond common law rights. Section 2 of the 1996 Act lists the work that can be done. The most common are the rights:

  (a) to demolish and rebuild the party wall;
  (b) to underpin the entire party wall;
  (c) to protect two adjoining walls, for example, by putting a flashing from the higher over the lower of the two;

(d) to cut into a wall, often to take the bearing of a beam, for a loft conversion or to insert a damp-proof course all the way through the wall;

(e) to raise the whole party wall, and if necessary, remove projections which would otherwise prevent the work.

4. The Notice

The building owner should give written notice about what he plans to do before the planned starting date for work to the party wall. The notice period depends upon the type of work that he proposes to carry out:

(a) if the building owner intends to build a party wall or a party fence wall on the line of junction between two buildings, he should serve a notice at least one month before building work commences: section 1(2) of the Act;

(b) if the building owner intends to build a wall along the line of junction, which is entirely on his own land, he should serve a notice at least one month before the work commences (section 1(5));

(c) if he proposes to excavate within a distance of three metres or six metres of any part of a building or structure belonging to an adjoining owner, he must serve a notice at least one month before beginning the excavation (section 6(5));

(d) if the proposed work is to an existing party wall, party fence wall or party structure, the notice period is at least two months before the commencement date for the proposed work (section 3).

It is not necessary to appoint a professional adviser to give notice on the building owner's behalf, although much difficulty can sometimes be avoided by doing so. There is no official form for giving notice under the Act, but the notice should include the following details:

(a) the name and address of the building owner;

(b) the address of the building, if different;

(c) a clear statement that the notice is a notice under the provisions of the Act;

(d) full details of what the building owner proposes to do (including plans where appropriate);

(e) when the building owner proposes to start the work.

Examples of party wall notices are given in the Appendix; see page 202. Notices under the Act must be issued by all the correct parties. In the case of *Lehmann v Herman* [1993] 16 EG 124, [1992] EGCS 122, a party structure notice served by only one of two joint tenants was held to be invalid.

A party structure notice and an excavation notice are valid for one year only. Such a notice ceases to have effect if the work to which it relates is not commenced within twelve months from the date on which it is served, or if the work is not undertaken with due diligence. If a notice lapses, it can be re-served.

5. The Effect of the Notice

Party wall or party fence wall notice
Where the building owner wishes to build a party wall or party fence wall, he must serve a notice under section 1(2). Section 1(3) provides that if the adjoining owner then serves a notice indicating his consent, the wall can lawfully be built without further ado. Thus, the building owner acquires a right to build it centrally over the boundary. Furthermore, section 1(3)(b) provides that the costs of building the wall will be shared by the two owners having regard to the use of the wall made, or to be made, by each of them.

If, having received notice, the adjoining owner agrees, in writing, that the work may start earlier than the date stated in the notice, the building owner does not have to wait for the full one or two months set out in the notice before starting work.

If the adjoining owner does not give consent, section 1(4) applies. It provides that the building owner can build the wall, but entirely at his own expense and on his own land. He is entitled to exercise statutory rights of entry to carry out the work. Section 8 of the Act gives the building owner special rights of entry on the adjoining owner's land in aid of works "in pursuance of the Act". If the building owner is not content to build the wall entirely on his own land, he must initiate the procedure under section 10 of the Act; see below.

If the building owner intends to build a boundary wall wholly on his own land (a fence wall) he must serve a notice under section 1(5) of the Act. A fence wall is built wholly on the building owner's land, apart from the footings. The building owner must build at his own expense and compensate the adjoining owner for any damage caused by the building of the wall and the placing of footings and foundations in his land.

Party structure notice

Where the boundary has already been built on, for example, where an external wall of a building stands on one owner's land with footings projecting into the neighbour's land, or there is a party fence wall, section 2 of the Act applies, giving the building owner certain rights to make good, repair, demolish and other activities. The building owner must first serve a notice under section 3 of the Act (a "party structure notice"), unless he can obtain the written consent of all adjoining owners to the works, or he has himself been served with a notice requiring him to undertake remedial works to a dangerous structure.

On receipt of the party structure notice, the adjoining owner can react in a number of ways. If he serves a counter-notice within fourteen days of service of the party structure notice, indicating his consent, there is no dispute and the work can proceed. He may also agree that the works may start before the period of notice expires.

Alternatively, he may, within one month of service of the notice, serve a counter-notice under section 4. Such a counter-notice has two purposes. First, the adjoining owner can require modifications to the proposed building works for his own convenience. For example, if the building owner proposes to reduce the height of an existing wall, the adjoining owner can require him to maintain its original height. Secondly, the adjoining owner may specify modifications to the proposed special foundations for the party structure. If so, he must be prepared to pay for the works which he requires (section 11(9)). The exception is underpinning work required by the adjoining owner; section 6(3) requires that underpinning is paid for by the building owner.

If the adjoining owner neither consents nor serves a section 4 counter-notice, a dispute is deemed to have arisen under section 5 of the Act which must be resolved under section 10; see below.

Protection for the adjoining owner

Section 7 of the Act provides valuable protection for the adjoining owner. Section 7(5) requires that work executed in pursuance of the Act must comply with statutory requirements, such as the Building

Regulations and regulations concerning site safety. It further requires that the building owner must not deviate from the agreed plans, except by agreement with the adjoining owner or the parties' surveyors. Furthermore, section 7(1) of the Act provides that the building owner may not exercise any right conferred on him in a manner or at a time which causes unnecessary inconvenience to the adjoining owner.

6. Dispute Resolution

The best way of settling any dispute is by discussion between the neighbours concerned. If the parties cannot reach agreement, the next step is to utilise the dispute resolution procedure set out in section 10 of the Act. Ideally, the parties would jointly appoint an agreed surveyor to adjudicate and draw up an "award", setting out the parties' rights and liabilities. The agreed surveyor should preferably be someone other than the surveyor appointed to supervise the building works in question.

The adjoining owner may decide to reserve his position by electing not to respond to the notice, and by instructing his own surveyor. The surveyors for the building owner and the adjoining owner would then draw up the award together, nominating a third surveyor who would be called in only if the two surveyors could not agree. The surveyors appointed under the dispute resolution procedure of the Act must behave impartially and consider the interests of both sides. They do not act as advocates for those appointing them.

Lastly, if the adjoining owner refuses to appoint an agreed surveyor under the dispute resolution procedure, the building owner can appoint a surveyor on the adjoining owner's behalf so that the procedure can go ahead.

Appointment of surveyors

If surveyors are to be appointed, it is important for the parties to instruct experienced party wall surveyors. The Royal Institution of Chartered Surveyors can provide names of specialist surveyors in particular areas. It can be contacted at Surveyor Court, Westwood Way, Coventry CV4 8JE; telephone (0870) 333 1600; www.rics.org. There is also the *Pyramus and Thisbe Club*, an organisation with countrywide membership, drawn from surveyors interested in party walls. The club was founded in 1974 in response to the widespread misreporting of the case of *Gyle-Thompson v Wall Street (Properties)* (see below), and played a pivotal role in framing the 1996 Act. It can be contacted at Rathdale House, 30 Back Road, Rathfriland BT34 5QF; telephone (028) 4063 2082; www.partywalls.org.uk.

The award
The agreed surveyor, or the parties' surveyors, seek to resolve the dispute by the formulation a Party Wall Act award, which:
   (a) sets out the work to be carried out;
   (b) states when and how it is to be carried out (for example not at weekends);
   (c) specifies any additional work required, for example to prevent damage to the foundations of the adjoining building;
   (d) records the condition of the adjoining owner's building before the work commences so that any damage can be properly attributed and made good;
   (e) provides for inspection of the works by the parties' surveyors as they progress, to ensure that the works are in accordance with the award.
The parties should keep a copy of the award with their property deeds.

Costs
Usually, the building owner who first planned the work pays all costs associated with drawing up the award. However, parties to the award who disagree with its terms may appeal against the award to the court. *Young v Bemstone Ltd* [2002] EWHC 2651 (TCC) was such a case. A developer was building new houses on the line of junction between its site and the site upon which the claimant's house stood. No party wall notice pursuant to section 1 of the Act was served on the adjoining owner before excavation works, to lower the level of the developer's site significantly, began. Cracks appeared in the claimant's house. The claimant maintained that the works had damaged the house and a dispute arose for the purposes of the Act. Both sides appointed their own surveyors in accordance with the dispute resolution procedure in section 10(b) of the Act and a third surveyor, appointed to decide the matter, made an award. The owner appealed and the developer cross-appealed against the award under section 10(17) of the Act. The court ruled that, on the evidence, moderate to severe damage had been caused to the house by the works that had been carried out on the

developer's site. The owner, as the successful party, recovered the costs of the whole award procedure and of the appeal.

Each side has fourteen days to appeal to the county court against an award. An appeal is appropriate only if an owner believes that the surveyors have acted beyond the scope of their authority.

7. Failure to Serve Notice

Most disputes arise because works to a party wall are undertaken without proper notification to the adjoining owner(s). The adjoining owner(s) may then apply to court for an injunction to prevent work continuing. The question arises whether the procedure under the Party Walls etc Act 1996 should be set in motion retrospectively. In the cases of *Woodhouse v Consolidated Property Corporation* (1993) 66 P&CR 234, [1993] 19 EG 134 (CA) and, more recently, *Louis v Sadiq* [1997] 1 EGLR 136, (1997) 74 P&CR 325 (CA), the answer was that it should not, but these cases were decided under the London Building Acts (Amendment) Act 1939, which was the precursor to the 1996 Act. Now, section 10(10) of the 1996 Act enables surveyors to deal with any matter to which the 1996 Act relates and is in dispute between the building owner and adjoining owner. However, the definition of a building owner is "an owner of land *who is desirous of* exercising rights under the Act". It is arguable that an owner who has already carried out the works does not fall within this definition, and that the matter cannot therefore be resolved within the procedures laid down by the 1996 Act.

Perhaps a sensible solution, where work has been carried out without following the procedure under the 1996 Act, would be for the building owner to engage a surveyor to negotiate and resolve the issues with his neighbour(s). The adjoining owner could also engage a surveyor. Each surveyor would inform his client that the provisions of the Act would now apply, and obtain authority from the client to agree costs and expenses, rights of entry and the need to make good. A document, recording the exact extent and nature of the works and the date they were completed, would then be drawn up.

The decision of the Court of Appeal in *Roadrunner Properties Ltd v Dean and Another* [2003] EWCA Civ 1816, [2004] 1 EGLR 73 demonstrates that the court will not give a building owner who has failed to serve a notice an advantage over an adjoining owner in a situation where the building owner can provide expert evidence, but the adjoining owner has not been able to instruct a surveyor to report on the condition of the property before, during and after the work. In this case, the defendant building owner undertook work to a party wall without serving the statutory notice of the proposed work on the claimant, the adjoining owner. The defendant had cut a "chase" (a channel) into the wall in order to fit piping for a radiator. The work had been undertaken by a building company, which had contracted the work to an agency labourer, who had used a heavy-duty "Kango" hammer drill, capable of digging up a roadway. The claimant alleged that damage had been caused to his property as a result of work done to the joint wall. Damages were sought under the heads of nuisance and/or negligence on the part of the defendant and/or the building contractors. It was alleged that the use of the Kango was inappropriate. The Act applied to the wall and the works, but as the claimant had never received notification of the works, he was unable to instruct a surveyor to assess the condition of the building before, during and after the works. The judge's ability to address the cause of the damage was therefore greatly reduced. The parties both instructed their own expert witnesses. The two experts ascribed the damage to different causes and the trial judge favoured the defendant's expert's explanation on the balance of probabilities.

The Court of Appeal reversed the first instance decision. It held that, since the claimant had been denied the opportunity to adduce more cogent evidence, due to the defendant's breach of his obligations under the Act, the court should take a robust view on causation, and reject hypothetical and circumstantial explanations devised after the event by defendants whose own actions had prevented the claimant from ensuring proper evidence was available.

8. Costs

Responsibility for paying for the building works is usually either agreed between neighbours, or set out in the surveyors' award. The general principle in the 1996 Act is that the building owner, whose scheme of work it is, pays for it. There are, however, cases where the adjoining owner may pay part of the cost, for example:

    (a) where he has requested that additional work should be done;

    (b) where work to the party wall is needed anyway because of

defects or lack of repair for which the adjoining owner may
be responsible.

Where the dispute resolution procedure is adopted, the award may
deal with the apportionment of the costs of the work and be used to
resolve the question of costs.

An adjoining owner who suspects that there is a real risk that he
will be left in difficulties because the building owner will stop work
before finishing the job, can ask for a sum of money to enable him to
restore the party wall to its original condition if the building owner
fails to complete the work. The money would remain the building
owner's throughout but if the adjoining owner needed to have a wall
rebuilt, he could utilise that security to pay for the rebuilding.

9. Access to Neighbouring Property

Under the 1996 Act, the building owner has rights of access to the
neighbouring property. The adjoining owner must, when necessary,
give access to the building owner's workmen, architect and surveyor,
and to any surveyors appointed as part of the dispute resolution
process. The Act provides for fourteen days' notice of intention to
exercise these rights.

It is an offence to refuse entry to, or to obstruct, someone who is
entitled to enter premises under the Act, if the offender knows that the
person is entitled to be there. If the adjoining property is empty, the
building owner's workmen may enter the premises if accompanied by
a police officer.

10. New Party Walls and Party Fence Walls

Gyle-Thompson v Wall Street (Properties) Ltd [1974] 1 WLR 123,
[1974] 1 All ER 295 concerned the rights of owners where the
junction line was built upon and the building owner proposed to
demolish and rebuild a party fence wall at a reduced height. It is also
important because an award was purportedly made by a third surveyor
without party structure notices having been served on the claimants.
The case was decided under the London Building Acts (Amendment)
Act 1939, but the principles are the same under the 1996 Act.

The defendant was the owner of a warehouse, one wall of which
formed the rear boundary of houses owned by the claimant, each

having a garden that ran down to the wall. The defendant was in the process of demolishing the warehouse with a view to redeveloping the site. It planned to reduce the height of the wall in question, but discovered that it was a party wall. Each side appointed surveyors. The defendant produced plans for reducing the height of the wall by nine feet, which was unacceptable to the claimant. The defendant's surveyor served party structure notices under section 47(1) of the 1939 Act on the claimant's surveyor, who failed to pass on copies to the claimant, believing that the defendant's surveyor had sent the originals to the claimant.

Meanwhile, the claimant's surveyor and the defendant's surveyor had appointed a third surveyor. The three surveyors met. The defendant's surveyor and the third surveyor were in favour of the agreed works and decided to make an award accordingly under section 55(i) and (k) of the 1939 Act. The claimant's surveyor maintained his objection. The defendant's surveyor wrote to the claimant, informing it of the intended award, and notifying it of the right, under section 55(n) of the 1939 Act, to appeal to the county court within fourteen days of the delivery of the award.

The award was drawn up and signed by the defendant's surveyor. Five days later, copies of the party structure notices were sent to the claimant. A week after that, the third surveyor signed the award, and within a further two weeks, the defendant began to demolish the wall. The claimant applied for an interlocutory injunction. No copy of the award was delivered to the claimant until three days after the defendant started to demolish the wall.

The court held that the claimant was entitled to the injunction. Paragraphs (a) and (k) of section 46(1) did not give the building owner the right to demolish a party fence wall and rebuild it to a reduced height. In the absence of an express right to lower a party fence wall, the right to "demolish and rebuild" conferred on a building owner required reconstruction of the wall to the same height. It followed that the defendant had claimed a right it did not have, and the two surveyors had made an award that they did not have power to make. Accordingly, the award did not determine the right of the defendant to carry out the works and the claimants were able to bring proceedings in the High Court. Their remedy was not limited to a challenge to the award in the county court. In any event, the award was invalid as the party structure notices were not validly served on the claimant.

11. Excavation

The Party Wall etc Act 1996 applies where a neighbour wishes to excavate near his neighbour's buildings. If the building owner plans to:

(a) excavate or construct foundations for a new building or structure within three metres of a neighbouring owner's building or structure, and that work will go deeper than the neighbour's foundations; or

(b) excavate or construct foundations for a new building or structure within six metres of a neighbouring owner's building or structure where that work will cut a line drawn downwards at 45 degrees from the bottom of the neighbour's foundations,

he must inform the adjoining owner by serving a notice accompanied by plans. The notice must state whether he proposes to strengthen or safeguard the foundations of the building or structure belonging to the adjoining owner. The notice must be served one month before the planned start date for the excavation and is valid for one year only.

Section 6(9) of the 1996 Act provides that the adjoining owner is entitled to request particulars of the work, including plans and sections of the work, after it has been completed. The purpose of this is, presumably, to enable an adjoining owner to plan any future work of his own, or to take appropriate remedial steps if a structural problem occurs in his own building. The provision creates a statutory duty on the building owner to provide these particulars, which would be enforceable by a mandatory injunction by the court.

If the adjoining owner gives a notice within fourteen days agreeing to the excavation, the work may proceed. If he does not respond or objects, a dispute has arisen and the resolution procedure set out above should be used.

12. Limitations of the Act

The 1996 Act does not contain any provisions that could be used to settle a boundary dispute. It does not change the ownership of any wall or the position of any boundary. Boundaries can still run through the centre of a wall and each owner can technically own half of a wall. What the 1996 Act does is to set out the rights of an owner in relation to work undertaken to a party wall, and the obligations upon a building owner before he can start work.

Unfortunately, the 1996 Act contains no enforcement provisions for failure to serve a notice. However, if work is started without proper notice having been given, adjoining owners may seek to stop the work through a court injunction, as demonstrated by the *Gyle-Thompson* case, above.

Furthermore, following *Roadrunner Properties*, it is arguable that if the building owner fails to serve a notice, the burden on him to disprove a link between damage to a building and the work is greater than the burden on the adjoining owner to prove that link. This contrasts with the usual situation at common law where the burden of proof generally falls squarely on the claimant to prove such a link on the balance of probabilities.

The *Roadrunner* case should make building owners think twice before embarking on building works without serving a Party Wall Act notice, as they may have to defend costly proceedings to prove that they are not responsible for damage to an adjoining property.

13. Successors in Title

The 1996 Act is concerned with owners of pieces of adjoining land. It contains no general provision explaining how successors in title are affected, if at all. There may be circumstances in which it is important to ascertain how a party wall matter affects a successor in title.

If the original owners have reached an agreement outside the procedures of the 1996 Act, the effect on successors depends on the ordinary principles of common law. If the agreement is by deed, it may grant rights in the land, such as easements, which bind successors.

If the agreement arises from the service of a notice of consent under section 5 of the Act, the benefit is assignable to the successor of the building owner, and the adjoining owner's successor is bound by statutory rights of entry.

If there is a dispute and a sale of one of the pieces of land takes place before an award is made, it is arguable that a new owner could insist on the whole procedure being started again from the beginning.

It seems harsh for an incoming adjoining owner, who refuses to take part in existing proceedings, to be bound by the decisions of surveyors he has not chosen. Conversely, to start the proceedings again from scratch could severely prejudice the building owner by delay. Provided that the new adjoining owner purchased with knowledge of the dispute, it seems that he falls within the definition of an adjoining owner in the Act and could be substituted as a party to the dispute, with provision for him to appoint his own surveyor. On that basis, it is arguable that he would not need to be served with a new notice and an award would bind him whether or not he participates in the process.

However, if he purchased the property in ignorance of the dispute, he may be entitled to insist upon a new notice being served upon him. If an appeal against an award is brought in the county court, these proceedings can be protected by a notice registered against the relevant title under the Land Registration Act 2002, section 87. This would then bind any incoming purchaser of the land, whether or not he has notice of the dispute.

14. Checklist

1. The Party Wall etc Act 1996 applies if a neighbour is about to carry out work or is already engaged in work which falls into one of these categories:
   (a) work on an existing wall or structure shared with a neighbour's property; or
   (b) building a free-standing wall or wall of a building up to or astride the boundary wall with his neighbour's property; or
   (c) excavating near a neighbouring building.
2. Notice must be served within the correct statutory time limit:
   (a) one month to build a new party wall or party fence wall, or to build a wall entirely on the building owner's own land on the line of junction;
   (b) two months before commencing work to an existing party wall, party fence wall or party structure.
3. Upon receiving a notice, the adjoining owner may either give consent in writing; serve a counter-notice within fourteen days; or not respond to the notice, thus reserving his position and enabling him to instruct his own surveyor.
4. The parties' surveyors prepare the award.
5. Generally the building owner pays the costs. Where the work confers a benefit on the adjoining owner, or is undertaken at his

request, the award may stipulate that he contributes to the costs.

6. An appeal against the surveyor's award may be brought in the county court within fourteen days after it is made.

7. The building owner has a statutory right of entry to the neighbouring property on fourteen days' notice. A building owner may not exercise any right conferred on him by the Act in such a manner or at such a time as to cause unnecessary inconvenience to the adjoining owner.

8. An adjoining owner is protected in that the work must comply with statutory requirements. Plans and particulars must be agreed between the parties or determined by an award. Such plans must be adhered to. The building owner must not cause unnecessary inconvenience in exercising his rights.

Chapter 4

Trespassers and Squatters

1. Introduction

The tort of trespass is committed when one person enters onto the land of another without the landowner's consent or without lawful justification. One of the incidents of land ownership in England and Wales is the freedom of the owner to exclude anyone else from entering onto his land.

A landowner is entitled to take reasonable measures to protect his land from trespassers by, for example, inserting spikes or broken glass into the top of a wall, or by having barbed wire running along the top of the wall (see, for example, *Gibson v The Plumstead Burial Board* (1897) 13 TLR 273). Such measures must not, however, amount to a nuisance, so, for example, the feature in question must be sufficiently high that it does not interfere with ordinary passers-by (*Stewart v Wright* (1893) 9 TLR 480). To avoid liability under section 1 of the Occupiers' Liability Act 1984, the landowner must also put up warnings that such steps have been taken.

At common law, a landowner is entitled to eject from his land anyone who has no right to be there, provided that he uses no more than reasonable force in so doing. This right has, however, been modified by statute, as will be seen later in this chapter. Further, it was held in *Burton v Winters* [1993] 1 WLR 1077, [1993] 3 All ER 847 (CA) that "self-redress is a summary remedy which is justified only in clear and simple cases, or in an emergency". It is also an offence under the Criminal Law Act 1977 for a person to use or threaten to use violence to secure entry to property if there is someone present on that property who is opposed to the entry, although this does not apply to displaced residential occupiers and their agents – section 72, Criminal

Justice and Public Order Act 1994.

Self-help, therefore, is generally not the best way forward. The risks include the possibility that a court may grant an injunction to allow the unlawful occupier to return to the premises pending a full court hearing, and the prospect of a long, costly legal battle during which the landowner is deprived of the property. Even if the landowner is ultimately successful, it is unlikely that he will be able to secure an effective costs order against the other party.

If a landowner is found to have unlawfully evicted a residential tenant or licensee he may be prosecuted under section 1 of the Protection from Eviction Act 1977. This is likely to result in a heavy fine or even a prison sentence if the illegal action was particularly serious or if the defendant has a previous conviction for the same or a similar offence.

An unlawfully evicted tenant may seek exemplary damages from the landowner, and an unlawfully evicted licensee may seek aggravated damages. If the displaced tenant decides not to require the landlord to re-admit him, he may seek damages under the Housing Act 1988 equivalent to the difference between the value of the property subject to the occupation and the value of the property without the occupier. This could be a substantial sum.

The wiser course is to issue proceedings in the local county court for an order for possession against the trespasser. Where the occupied land does not comprise residential property only two clear days have to elapse between the service of the application and the hearing (Civil Procedure Rules 1998, rule 55.5). A "clear" day means that the day on which service is effected and the day of the hearing are to be ignored: see rule 2.8(3). For residential premises, at least five clear days must elapse between service and hearing. These are the minimum periods. They can be abridged by the court in cases of emergency, or where the trespasser has committed an assault or caused damage to property.

Some county courts fix a hearing for the earliest possible date under the rules, in which case a possession order can be obtained reasonably quickly. Other county courts are less accommodating; here, the temptation to the landowner to resort to self-help may be great, but must be resisted, particularly if the trespassers are residing on the premises.

Some firms of bailiffs are prepared to assist landowners in removing trespassers from land by posting on the land a notice of their intention to tow vehicles from the land if they are not removed voluntarily by a certain time. This is often successful, as the trespassers do tend to move on of their own accord when or before the tow truck arrives, but the landowner risks finding himself on the wrong side of the law if his agent's activities go beyond the exercise of reasonable force. Further, there is nothing to prevent the trespassers from returning if no court order has been obtained. On the other hand, with the benefit of a possession order, there is an expedited procedure for returning to court for a warrant of restitution where a trespasser has been evicted from the land pursuant to a warrant of possession but returns shortly afterwards (order 26, rule 17(4) and (5) of the County Court Rules 1981 (SI 1981 No. 1687)).

2. Examples of Trespass

A landowner can commit a trespass on his neighbour's land by, for example, placing objects on the neighbour's land. Thus, a ladder propped up against the neighbour's wall (*Westripp v Baldock* [1939] 1 All ER 279), and placing rubbish against a neighbour's wall (*Kynoch Ltd v Rowlands* [1912] 1 Ch 527), constitute a trespass. Perhaps more commonly, a landowner may attach his building, or an extension to his building, to a neighbour's property, thus committing a trespass. The property does not need to be physically attached to the neighbouring land or building to amount to a trespass; it may simply be a matter of eaves or guttering overhanging beyond the line of the boundary between two properties which constitutes the trespass.

A person may become a trespasser even though he may have lawfully entered upon and remained in occupation of the land but his right to remain in occupation has terminated. This is the case where a tenant remains in occupation after the tenancy has come to an end and the tenancy is one in respect of which there is no statutory security of tenure at the end of the term. Again, a person becomes a trespasser if he has entered onto land as a licensee (that is, with the consent of the owner) and that consent has been withdrawn or terminated. Where former tenants or licensees are residing in the property the landowner cannot simply eject them. Section 3(1) of the Protection from Eviction Act 1977, as amended by the Housing Act 1988, obliges the landowner to take legal proceedings to enforce his right to recover possession. This section does not, however, apply to certain tenancies and licences, such as those granted otherwise than for money or money's worth, and those where the tenant or licensee shares living accommodation with the landlord whose only or principal home is part of the shared accommodation (section 3A, Protection from Eviction Act 1977). Holiday lettings are also excluded (section 3A(7)(a)).

It is a trespass for a person to cut across a neighbour's land to gain access to his own property, usually because this is a shorter or more convenient route.

Another common instance of trespass is where a neighbour encloses within his own garden part of the garden of his next-door neighbour. This may occur because a fence has blown down and, by accident or error, the new fence is erected in the wrong place, or the neighbour has tried to gain a few inches of land. It may be that where gardens are separated by a hedge, the route of the hedge alters over time because of the way it is left to grow, or perhaps pruned or hacked back on one side. The owner whose land has been purloined in this way may or may not decide to object. If he does not object for a number of years, he may find that he is no longer entitled to do so, the land becoming that of the neighbour, who acquires it by adverse possession. This is dealt with in detail later in this chapter.

Farmers or owners of open land in the countryside may encounter those who wish to ramble across their land even though they do not have the farmer's consent. Those wishing to do this are most likely not neighbours, but hikers and ramblers who are not trespassers if they fall within the relevant provisions of the Countryside and Rights of Way Act 2000, which confers public rights of access to the countryside. The detailed provisions of this Act are beyond the scope of this book, but section 2(1) enables "any person . . . to enter and remain on any access land for the purposes of open-air recreation", so long as no damage is caused and the restrictions in schedule 2 to the Act are observed. Those restrictions include such matters as lighting fires, feeding livestock and taking, killing, injuring or disturbing any animal, bird or fish. "Access land" is any land shown as open country or as a registered common on maps created for this purpose. It also includes unmapped registered common land and managed land in excess of 600 metres above sea level.

3. Damages for Trespass

To establish trespass, it is not necessary to prove that there has been an actual loss to the claimant, but if there is no actual loss then nominal damages only will be awarded in any proceedings for trespass. Examples of trespass without actual loss include where a trespasser has simply walked over another's land, or where some article (such as a ladder) has been resting against a neighbour's wall without causing damage. Often, the main aim of the proceedings in such cases is not damages, but an injunction preventing the trespass continuing or recurring.

Where actual physical damage to the land can be proved, the measure of damages is the diminution in value of the land as a result of the trespass. If, however, the landowner has put the damage right or intends to do so, then the cost of repair and reinstatement may be ordered. Where a trespasser has actually had use of premises, the landowner may seek compensatory damages for the trespasser's use and occupation of the land. This is usually on the basis of what the landowner could have obtained in rent if he had let the property to the trespasser.

If the trespasser was originally a tenant, but has stayed on after his tenancy has ended, the damages take the form of "mesne profits", but are not conceptually different from damages for trespass generally, with one exception. Mesne profits may be calculated, at the landlord's election (and subject to the court's agreement), as the same sum as was last payable under the tenancy, whether or not that is the current letting value: *Swordheath Properties Ltd v Tabet* [1979] 1 WLR 285, [1979] 1 All ER 240 (CA).

4. Injunctions

The relief afforded by an injunction is likely to be foremost in the client's mind when he first consults a solicitor to say that, for example, his neighbour has erected a new boundary fence in the wrong place and on his land, or is drilling into his wall to key in an extension that the neighbour is building onto his own house. If the neighbour is indeed in the wrong and cannot be persuaded to desist or refrain from pursuing his course of action, the solicitor may need to act quickly to obtain an order of the court requiring the neighbour to stop what he is doing.

Interim injunction

An injunction is usually claimed as one of the forms of relief sought in proceedings for damages for trespass, and an interim injunction may be obtained by making an application in the course of those proceedings before the final hearing. The procedure is governed by the Civil Procedure Rules, part 25 and the Practice Direction thereto.

If the matter is urgent, an application may be made without notice to the defendant. The claimant must give an undertaking to the court that if a full injunction is not granted at the final hearing of the claim, the claimant will pay to the defendant such damages as the court may order to compensate him for the interim injunction having been put in place. The claimant must therefore be on strong ground before seeking an interim injunction and must be prepared to pay what may, in some circumstances, be substantial damages if, at the final hearing, the judge decides that the interim injunction was wrongly granted.

An interim injunction obtained without notice is granted for a short period only. The defendant is usually given permission to apply on short notice if he disagrees with the interim order and the matter is so urgent that it cannot wait until the return date to come back before the court.

An interim injunction is a temporary remedy granted where it is considered necessary to preserve the *status quo* until the matter can be fully argued at trial. The judge has a discretion whether or not to grant the remedy. At the hearing of an application for an interim injunction, the court is not concerned with the detail of the case; it is sufficient for the claimant to show that there is a serious question to be tried. Unless the judge decides that the claimant has no real prospects of success, or that the claim is frivolous or vexatious, he must go on to consider whether or not the balance of convenience is in favour of granting the injunction: *American Cyanamid Co v Ethicon Ltd* [1975] AC 396, [1975] 2 WLR 316, [1975] 1 All ER 504 (HL). Like other injunctions, an interim injunction is not granted if damages would be an adequate remedy.

In cases of trespass, the claimant can avoid this balancing process if he has a clear enough case to proceed for summary judgment under part 24 of the Civil Procedure Rules. An injunction to restrain trespass, on clear facts, is granted "as of right", not on the balance of convenience: see *Patel v W H Smith (Eziot) Ltd* [1987] 1 WLR 853, [1987] 2 All ER 569 (CA).

Mandatory injunction

An injunction is usually an order that the person to whom it is addressed shall cease doing something. There are occasions, however, when the order – a mandatory injunction – requires the addressee to do something positive. Such injunctions can be made pursuant to an interim application, but only if it can be shown that:

    (a) there is a probability that damage may be inflicted if the order is not made;

    (b) there is a means by which the addressee can take remedial steps; and

    (c) it is likely that the order, or a similar one, will be granted at trial.

See *Hooper v Rogers* [1975] Ch 43, [1974] 3 WLR 329, [1974] 3 All ER 417 (CA). For example, if a next-door neighbour starts to key his new extension into the client's wall and removes some brickwork in the process, in addition to an injunction restraining the neighbour from taking any further steps towards keying in the extension until the trial of the action, a judge might also award a mandatory injunction. The mandatory injunction might require the neighbour to do such works as are necessary to remove such of the structure as is interfering with the client's property and to make good the wall. The terms of a mandatory injunction should be clearly set out so that the person against whom it is granted knows precisely what he is expected to do.

Rule 25.10 of the Civil Procedure Rules states that if an interim injunction is granted and the case is subsequently stayed, the injunction is discharged immediately unless the parties have agreed the stay, or the court orders that the injunction is to continue. In addition, if the claim is struck out, any interim injunction ceases fourteen days after the date on which the strike-out is ordered, unless the claimant applies within that time to reinstate the claim (rule 25.11).

If the party to whom an injunction is addressed fails to comply with its terms, the party in whose favour it was granted may enforce the order by applying to commit the defendant to prison for contempt of court. This is governed by rule 29 of the County Court Rules and rule 52 of the Supreme Court Rules. The party applying to commit must be able to prove that the terms of the injunction had been brought to the other party's attention. This is done by an affidavit that the order was served personally on the person required to comply with the order of the court.

Any other evidence, for example of the breach of the order, must likewise be by way of affidavit, rather than witness statement. Unless the court orders otherwise, the hearing must take place at least fourteen days after service of the application for committal. Unless the breach is flagrant, the court is likely to suspend execution of the committal order for a period, on terms requiring the contemnor to do what was required by the injunction. Under section 14 of the Contempt of Court Act 1981 a court can commit a person to prison for contempt of court for a fixed period not exceeding two years.

For a specimen form of particulars of claim in the case of the obstruction of a right of way and trespass over a boundary, see page 198.

5. Defences

It is not a defence for a trespasser to claim that he entered onto the owner's land by mistake, thinking that it was his own, or that he had a right to be on the land. There is no common law right for a person to enter upon his neighbour's land for the purpose of repairing his own property, although such a right is now provided, in certain circumstances, by the Access to Neighbouring Land Act 1992 (see below).

In certain circumstances it may be permissible, and therefore provide a defence to an action in trespass, to enter onto another's land to abate a nuisance, such as to extinguish a fire, provided that the trespasser has not created the nuisance in the first place. A person may also enter another's land to recover goods taken there by the wrongful act of the owner of the land (*Patrick v Colerick* (1838) M & W 483).

Other defences might be that:

(a) it was not the defendant who entered onto the claimant's land;

(b) the claimant is not entitled to possession and therefore has no right to bring an action in trespass;

(c) the land does not belong to the claimant;

(d) the defendant has acquired title by adverse possession – see below.

6. Travellers

Travellers are nomadic people who live in motor homes or caravans which are towed from place to place, often by large vehicles. Local authorities are advised by the government (see paragraphs 19 to 22 of the Department of the Environment's Circular 18/94, *Gypsy Sites Policy and Unauthorised Camping*) to provide sites for the use of such travellers, but often insufficient facilities are available, or the travellers choose not to use the sites that are available. They may instead occupy other land, setting up camp there until they decide to move on or the landowner obtains a possession order.

The sort of land that attracts travellers is farm land, large car parks near factories, or local authority open spaces. The average homeowner is unlikely to have a sufficiently large or convenient area of land to be attractive to travellers, but a farmer could well find his field being occupied, and anyone living in the vicinity of land on which there is a travellers' encampment is likely to be affected indirectly. The lack of facilities in such locations may lead to the dumping of rubbish and other detritus, causing landowners to complain about the cost of clearing up once the travellers have departed.

Section 61 of the Criminal Justice and Public Order Act 1994 gives the police certain powers to move travellers on. It provides that a "senior police officer" may direct persons to leave land if he reasonably believes that two or more persons are trespassers and "are present there with the common purpose of residing there for a period". The police must be satisfied that the owner has asked the trespassers to leave and that they are causing damage, using threatening behaviour or have six or more vehicles on the land. If the trespassers do not leave they commit an offence. Section 68 of the same Act creates the offence of "aggravated trespass" where persons trespass on land in order to disrupt lawful activity.

In practice, the police are usually reluctant to exercise the powers under the Criminal Justice and Public Order Act 1994, leaving the landowner with the costly task of obtaining a possession order against "persons unknown" in the county court. The procedure is exactly the same as obtaining a possession order against any trespasser and is set out in Part 55 of the Civil Procedure Rules 1998 and its associated Practice Direction.

7. Access to Neighbouring Land

As mentioned above, a landowner does not have any right at common law to enter onto his neighbour's land to carry out repairs to his property, and so needs his neighbour's permission to do so. This is unsatisfactory because the neighbour may unreasonably refuse such a request, or his whereabouts may be unknown, or for some other reason he cannot be contacted when the need for access arises. To overcome these problems, the Access to Neighbouring Land Act 1992 was enacted. By section 1(1) of that Act:

"A person—

(a) who, for the purpose of carrying out works to any land (the 'dominant land'), desires to enter upon any adjoining or adjacent land (the 'servient land'), and

(b) who needs, but does not have, the consent of some other person to that entry,

may make an application to the court for an order under this section ('an access order') against that other person."

Subsection 2 provides that the court will make an access order if, and only if, it is satisfied:

"(a) that the works are reasonably necessary for the protection of the whole or any part of the dominant land; and

(b) that they cannot be carried out, or would be substantially more difficult to carry out, without entry upon the servient land."

This is subject to subsection (3), which provides that a court may not make such an order where it is satisfied that:

"(a) the respondent or any other person would suffer interference with, or disturbance of, his enjoyment of the servient land, or

(b) the respondent, or any other person (whether of full age or capacity or not) in occupation of the whole or any part of the servient land, would suffer hardship."

The hardship must be unreasonable to prevent an order being made.

If an order is made, it specifies the works that may be carried out, the extent of the servient land that may be entered upon and the date on which, or the period during which, the land may be entered upon (section 2(1) of the 1992 Act). The order may set out terms to avoid or restrict the damage, loss, inconvenience or loss of privacy that the entry may cause. Further, it may specify:

(a) the way in which the works are to be carried out;

(b) the days and times of day when the work may be done;

(c) who may carry out the work; and

(d) the precautions that the applicant must take

(section 2(3)).

The court has power to order compensation for loss, damage or injury, for loss of privacy and for substantial inconvenience (section 2(4)). The order may also require payment for the privilege of the right of access, irrespective of loss or damage; the method of calculating the amount of any such payment is specified in section 2(6) of the 1992 Act.

8. Acquisition of Title by Adverse Possession

The law of adverse possession may be summarised thus: if a landowner fails, for long enough, to prevent a trespasser from using his land, the trespasser gains legal title to the land he wrongfully occupies. This is not necessarily restricted to small areas of land such as those along the boundary between two properties. Quite extensive areas of land have been acquired in this way, irrespective of whether or not the original landowner and the person acquiring the land are neighbours.

J A Pye (Oxford) Ltd v Graham

The Land Registration Act 2002 has made changes, but the position concerning cases before the Act came into force has been the subject of litigation. In *J A Pye (Oxford) Ltd v Graham* [2002] UKHL 30, [2003] 1 AC 419, [2002] 3 WLR 221, [2002] 3 All ER 865, Mr Graham had grazing rights over a part of the claimant company's land. This land was totally enclosed by hedges, and access to it was through a gate which Mr Graham kept locked, although access could be gained elsewhere on foot. The grazing agreements came to an end on 31 December 1983 and in June 1984 the company sold the standing crop of grass to Mr Graham. Mr Graham continued to use the land for approximately the next fourteen years exactly as before, but without the owner's permission. On several occasions he asked for a new grazing agreement, but in 1984 the company refused and in 1985 the request went unanswered. Nevertheless, Mr Graham continued to use the land just as if it were part of his own farm. He kept cattle on the land and treated the grass. He trimmed the boundary hedges regularly and maintained the boundary fencing.

On 30 April 1998 the company issued an originating summons seeking cancellation of the caution which Mr Graham had registered against the title. In 1999 it commenced possession proceedings, claiming that Mr Graham's repeated requests for a new grazing agreement meant that he could not have had the necessary intention to dispossess the company. Mr Graham contended, however, that the company's action for possession was statute-barred by section 15(1) of the Limitation Act 1980. That section provides that:

"No action shall be brought by any person to recover any land after the expiration of 12 years from the date on which the right of action accrued to him or, if it first accrued to some person through whom he claims, to that person . . ."

Paragraph 1 of schedule 1 to the Act provides:

"Where the person bringing an action to recover land, or some person through whom he claims, has been in possession of the land, and has while entitled to the land been dispossessed or discontinued his possession, the right of action shall be treated as having accrued on the date of the dispossession or discontinuance."

Section 17 of the Limitation Act 1980 provides that, where the land is unregistered, on the expiration of the limitation period regulating the recovery of land, the title of the paper owner is extinguished. For registered land which is unaffected by the provisions of the Land Registration Act 2002, the title of the paper owner is not extinguished, but the registered proprietor is deemed to hold the land in trust for the squatter. The effect of the Land Registration Act 2002 on the law of adverse possession is discussed later in this chapter.

The issue in *J A Pye (Oxford) Ltd v Graham* was whether the company was "dispossessed" of the land at least twelve years before it started proceedings for possession and, if so, whether Mr Graham had remained in possession of the land for a period of twelve years. The judge at first instance found in favour of Mr Graham. The Court of Appeal reversed this decision, finding that Mr Graham did not have the necessary intention to possess the land to the exclusion of the owner, but, on further appeal, the House of Lords restored the decision at first instance. Before this case, there had been authority to the effect that where land was being held by the owner for its development potential, ouster of the owner from possession could be established only where the owner had been prevented from doing with the land what he might have been expected to do in his own interests, and that acts of trespass which did not prejudice the purpose for which the land was held did not amount to dispossession. See, for example, *Wallis's Cayton Bay Holiday Camp Ltd v Shell-Mex and BP Ltd* [1975] QB 94, [1974] 3 WLR 387, [1974] 3 All ER 575 (CA).

In *J A Pye (Oxford) Ltd v Graham*, however, Lord Browne-Wilkinson, in the House of Lords, held that only one party can be in possession of land. If the squatter is in possession then the owner of the paper title cannot be in possession. Legal possession requires two elements: factual possession and the intention to possess. As far as the factual possession is concerned, he agreed with Slade J in *Powell v McFarlane* (1979) 38 P&CR 452 (Ch D) – the strange case of "Ted's cow" – who said that "an appropriate degree of physical control" suffices. What amounts to an appropriate degree of physical control will vary depending on the particular circumstances of the case, but the test would usually be satisfied where the alleged possessor had been dealing with the land as an occupier owner might have been expected to deal with it, and nobody else had done so. In Pye's case, the land was within the physical control of the Grahams and they farmed it in exactly the same way as their own land.

As for the necessary "intention to possess", Lord Browne-Wilkinson again approved a *dictum* of Slade J in *Powell v McFarlane*, where he said that the intention to possess requires an:

> "intention, in one's own name and on one's own behalf, to exclude the world at large including the owner with paper title, so far as is reasonably practicable and so far as the process of the law will allow".

Furthermore, what is required is an intention to "possess", not to own. Six factors were considered by the judge at first instance to evidence an intention to possess. They were:

(a) the activities of Mr Graham on the land;

(b) that for many years before 1984 grazing was a normal farming use for the land;

(c) that although Mr Graham had not enclosed the land himself, the whole world, including the company, was excluded from it save on foot;

(d) that Mr Graham tended the land in exactly the same way as the rest of his farm;

(e) the refusal of the company to grant a further grazing licence, which meant that anything done on the land thereafter by Mr Graham could not have been done with a view to obtaining such a further licence;

(f) the fact that the company had applied for planning permission to develop the land. Any agricultural use of the land by Mr Graham thereafter was inconsistent with the intended future use by the company.

By restoring the judgment of the judge at first instance, the House of Lords did not demur from the findings that these were relevant factors in this particular case, evidencing an intention to possess.

Both the Law Lords and the court at first instance concluded that Mr Graham had succeeded in establishing title to the land in question by adverse possession (a phrase actually disapproved of in the House of Lords). But they came to that conclusion with great reluctance because, in the event, planning permission was granted for development of the land and Mr Graham's estate (Mr Graham himself having been killed in a shooting incident) benefited from a windfall by ending up as the owner of the land with an estimated value of £21 million, without having paid anything for it. Lord Bingham said that this was a conclusion he came to "with no enthusiasm".

As this book goes to press, in November 2005, the European Court of Human Rights (*J A Pye (Oxford Ltd v United Kingdom*, application no 44302/02) has found (by a majority of four to three) that the operation of section 75(1) of the Land Registration Act 1925 and section 15 of the Limitation Act 1980 violated the company's rights under article 1 of the first Protocol to the European Convention on Human Rights (the right to peaceful enjoyment of possessions). The judgment recognises that the position has now been altered by the Land Registration Act 2002 (see below) and it is submitted that the effects of the decision of the ECHR are confined to cases arising before the 2002 Act came into force and to registered land.

Occupation with consent or acknowledgement of ownership
It is perhaps self-evident, but it is sometimes overlooked, that there can be no "adverse possession" where someone is occupying land with the owner's permission, or where a squatter has acknowledged the owner's title to the land. In the recent case of *Colin Dawson Windows Ltd v Howard* [2005] EWCA Civ 9, the claimant's case

failed because for a number of years it had been negotiating with the defendants to purchase the property in question. The Court of Appeal found that the inference to be taken from the correspondence which had passed between the parties was that the claimants could remain on the property only while the negotiations for the sale and purchase continued. In those circumstances the claimants' possession of the land was not adverse to that of the paper owner.

The Land Registration Act 2002
The case of *J A Pye (Oxford) Ltd v Graham* was not affected by the Land Registration Act 2002 because title had been established by twelve years' adverse possession before the 2002 Act came into force on 13 October 2003. Squatters in a similar position have until 13 October 2006 to apply for registration under transitional provisions. For those whose requisite period of possession ends after 13 October 2003, the 2002 Act applies, unless the land is unregistered, in which case the old law governs the situation.

Schedule 6, paragraph 1(1), to the 2002 Act states that a person may apply to the land registrar to be registered as the proprietor of a registered estate in land if he has been in adverse possession of the estate for a period of ten years ending on the date of the application. The application is made on form ADV1. The squatter has to supply evidence in support of the application by way of statutory declaration made within one month of the application. The registrar gives notice of the application to the registered proprietor, any registered mortgagee, the proprietor of any superior leasehold estate and any other person who has identified himself as a person interested in the property. All these persons are given an opportunity to object, and have sixty-five business days in which to do so. If there is no objection, the squatter is registered as proprietor.

There are two ways in which the registered proprietor may object. The first is to return Land Registration Form NAP, on the basis that the recipient of the notice does not accept that the squatter has been in adverse possession, or accepts that the squatter has been in adverse possession but not for the requisite period as claimed. If the objection appears not to be groundless and the parties cannot agree, the case is referred to the Adjudicator to Her Majesty's Land Registry for a determination. The adjudicator may in turn refer the matter to the court. The burden of proof is on the objector and, if he is unsuccessful, the squatter is automatically registered as owner.

The other way of opposing the application is for the recipient to serve a counter-notice requiring the matter to proceed under paragraph 5 of schedule 6 to the Act. Under this procedure, the squatter's application is rejected automatically unless the squatter can show:

    (a) that there is an equity by estoppel such that the squatter should not be prevented from being registered as proprietor. This would be the case, for example, if the registered proprietor has led the squatter to believe that the squatter owned the property and the squatter has acted to his detriment in reliance upon that encouragement or belief; or

    (b) that the squatter is entitled for some other reason to be registered as proprietor, for example where the property was held on a bare trust for the squatter; or

    (c) that the squatter reasonably believed, for at least the last ten years of the period of adverse possession, that the land belonged to him with other adjoining land, and the exact line of the boundary between the land claimed and the adjoining land has not been determined. In this case the land claimed by the squatter must have been registered for more than one year prior to the date of the application.

In cases where one owner claims title to his neighbour's land after a hedge, fence or wall enclosing garden land is moved, it is unlikely that the owner who actually moved the boundary would be able to claim to have reasonably believed, for the last ten years of adverse possession, that the land belonged to him. It is more likely that this could be claimed by a successor in title to the squatter, who came to the land with the changed boundary already in place, not knowing that it had been moved.

The squatter has to make clear in his application that he claims to rely on one of the three conditions set out in (a) to (c) above, and must file a statutory declaration in support of the claim. The burden of proof is on the squatter. It is therefore recommended that, when completing form ADV1, an objector ticks the box bringing paragraph 5 of schedule 6 into consideration, in addition to any objection on the merits of the claim to adverse possession.

If the squatter fails to establish one of the three conditions, he may make a second application two years later, provided he has been in adverse possession since the date that his original application was rejected (paragraph 6 of schedule 6 to the 2002 Act). A further statutory declaration is required from the applicant. The squatter will then be registered as proprietor unless possession proceedings are pending or a possession order has been made (except where such an order has remained unenforced for more than two years), or the squatter's occupation has been regularised by means of a lease or licence (paragraph 6(2) of schedule 6).

Thus, the Land Registration Act 2002 provides a landowner with a greater degree of protection from being deprived of his land by a squatter than was available under the previous law. In the absence of one of the three special conditions referred to above, the landowner can prevent the squatter from being registered as proprietor, provided he acts either to obtain a possession order or to grant a lease or licence within the two-year period after an application is first rejected. The landowner must, though, be vigilant to take the appropriate action within the two-year window of opportunity provided by the 2002 Act.

Human rights aspects

It was unsatisfactory that there should be three different regimes: one for registered land, another for unregistered land, and a third for registered land where the period of twelve years' adverse possession had already elapsed before 13 October 2003. The recent decision of a deputy judge of the High Court in *Beaulane Properties Ltd v Palmer* [2005] EWHC 1460 Ch, [2005] 3 WLR 554 appeared to create a fourth regime relating to registered land where the matter falls to be decided after the introduction of the Human Rights Act 1998, but where the period of adverse possession was completed prior to 13 October 2003. Only a limited number of cases fall into this category.

As stated above, it was held in *J A Pye (Oxford) Ltd v Graham* that adverse possession means factual possession and an intention to possess without the consent of the owner. That case was decided on the basis of the law before the Human Rights Act 1998, because the twelve-year period of possession ended before the 1998 Act came into force on 2 October 2000. The UK courts proceeded on the basis that the 1998 Act was not retrospective and so played no part in the decision. The European Court of Human Rights, however, found that the Convention rights were engaged and that the law on limitation which operated in the *Pye* case breached the landowner's rights under article 1 of the first protocol to the Convention.

In *Beaulane*, the possession period expired after 2 October 2000 but before the Land Registration Act 2002 came into force on 13 October 2003. The 1998 Act had, therefore, to be considered. The judge found that extinguishing an owner's title under section 75 of the Land Registration Act 1925 was a deprivation of possession within the meaning of that phrase in the European Convention on Human Rights, and that the justification for doing so, namely to avoid uncertainty of title, was irrelevant where registered land was concerned.

The judge went on to consider how the legislation could be construed to avoid its being incompatible with Convention rights. He decided that the intention behind section 75 of the 1925 Act was to regularise minor matters such as those arising from inaccurately placed boundary features. Also, the law in 1925 concerning adverse possession was, as the Court of Appeal in *Pye* had found, that to establish adverse possession, the claimant's possession had to be incompatible with the owner's intentions for the land. In *Beaulane*, therefore, the judge held that possession for the purpose of section 75 of the Land Registration Act 1925 should be construed in this same way. Thus, pursuant to *Beaulane*, any case of possession which is not incompatible with the paper title owner's intentions for the land does not count towards the period of possession to make it adverse and deprive the registered owner of title to the land.

In the event, the decision in *Beaulane* appears to be consistent with that of the European Court of Human Rights in *Pye*.

Precautions

The purpose of the changes introduced by the Land Registration Act 2002 was to improve the situation for landowners so that they should not in future lose their land through inadvertence. To ensure that he is notified of any such application, the registered proprietor of the land should ensure that the Land Registry is aware of his current address in respect of every title he owns. The owner of unregistered land should ensure that proceedings for possession are taken, against any occupier of land who does not have the owner's express permission, before the expiry of twelve years from the date this state of affairs first occurred.

9. Evidence

The acquisition of title to land by adverse possession and boundary disputes (see Chapter 2) are often interlinked. A houseowner who is involved in a dispute with his neighbour over the route of the boundary between their gardens may claim that he has been in possession of the land in dispute for over twelve years and that his neighbour cannot now claim to own it and take it back. The evidence that will need to be gathered in such cases is dealt with in Chapter 2 of this book.

10. Checklists

Proceedings against trespassers
1. Ascertain whether the client can prove ownership of the land in question and, if so, by what means.
2. Ascertain whether the client is entitled to possession, thereby having the right to sue.
3. If the matter is urgent, consider applying for an interim injunction if the offender does not agree to desist pending agreement or order of the court.
4. Ascertain whether the client can give an undertaking as to damages, and whether it would be advisable to give such an undertaking as a prerequisite to obtaining an interim injunction.
5. Consider whether an injunction is necessary, or whether damages would be an adequate remedy.
6. If a mandatory interim injunction is required, the terms must be carefully considered so that what is required to be done is clear.
7. Marshall the evidence of trespass. Photographs may be useful in some circumstances.
8. Although damage is not necessary to constitute a trespass, if it is alleged, expert evidence of the damage itself, and of the quantum of the loss, is likely to be required.

Adverse possession
1. If the squatter had been in continuous possession for at least twelve years prior to 13 October 2003, the law in force before the Land Registration Act 2002 applies.
2. If title to the land is not registered, the law as it was prior to the Land Registration Act 2002 applies.
3. If the Land Registration Act 2002 applies, establish whether or not

the squatter has been in adverse possession for at least ten years.

4. Establish whether the squatter has been in possession of the land; whether the squatter has exercised sufficient control of the land; and whether the squatter has shown an intention to possess the land, for example, by fencing off the land; barring access to other people including the landowner; repairing fences; trimming hedges; clearing ditches; or ploughing or fertilizing the land. If he has done any of these acts, he is likely to have been in possession for the purpose of acquiring title after the requisite period of time.

5. If the squatter applies for registration under the 2002 Act, the paper title owner must respond within sixty-five business days.

6. The paper title owner may object under paragraph 5 of schedule 6 to the Land Registration Act 2002 and/or on the merits. The squatter may then seek to prove one of the three grounds to enable him to be registered as proprietor straightaway.

7. If the squatter is applying for a second time after his original application was rejected because he could not prove one of the grounds in paragraph 5 of schedule 6, two years must elapse with his continuing to be in possession without either possession proceedings being brought against him, or a lease or licence granted.

8. If the old law applies, twelve years' adverse possession must have elapsed prior to 13 October 2003 and application for registration must be made by the squatter before 13 October 2006.

Chapter 5

Rights of Way

1. Introduction

A right of way is an easement, that is to say, a right enjoyed by the owner of land (the "dominant tenement") over the land of another (the "servient tenement") which exists for the benefit and enjoyment of the land to which it is attached, but does not amount to a right to possess the servient tenement. It is more than a personal licence to the owner; it runs with the land and therefore benefits the present owner of the land and his successors in title. Like other easements it can be created expressly, by implication or by prescription.

Any interference with or obstruction of a right of way amounts to an actionable nuisance. Examples of actions that may constitute an interference or obstruction include parking on the land over which the right exists, erecting a gate across the right of way or building a structure on it. If a claimant believes that his right of way has been interfered with, it is necessary to:

    (a) check that the right exists;

    (b) establish how the right arose;

    (c) ascertain the nature and extent of that right; and

    (d) check whether there has been an interference or unlawful user; and, if so,

    (e) identify the appropriate remedy.

These issues are explored in this chapter.

2. Express Grant

General principles

The grant of a right of way can be contained in a conveyance or transfer of land or in a separate deed of easement. It is important to read the wording of the document carefully to identify the land over which the right exists, and the land which benefits from the right. The nature and extent of the right must be construed from the document and, in the event of a dispute, the matter may have to be brought before a court for determination. The court considers all the circumstances which existed at the time the instrument was executed and gives effect to the intention of the parties, if that can be divined. If not, then the grant is usually construed against the grantor (*Williams v James* (1867) LR 2 CP 577 at 581; *Morris v Edgington* (1810) 3 Taunt 24 at 30). In instigating or defending a dispute over a right of way, there is no substitute for reading the case law; although a body of legal principle has built up over many years, no two cases are the same, and each is considered on its own facts.

The circumstances that the court considers in construing the wording of the grant include the description of the dominant tenement; the place over which the right of way is granted; the starting and finishing points of the way; and the purpose for which the right is to be exercised. Since these are often considered together, it is more convenient to review the principles that can be derived from the cases as a whole, rather than to examine separately each of the circumstances that the court may consider.

It is settled law that, if the wording of the grant is not restrictive as to the mode or amount of user, then the right that is granted is a general right that allows whatever passage the physical layout and type of the land will bear. Therefore, a right to pass and repass which does not contain any reference to any particular mode of transport confers a right to pass with vehicles as well as on foot, provided that the way was suitable for vehicular use at the date of the grant: *Kain v Norfolk* [1949] Ch 163, [1949] 1 All ER 176, following the *dicta* of Sir George Jessel MR in *Cannon v Villars* (1878) 8 ChD 415 at 420. It is also settled law that, if the wording is silent as to purpose, the right can be exercised for any purpose, irrespective of the purpose at the date of the grant. See, for example *Alvis v Harrison* (1991) 62 P&CR 10, HL (Sc), in which the appellant was held to be entitled to exercise a right of way for the purposes for which the dominant tenement was used at the time the right was granted, but also for any other purposes that the dominant tenement might in the future fulfil, provided this was done reasonably and with the minimum burden to the servient tenement.

In some cases, however, the wording is qualified, for example, as to the mode of user (with or without vehicles, or on foot only, for instance); the amount of use (e.g., restricted to certain periods of the day); the precise location from which the right of way is to be accessed (through a particular gate, say); or the purpose for which the right is to be granted (such as, all reasonable purposes in connection with the use of the dominant tenement, or for certain defined purposes only).

The nature of the dominant and servient tenements
It may be necessary to identify the dominant tenement and to ascertain whether there has been any attempt to exercise the right for the benefit of a parcel of land in common ownership which is not the dominant tenement. For example, in *Peacock v Custins* [2002] 1 WLR 1815, [2001] 2 All ER 827 (CA), the claimants had a right of way over a roadway owned by the defendants expressed to be "at all times and for all purposes in connection with the use and enjoyment of the property hereby conveyed". The claimants owned another piece of land adjacent to the dominant tenement. The two parcels of land were farmed together as one by the claimants' tenant and the right of way was used for the benefit of both parcels. The trial judge found that this did not amount to using the servient tenement in excess of the rights granted, and so found for the claimant. This was overturned on appeal when the Court of Appeal found that the right was to use the way for the purposes of the dominant tenement only. Whether use of the right of way for the benefit of land that had not been expressly referred to in the grant amounted to exceptional user was therefore irrelevant.

There may also be a question whether the owner of the dominant tenement has attempted to enlarge the right, either by physically enlarging the dominant tenement itself or by excessive user, or by both. The basic principle, that the owner of the dominant tenement cannot seek to increase or change the user beyond the restrictions imposed in the grant, is derived from *Harris v Flower and Sons* (1904) 91 LT 816, (1904) 74 LJ Ch 127. In more recent cases, however, it has been sought to distinguish *Harris v Flower*. For example, in *National Trust v White* [1987] 1 WLR 907 (Ch D), the National Trust had a right of way over a track leading from the main road to its historic site "for all purposes". The Trust formed a car park next to the track and visitors used the track to walk from the car park to the site. The court held that the easement was being used not for the enjoyment of the car park but so as to visit the site; this was ancillary to the enjoyment of the site and the car park was not an enlargement of the dominant tenement. The case of *Alvis v Harrison*, while on a slightly different point, seems to have been decided in a similar spirit, recognising a need to allow some flexibility in the interpretation of a grant so as not to fetter the lawful use of land.

A case in which there were considerations similar to those in *National Trust v White* is *Chand v Linden Mews Ltd* [2002] EWCA Civ 590, [2002] 2 EGLR 76 [2003] 2 P&CR 4 (CA), although the outcome was different. The case concerned a small mews in west London which contained seven properties. Two of the residents formed a company, Linden Mews Limited, to purchase the freehold of the carriageway in the mews, and then charged the other owners substantial sums to park there. The owners resisted. The owners of numbers 4 and 5 also owned another piece of ground, referred to as the "garden ground", at the end of the mews, which they used for parking cars. In the ensuing litigation, the defendant counterclaimed against the owners of numbers 4 and 5 that, although those owners had a right to pass and repass over the carriageway from the highway to their respective properties, by foot and with vehicles, and a right to halt a single vehicle immediately adjacent to their houses for the purposes of loading and unloading, this right did not extend to a right of way over the carriageway to access the garden ground.

The Court of Appeal upheld the decision of the judge that parking was a separate use from access and it was a use that took place other than on the dominant tenement. Accordingly the principles in *Harris v Flower* and *Peacock v Custins* were followed. The court was not prepared to find, as had the court in the *National Trust* case, that the use was ancillary to the enjoyment of the dominant tenement.

There may be further complications if physical features have been eroded over time so that it is difficult to establish the exact starting and finishing points. For example, the access that existed when the right was granted may have disappeared, and it is then a question of construction whether the right had to be exercised from that access only, or from any part of the dominant tenement. So in *Lomax v Wood* [2001] EWCA Civ 1099, [2001] All ER (D) 80 (Jun) (CA) the claimants claimed a right of way (conveyed in an 1884 grant) over the defendant's adjoining land. The right granted permitted the claimants to use a road, part of which was in the defendant's title, known as "the occupation road", which joined the public highway. The claimants wanted to continue to have access to the occupation road from the three exits from their land that existed at the time they acquired their land. The defendant contended that the right of way did not include a right of access at any point where the claimants' land abutted the occupation road. The grant itself was worded in such a way as to terminate the right before the end of the occupation road. One of the exits that the claimants wished to use lay beyond the point at which the right terminated, and so the claimants had to cross the defendant's land to reach the occupation road. The judge found that the right could be explained only if it allowed access from the claimants' land onto the occupation road at at least one point of their choosing, because otherwise it would not have afforded to the claimants' predecessors in title any greater right than that which they already possessed. The Court of Appeal upheld his decision.

Limitations on mode of user
The description of the servient tenement, as it existed when the right was granted, is a relevant consideration: see *Cannon v Villars* (1878) Ch D 415. So, for example, if a driveway is too narrow to accommodate heavy goods vehicles, the user may be limited to cars and vans only.

Limitations as to purpose
There may also be limitations on the purpose for which a right of way is to be exercised. If the wording is not clear, again it is a question of construction requiring consideration of the nature of the dominant tenement. For example, a right of way granted to a factory includes a right to use it for all reasonable purposes connected with the business. This would include the right for heavy goods vehicles to go to and from the factory at reasonable times. In *Bulstrode v Lambert* [1953] 1 WLR 1064, [1953] 2 All ER 728, it was held that a right of way to "pass and re-pass with or without vehicles over and along [the yard] for the purposes of obtaining access to the building at the rear of the . . . premises and known as the auction mart" was a right of way for the purposes of an auction business, that is, a right to enter with goods and vehicles of any size appropriate to pass down the yard, and to keep the

vehicles in the yard for such time as was necessary to load and unload them.

Disputes between residential owner-occupiers often concern whether a right of way includes a right to park. It is now settled law that a right to park is capable of being an easement. *Bulstrode v Lambert* suggests that a right to pass and repass for the purposes of access implies a further right to stop for loading and unloading as this was necessary for the enjoyment of the right reserved. However, this was a finding based on the facts of that particular case and cannot be distilled into a general principle, although attempts to do so have been made. The basis of the decision was that the right to stop was necessary to the enjoyment of the right; it is not necessary for a residential occupier to have a right to park on a right of way in order to enjoy the right of way. Again, much depends on the wording of the actual document creating the right. The right to "use" a way may be wide enough to encompass parking, but a right to "pass and repass" may not, particularly if there is already space to park on the dominant tenement. So, in *London & Suburban Land and Building Co (Holdings) Limited v Carey* (1991) 62 P&CR 480 (Ch D), the court found no evidence that it was necessary for the enjoyment of an access way for vehicles to park or stop for loading or unloading on the access way, because the defendant owned a large forecourt that abutted onto the access way that could be used for that purpose.

Another factor relevant when considering the extent of the rights granted is the condition of the servient tenement at the time of the grant. It has been seen that, where the purposes for which the right is granted are unrestricted, the courts have been prepared to find that the purposes can be very wide, subject to the physical constraints of the way. The grant may, however, contain words that suggest that the purposes for which the right is to be exercised are to be those in existence at the time of the grant. In *Allan v Gomme* (1840) 11 A&E 759, the defendant transferred land to the plaintiff and reserved a right of way over the plaintiff's land to a stable and loft house and to a "space . . . used as a woodhouse". The space was an open piece of ground. The defendant then converted the loft and the woodhouse into a cottage and tried to exercise the right of way for the purpose of access to the cottage. The court found that the defendant could use the way only for the purposes of reaching a place that is "in the same predicament" as it was when the right was granted. This is not to say, however, that in all cases the purpose is restricted to the use that was made at the date of the grant. Indeed, it has been seen from *Alvis v Harrison* that where there are no words that restrict the purpose, the right is construed widely. The distinguishing factor is that the deed in which the right was granted specified the place to which the right of way was to lead. Once the woodhouse had been replaced by a cottage, the specific place contemplated by the grant no longer existed, so the right was no longer capable of being exercised. Of course, if the wording of the grant makes clear that the only purposes for which the grant may be exercised are those that existed at the date of the grant, then that may well limit the user accordingly.

3. Implied Grant

There may be occasions when it is necessary to imply a right of way where one has not been expressly granted, if the land cannot be enjoyed without it. A detailed exploration of such implied rights is beyond the scope of this work, but the basic principles are as follows.

One way in which rights can be implied is by the rule in *Wheeldon v Burrows* (1879) LR 12 ChD 31, which operates to ensure that, on the sale of part of a parcel of land, the purchaser acquires all easements necessary to the reasonable enjoyment of the property, a rule which is based on the proposition that a person may not derogate from his grant.

Also, under section 62 of the Law of Property Act 1925, a conveyance of land is deemed to include all ways and other easements appertaining to the land unless a contrary intention is expressed.

It is possible to exclude the effects of section 62 and of any right implied under the rule in *Wheeldon v Burrows*.

A "way of necessity" is implied on the sale of part of a parcel of land where no rights of way are reserved and where there is no other means of access to the land except over the servient tenement. In *Sweet v Sommer* [2005] EWCA Civ 227 the claimants owned Forge Meadow and their neighbours, the defendants, owned the Old Forge. Both parcels of land had previously been in common ownership, but when they were developed, the seller failed to reserve to himself rights of way in favour of Forge Meadow. Forge Meadow was later sold and the transfer included access with or without vehicles for all purposes across the Old Forge. The fact that the seller had no right to grant such access went unnoticed at the time, and the Land Registry registered the right of access on the title. The Old Forge and Forge Meadow were later sold to the claimants and defendants respectively, and it was subsequently discovered that the title to the Old Forge did not contain the right of way in favour of Forge Meadow. The Court of Appeal found that the earlier transfer created, by implied reservation, a vehicular right of way over the Old Forge because there was no other way of accessing the land, and ordered that the right be restored to the register.

4. Acquisition by Prescription

Rights of way are a form of easement that may be acquired by "prescription", that is to say, the use of a way over a sufficiently long period of time, without an express or implied right of way having been granted, matures into a legal right. At common law, title by prescription is derived from long user – "from time immemorial", that is, AD 1189. However, because of the development of the common law doctrine of lost modern grant and the advent of the Prescription Act of 1832, it is now rarely relied upon.

The doctrine of lost modern grant is a legal fiction, which presumes that at some time before the use of the easement commenced, an actual grant was made but was subsequently lost.

The Prescription Act provides that in the case of the use of a way, enjoyment for a period of twenty years gives a right of way. This can be challenged by evidence. Once the use has been enjoyed for a period of forty years, however, the right is "absolute and indefeasible". The exception to this is light, which requires only twenty years, rather than forty, to create a right that is beyond challenge (see Chapter 6).

The disadvantage of the Act is that it requires the periods of twenty and forty years to be calculated up to the date when the action is brought. This can be difficult if there has been a period of non-user. The doctrine of lost modern grant can found an easement on any continuous period of twenty years. It is therefore usual to plead the doctrine of lost modern grant as an alternative to the Prescription Act, and to include prescription at common law for good measure.

Under the Prescription Act, the easement claimed must be enjoyed as of right. In other words, it must be enjoyed openly, rather than furtively; continuously; without needing to apply force or committing an unlawful act; and with the knowledge of the servient owner but without his permission. It must also be enjoyed for the benefit of the dominant owner. It cannot be acquired by a tenant, although a tenant can, by exercising it, acquire it for the landlord: *Pugh v Savage* [1970] 2 QB 373, [1970] 2 WLR 643, [1970] 2 All ER 353 (CA).

The nature and extent of the right
When construing a right of way acquired by prescription, in contrast with the position when dealing with an express grant, the court has no words to interpret, and must therefore consider evidence of the user as well as the nature of the dominant tenement. Nevertheless, some of the principles derived from the cases on rights of way by grant can be applied to prescriptive rights of way. So, for example, if the evidence shows that the right has always been exercised on foot only, it may not be possible to obtain a prescriptive right of way for vehicles, particularly if a claimant could have used the way for the passage of vehicles but chose not to do so. In *Guise v Drew* (2001) 82 P&CR D 25 (Ch D), it was established that the defendant had acquired a prescriptive right of way that had been exercised primarily for residential purposes until 1980. Since then, the use had become predominantly commercial. The court found, following *Williams v James* (above) that the right of way could not extend to business purposes where that would place a greater burden on the servient tenement.

Prescriptive rights and common land
Common land is land over which "rights of common" (which include the right to pasture cattle and the like) may be exercised. Until recently, it was accepted that a right of way could be acquired by long user over any piece of land, whether privately owned or common land. However, in 1994, a decision of the Court of Appeal introduced an unwelcome change into the law. In *Hanning v Top Deck Travel Group Ltd* (1994) 68 P&CR 14, *The Times* 6 May 1993 (CA), the trustees of a common appealed against a decision that the defendant company had acquired a right by prescription to drive their buses along a track over Horsell Common to their maintenance depot. It was held that section 193(1) of the Law of Property Act 1925 precluded members of the public from acquiring any right to drive upon common land without lawful authority. The court found that, because the defendant

company had never been given lawful authority to drive over the land, a prescriptive right could not have arisen. This appeared to fly in the face of the Prescription Act, which legitimises the acquisition of rights of way by activities that have been carried out without the lawful authority of the owner of the land. The confusion arose out of the Court of Appeal's finding that if an activity was prohibited *by statute* without lawful authority, as opposed to simply being unauthorised by a landowner, that activity could not give rise to an easement.

The position went unchallenged for almost ten years until the case of *Bakewell Management Ltd v Brandwood* [2004] UKHL 14, [2004] 2 AC 519, [2004] 2 WLR 955, [2004] 2 All ER 305 (HL). Bakewell managed to acquire the freehold title of Newtown Common. Residents whose homes bordered the common obtained access to their houses across the common. Bakewell asserted that Newtown Common was land to which section 193 of the 1925 Act applied, and that the residents' use of the common was without lawful authority and therefore could not give rise to a prescriptive easement. Further, Bakewell sought to charge the residents who used the common to gain access to their homes for the privilege of doing so. At first instance the judge agreed with Bakewell and his decision was confirmed by the Court of Appeal, following *Hanning*. The House of Lords, however, found that *Hanning* and the decisions based on it were wrongly decided. It was always possible for landowners to give lawful authority (just as it would be even if an activity were not prohibited by statute) because the statute made it possible for them to do so. Accordingly, there was no difference between acquiring a prescriptive right where a landowner refused to authorise the use of a way *per se,* and where a landowner refused to authorise the use of a way that was prohibited by statute without lawful authority.

Statutory rights: the right to roam
As a result of *Hanning*, the Countryside and Rights of Way Act 2000 was brought into force. The Act defines "access land", to which the public has access, as including registered common land. This topic is beyond the scope of this book, although a brief summary of the law is to be found in Chapter 4.

5. Extinguishment

Unity of ownership and possession of the dominant and servient tenements extinguishes an easement: *Payne v Inwood* (1997) 74 P&CR 42 at 48 (CA).

An easement may be expressly released by deed. Otherwise there may be an implied release if it can be shown that the easement has been abandoned. However, the burden of proving abandonment is heavy, as the servient owner must show that the dominant owner has made it clear that he had a firm intention to abandon the easement and to bind his successors in title: *Gotobed v Pridmore* (1970) 115 SJ 78 (CA). Non-user on its own does not amount to abandonment, but it may be necessary for the dominant owner to give some indication of his intention to preserve the right during the period of abandonment: *Crossley v Lightowler* (1867) 2 Ch App 478. However, all that may be required is an explanation, and it may be that the use of the right was simply suspended for a period for the convenience of the owner of the servient tenement as a gesture of good neighbourliness. The court looks at the facts of each case to determine whether there has been any clear intention to abandon.

If any single principle can be derived from the cases, it is that the longer the period of non-user, and the more the dominant owner appears to acquiesce in an interruption or interference, the greater the explanation that will be called for to avoid extinguishment.

On the extinguishment of easements, see also page 91.

6. Interference

The cases referred to thus far have largely concerned the nature and extent of rights of way; whether or not there has been any unlawful user; and whether the dominant tenement is entitled to a particular mode of user or use for a particular purpose. The class of case that is most often encountered in private practice is, however, interference with or obstruction of a right of way, and frequently the cause of the problem is the parking of a vehicle or vehicles.

Establishing interference
The first point to establish is whether there has been wrongful interference. Wrongful interference with a right of way constitutes a nuisance, but not every obstruction amounts to an unlawful

interference. The test is whether the right of way can be substantially and practically exercised as it was before the obstruction.

So, in *B&Q PLC v Liverpool and Lancashire Properties Ltd* (2001) 81 P&CR 20, [2001] 1 EGLR 92, B&Q complained that the construction of a large extension by its landlord (the defendant) on the service yard would constitute an actionable interference with the right of way over the yard granted to B&Q by the lease to them. In deciding whether there would be an actionable interference, the court stated that the test was not whether what the grantee was left with was reasonable, but whether his insistence on being able to continue the use of the whole of what he contracted for was reasonable. The court found that vehicle-turning movements would be more difficult if the service area were reduced by the extension. It upheld B&Q's complaint that its right to pass over and turn within the yard would be materially less convenient, and granted an injunction in its favour. Interestingly, the court also found that an interference could still be actionable even when it was infrequent and relatively fleeting when it did occur.

Whether there has been substantial interference is a question of fact for the court to determine in each case. The evidence the court needs is usually oral evidence by the users of the right of way about their experience of the interference, supported by photographic and video evidence. A judicial site visit may be important if it is the only way in which a judge can form a view about, for example, turning circles. The court may be assisted by expert evidence, but a litigant should consider whether commissioning an expert is proportionate. In a case such as the B&Q action, it may very well be; in a dispute about parking on a residential driveway, it may not.

If an expert is likely to be of assistance, the relevant expertise (in considering an interference with a vehicular right of way) may be found in an accident investigation consultancy. Many of these employ former police officers with relevant experience. The Institute of Traffic Accident Investigators (www.itai.org; tel: 01332 292447) can provide details of experts, who may also be civil engineers, with experience of highways and transportation planning. An expert should be able to take measurements using a calibrated EDM (electronic distance measurement) theodolite, and then use a computer simulation program to predict the space needed to manoeuvre vehicles. The individual turning circles of the vehicles in use can then be taken into account in establishing whether a vehicle's passage along a road or driveway is impeded by the obstruction complained of.

A further consideration is the identity of the persons entitled to use the right of way. Again, this is a question of construction, but in the case of a right of way to a dwelling house the right extends to visitors, family members and contractors.

Shared driveways

A problem which can be particularly difficult to solve is where two neighbours (A and B in the examples below) share a driveway. The factual matrix can take a number of forms:

(i)   A owns the driveway but B has a right of way over it. B complains that A interferes with the right of way by continually obstructing it with his cars and those of his visitors.

(ii) A owns the driveway and B has a right of way over it. A complains that, in exercising his right of way, B impedes A's access to his own property over the driveway he owns.

(iii) Neither A nor B owns the driveway but each has a right of way over it. It may or may not be possible to trace the owner.

In addition to the general comments set out above, certain specific considerations apply to each of these three scenarios.

In (i), it is open to B, if A obstructs the way, to go around the obstruction if it cannot be easily removed. In doing so he is entitled to deviate over any part of A's property, but he must do so in a reasonable way and confine himself to A's property. He cannot trespass onto the property of another. However, this state of affairs should not be allowed to persist indefinitely as B may be found to have acquiesced in the change of route and therefore lose his entitlement to have the obstruction removed. If, however, the way is rendered impassable by the acts of someone other than A, then B is not entitled to deviate.

In situation (ii), if B exercises his right of way in such a way as to interfere with A's use of his land, the cause of action may be trespass as well as nuisance. If the right of way were expressly restricted to passage by foot, then the parking of a vehicle on the way would constitute a trespass. If the right of way is wide enough to encompass parking (either expressly or impliedly because it is necessary for the enjoyment of the right), then the court will have to balance B's right to use the way against the rights of A arising from his ownership of the way, and determine whether B's use is excessive. A's property is, of course, burdened by the easement and therefore A cannot expect to have exclusive use of the way. On the other hand, B can exercise his right of way only within the limit of the grant or the prescriptive right. A perusal of the cases considered earlier in this chapter should assist in determining the principles that the court applies when determining whether use is excessive.

Turning to situation (iii) – where neighbours share a private driveway to their properties, each having a right of way over that driveway, but neither of them owning it – if it is possible to trace the owner, the claimant who complains that his right is being infringed may be able to persuade the owner to take action in trespass against the offending neighbour. In practice, the owner is unlikely to be interested, content for the parties to resolve their differences between themselves. The court would then have to balance the competing rights of the parties, just as it would have to do if the owner cannot be traced, and considerations similar to those in situation (ii) would apply.

7. Remedies

Injunction and/or damages

A claimant who believes his right of way has been substantially interfered with may sue for an injunction to restrain the interference, or for damages. In many cases an injunction is appropriate, but only if the claimant actually suffers damage. In *Mayflower Estates Ltd v Highnorth Ltd and Others* [2001] All ER (D) 13 (Ch D), the claimant was refused an immediate injunction because there was little evidence of continuing interference with its rights at the time at which proceedings were issued.

In some cases an interim injunction is appropriate, for example where it is intended to build on the whole of the right of way; in others, a final injunction may be granted at trial but an interim injunction may not be necessary. In cases where there has been interference, but the claimant can negotiate around the obstruction (for example, where cars are left inconveniently parked), it may be preferable to await the outcome of the trial rather than seek an interim injunction (see page 48 for the risks attaching to an application for an interim injunction).

The court will have to decide, when considering what relief is appropriate, whether damages would be an adequate remedy. Damages are often not adequate; if the court finds that there has been substantial interference, the only way in which that interference can be prevented is to remove the cause of it. Damages may compensate the claimant for past nuisance, but do not prevent that nuisance from recurring.

Depending on the nature of the interference, the court may decide not to grant a final injunction, but instead make a declaration of the activities which will constitute an interference with the right of way in future; and may award damages for past transgressions. The claimant would then have to issue a fresh claim if the defendant carried out any of the prohibited activities, and might then be successful in obtaining an injunction.

In *Forestry Commissioners for England and Wales v Omega Pacific Ltd* [2000] All ER (D) 17, *The Times*, 13 January 2000, the only way the claimants could obtain access to land over which they had an express right of way was through a locked gate (to which they held no key) by prior arrangement and after disclosure of their names. The court granted a declaration that, on the proper construction of the grant, the right of way could not be limited in this way and that the defendant's actions constituted a substantial interference. The court did not, though, grant an injunction to prevent future obstruction because there was no evidence that the defendants either had, or would, refuse entry to the claimants. Applying this finding to a case concerning the obstruction of a vehicular right of way by a neighbour's parked cars, an injunction may not be granted if there is no evidence that the neighbour would not move his car if asked to do so.

If the nuisance is not continuing, damages may be awarded to compensate the claimant for the interference he has suffered, or the court may decide to award damages as well as an injunction. The measure of damages is the tortious measure, namely compensation for the loss which is the natural consequence of the interference. If the claimant is, by the act of the defendant, deprived entirely of his right of way (for example if it has been ploughed up by horses or heavy vehicles to such an extent that it is impassable), the measure of damages is the diminution in the value of the right as a result of the damage, rather than the true reinstatement cost (although they may in practice be the same). Thus, a hypothetical purchaser of the right may require a reduction in the purchase price to reflect the cost of having to reinstate it before it can be used. If the right of way has been obliterated entirely by the act of the defendant (for example because a building has been erected on it) then, in the absence of an injunction requiring the removal of the building, the measure of damages would be the loss in value resulting from the fact that the dominant tenement no longer has the benefit of a right of way.

The claimant may also be entitled to consequential damages for damage that is foreseeable, for example, if the result of an interference is that perishable goods cannot reach a warehouse or supermarket and perish, the claimant may be entitled to compensation for the value of the goods.

On the other hand, there may be cases where no actual quantifiable damage has been suffered, but the claimant has been inconvenienced by the obstruction. In such cases the amount of the damages recoverable must be reasonable.

If no damage is actually caused by the obstruction, then nominal damages only will be awarded.

Abatement

The grantee of a right of way is entitled to "abate" the nuisance, that is, remove whatever it is that is obstructing the right of way. This right is not, though, as wide as might first appear, and the modern approach is to discourage self-help. In *Burton v Winters* [1993] 1 WLR 1077, [1993] 3 All ER 847, it was held that self-redress for trespass by encroachment was restricted to simple cases that do not justify the expense of legal proceedings, and urgent cases requiring an immediate remedy.

8. Settlement

As with boundary disputes (see Chapter 2), unless there are important commercial interests that need to be protected, litigants should be looking to settle disputes over rights of way. This is particularly true in the case of neighbouring properties sharing a driveway. It can be constructive to agree, for example, that only certain areas of the driveway should be used for parking, or that parking may take place provided the driver is available and willing to move a vehicle if requested to do so. Too much detail is to be avoided, as the agreement may prove unworkable in practice if there are too many restrictions.

9. Checklists

Express grant

1. If there are no express restrictions as to mode of user, ascertain the user contemplated at the time of the grant and identify any physical restrictions that limit the mode of user.
2. If there are express but unclear restrictions as to purpose, consider whether the purpose sought is necessary to the enjoyment of the right.
3. If there has been an attempt to enlarge the right, consider whether:
   – this was by enlargement of the dominant tenement or excessive user;
   – the right being exercised is for the benefit of land other than the dominant tenement;
   – the way is being accessed from a different point or used to reach a different place from that which was contemplated by the grant;
   – the use is ancillary to the enjoyment of the dominant tenement.

Implied rights

1. The rule in *Wheeldon v Burrows* or section 62 of the Law of Property Act 1925 may apply.
2. Consider whether the way is necessary to the enjoyment of the land.

Prescriptive rights

1. Establish the period of user – twenty years or more, or forty years or more.
2. Establish when the period started to run and when it ceased running.
3. Establish whether the user has been restricted to a particular mode or purpose.
4. Establish whether the user been exercised "as of right".

Interference
1. Consider whether there been a substantial interference with the right of way, that is, whether the right can be substantially and practically exercised as it was before the obstruction.

Evidence
1. Obtain oral, photographic and video evidence.
2. Obtain expert evidence if relevant and if the cost is justified.

Remedies
1. Injunction and/or damages; consider whether damages will suffice.
2. Abatement is appropriate only in urgent cases or where the expense of legal proceedings is not justified.

For a specimen particulars of claim for the obstruction of a right of way and trespass over a boundary, see page 198.

Chapter 6

The Right to Light

1. Introduction

The expression "right to light" can be misleading. There is no general right at common law to have natural light fall on land or any premises. The "right to light" really means the acquisition of a specific right to have a certain amount of light to a specific window or aperture in a building. As a right to light is a species of easement, then, as with rights of way, it is necessary to establish that the right has been acquired as an easement. Such rights are acquired either by express or implied grant, or by reservation, or by presumed grant, most commonly by prescription. In other words, the same broad, general principles that apply to the acquisition of rights of way (see Chapter 5) also apply to the right to light.

Most disputes about light concern prescriptive rights rather than express rights, and arise in a variety of circumstances. The most common is where light through windows is blocked by a new development or extension on adjoining land, but increasingly, both in the residential and commercial sectors, there are challenges arising from high hedges and trees. Glasshouses belonging to commercial growers can be at risk from the erection of new buildings or trees growing unusually tall. (The problems caused by high hedges, and particularly *leylandii,* has led to the development of separate, special rules which are dealt with in Chapter 8.)

The easement of light that comes into existence through prescription is often referred to "ancient lights" where "lights" means "windows" rather than light itself.

Interference with a right to light founds an action in nuisance; see Chapter 7.

2. Acquisition by Prescription

The general principles by which an easement can be acquired by prescription are discussed in Chapter 5 on rights of way. In this chapter, the additional rules which apply only to rights of light, and the way in which the general rules apply to this easement, are discussed.

Section 3 of the Prescription Act 1832 applies only to rights to light. It requires twenty years' uninterrupted use before the property receiving the light acquires an absolute and indefeasible right to continue enjoying such light, even though there is no express written agreement. By contrast, section 2 of the 1832 Act, which applies to all other easements, provides that twenty years' enjoyment gives rise to an irreversible presumption only (which can be displaced by evidence), but that forty years' use is required for a right to be unchallengeable even where there is evidence that casts doubt on it.

It is important to appreciate that the twenty-year period does not, on its own, give rise to a right to light. For the right to crystallise, proceedings must be brought, and the period of user is calculated back from that point.

It is not necessary to show actual enjoyment of light to establish a prescriptive right, so it is immaterial whether or not the land is occupied throughout the whole of the twenty-year period. In *Courtauld v Legh* (1869) LR 4 Exch 126, a house under construction was structurally complete but it was neither finished internally nor fit for human habitation. Nevertheless, it was held that the owner was entitled to bring an action for obstruction of the windows because the windows had been put in and could be open and shut even though the house was not finished and there was no one living in it during the twenty-year period.

As well as the twenty-year rule, there are other important distinctions between a right to light acquired by virtue of section 3 of the 1832 Act and the acquisition of other easements, for example:

(a) to acquire a right to light, it is not necessary for the owner of the servient tenement at the commencement of the period to be the freehold owner;

(b) a right to light can be acquired by a leasehold owner as well as by a freehold owner;

(c) the use of the light does not need to be "as of right", as with other easements. All that is required is twenty years' use and enjoyment without written interruption and without written consent (*Colls v Home and Colonial Stores Limited* [1904] AC 179 at 205). Thus, the right can be acquired even if it has been enjoyed by force, or with occasional permission, or if the enjoyment has been deliberately concealed from the servient owner.

3. The Nature and Extent of the Right

The right to light has been referred to as a "negative" rather than a "positive" right; that is, it is a right not to have the passage of light obstructed. The cases are therefore concerned with the extent to which an owner of such a right is entitled to prevent his neighbour from building so as to obstruct light. An owner has been held to be:

> "entitled to sufficient light, according to the ordinary notions of mankind, for the comfortable use and enjoyment of that house as a dwelling-house, if it were a dwelling house, or for the beneficial use and occupation of the house, if it were a warehouse, a shop or other place of business." (*City of London Brewery v Tennant* (1873) LR 9 Ch App 212 at 216-217).

Thus, the courts are concerned, not with preserving the level of light, no matter how great, but with maintaining an appropriate minimum level of light. In *Colls v Home and Colonial Stores* (above), the respondents were the lessees of a building in which they carried on their business; the appellant proposed to build on the opposite side of the street. At first instance, the judge found that there would be no material interference with access to light. The Court of Appeal disagreed and granted an injunction against the respondents. The House of Lords posed the question, after the enjoyment of light for twenty years, would the dominant owner "be entitled to all the light without any diminution whatsoever?" Their Lordships found that the simple fact that the dominant owner is left with less light than he had before does not necessarily found an actionable obstruction: the question is, as posed in *City of London Brewery v Tennant,* not how much the available light had been diminished by the nuisance, but, rather, whether there was sufficient light left for the ordinary purposes to which property was put.

In *Price v Hilditch* [1930] 1 Ch 500, the light to a scullery was substantially diminished. The court considered whether the right to light was limited by the use to which the scullery had been put in the past and found that it was not. The issue was only whether the light left was:

> "what is required for the ordinary purposes of inhabitancy or business of the tenement according to the ordinary notions of mankind, and that the question for what purpose [the dominant owner] has thought fit to use that light, or the mode in which he finds it convenient to arrange the internal structure of his tenement, does not affect the question." (*per* Maugham J at 506-7).

Conversely, if an unusually high degree of light has been enjoyed for the requisite period and is required for the activities carried on in the building, then it is possible to acquire a right to unusually good light. In *Allen v Greenwood* [1980] Ch 119, [1979] 2 WLR 187, [1979] 1 All ER 819 (CA), a domestic greenhouse had been used for over twenty years. The defendant's obstruction left sufficient light for working in the greenhouse, but it was no longer possible to grow plants in it. The court found that the claimants were entitled to an extraordinary degree of light in this case, including the rays of the sun and not just the amount of light required for illumination, not because there was insufficient light left for "ordinary purposes" of a greenhouse, but because they had established twenty years' use of a higher than usual degree of light and the defendants had reasonable knowledge of it.

4. Evidence

Measuring diminution in the amount of light is a matter for expert evidence from a specialist rights of light surveyor. As with boundary surveyors, the best starting place is the Royal Institution of Chartered Surveyors. Some developers engage a rights of light surveyor before starting a development to negotiate with the owners of neighbouring properties on their behalf. In cases involving prescriptive rights, however, their usual function is to act as expert for one side or the other in a dispute, or as a single joint expert.

The following is a very brief summary of the work of a rights of light surveyor. The surveyor's task involves measuring the amount of light from an overcast sky from a given point in a room, sometimes referred to as the "table test", as it measures the amount of direct sky which will reach a hypothetical table at a convenient height for reading. This measurement is called the "sky factor percentage". The surveyor then plots this against what is recognised as the minimum amount of daylight required to undertake such tasks as reading and other close work. The result is a "Waldram graph" or "Waldram diagram" (named after the expert who devised it), which demonstrates the "before" and "after" conditions in the room. The loss is then assessed by the "50/50" working rule; that is, if 50 per cent of the room contains adequate light after the obstruction, there is no actionable loss.

A court would of course consider such expert evidence, but does not necessarily follow the "50-50" rule adopted by surveyors. In *Sheffield Masonic Hall Co Ltd v Sheffield Corp* [1932] 2 Ch 17 (in which Mr Waldram gave evidence as expert), the table test was described as capable of giving a "wholly false" view (*per* Maugham J at 25).

Some older cases contain references to an angle of 45 degrees of unobstructed light as the upper limit, so that there would be no nuisance if 45 degrees of sky were left after the obstruction. However in *Colls v Home & Colonial Stores*, it was stated that there was no such rule of law (*per* Lord Lindley at 210).

The court would also take into account evidence of lay witnesses, although it has been held that "their evidence is necessarily subjective, and the recollection of laymen of the amount of light formerly enjoyed is notoriously unreliable"; and that laymen are "incapable of distinguishing between direct and reflected light": *Carr-Saunders v Dick McNeil Associates* Ltd [1986] 1 WLR 922, [1986] 2 All ER 888 at 890 (Ch D). More recently, in *Midtown Ltd v City of London Real Property Company Ltd* [2005] EWHC 33 Ch, evidence given by employees working in an office building was derided by Mr Justice Peter Smith, who referred in his judgment to the witnesses having "stressed in vague and subjective ways the advantages of natural light" and stated that "What they were talking about was in reality the view and airiness, which are not factors that are relevant". Although the judge admonished a barrister in the case who had referred to one of the witness's evidence as "twaddle", he had some sympathy with that view.

The judge might very well benefit from a site visit to gain an impression of the light, which he can consider in conjunction with the other evidence. This can, though, be a double-edged sword, particularly if, from the defendant's point of view, he visits on a particularly dull day. Further, the judge has no means of comparison with the light before the obstruction, or after a development. For that reason, would-be claimants should be encouraged to take photographs or video recordings of the affected room during different sorts of weather conditions, and at different times of the day.

5. Light from Other Sources

If a room receives natural light from a number of different sources, for example a window and a skylight, the claimant may complain that the light through one source is obstructed even though the other light source remains clear. However, provided that the net light is unaltered, the owner of the servient tenement is entitled to build; see, for example, *Davis v Marrable* [1913] 2 Ch 421. The effect of artificial lighting is ignored, because artificial light can always be used to counteract an ill-lit room. If the law took artificial light into account, there would never be an infringement of the right to light: *Midtown Limited v City of London Real Property Company Limited* (above).

6. Express Grant

Although many disputes concerning light arise from a prescriptive claim, express rights can also give rise to litigation. The wording of the grant is crucial, and often confers a much wider right than could be acquired under section 3 of the 1832 Act. The redevelopment of the former GLC County Hall in London was the focus of such a dispute in the case of *Frogmore Developments Ltd v Shirayama Shokusan Co Ltd* [2000] 1 EGLR 121 (Ch D). The former County Hall building and certain other land known as "the East Land" was owned by the London Residuary Body, which in 1993, let the building, but not the East Land, to Shirayama. The lease expressly granted "the right to the free and unobstructed passage of light and air to the premises at all times". Two years later, the London Residuary Body transferred the East Land to Frogmore, but reserved out of that transfer "the right to the free and unobstructed passage of light and air to the premises at all times" for the benefit of retained land, the Riverside Building. Frogmore proposed to develop the East Land and to build a new building, which would substantially diminish the light into the Riverside Building. Frogmore argued, somewhat ingeniously, that when the lease was granted, it had been intended that another building would be erected on the East Land, although it never was. Therefore, Frogmore argued, the defendant should be entitled only to such light as would have survived had that other building been constructed. The court disagreed, finding that the factual possibility of there being another building could not displace the very clear wording of the grant in the lease. It did not mean that the East Land could not be developed, however, merely that Frogmore would have to revise its proposal so as not to infringe Shirayama's light.

7. Relationship with Planning Laws

As with boundaries and rights of way, the relationship between the public planning laws and the private law of nuisance and trespass often causes confusion and misunderstandings among property owners. The fact that planning permission has been granted for a particular structure does not necessarily mean that the erection of that structure will not infringe another's private legal rights. Equally, the fact that permission is not granted for a particular structure does not mean that the erection of such a structure in breach of planning controls would necessarily infringe those private rights.

On the question of light, the planners use a central report produced by the Building Research Establishment entitled *Site Layout Planning for Daylight and Sunlight: A guide to good practice.* This contains strict guidelines designed to preserve daylight to existing buildings, but it is only a factor to which the planners must have regard. Their view is neither decisive nor determinative of parties' rights to light. While decisions to refuse planning permission may be made on the grounds of loss of light, even in the absence of any express, implied or prescribed right, the existence of a right to light does not necessarily mean that planning permission will be refused. The planning process is concerned with the public interest rather than private interests, and while the two may coincide, they do not always do so.

This was most recently highlighted in *R v (1) The Mayor and Commonalty and the Citizens of London (2) Royal London Mutual Assurance Society, ex parte the Master Governors and Commonalty of the Mystery of the Barbers* LTL 28/5/96, [1996] EGCS 101, *The*

Times, 28 June 1996. This case concerned an application for judicial review of planning permission granted to the second respondents to redevelop a property adjacent to that of the applicant. The first respondents owned the freehold of the applicant's property, and by a deed of transfer dated 12 June 1969 covenanted "not to erect or suffer to be erected anything which shall cause any obstruction to the light or air passing through any of the windows" of the claimant's property. It was held that section 237(1) and (2) of the Town and Country Planning Act 1990 empowered a local authority which has acquired land for planning purposes, to authorise building on that land provided it is done in accordance with planning permission, even if it may have involved a breach of covenant.

8.   The Rights of Light Act 1959

Under Section 3 of the Prescription Act 1832, the use of light must be enjoyed for the full period of twenty years without interruption if the right to light is to accrue. Section 4 of that Act defines an interruption that will prevent a prescriptive right from arising as one that is "submitted to or acquiesced in for one year after the party interrupted shall have had or shall have notice thereof".

The traditional method of interrupting use of light was to erect a screen, but with the advent of tighter planning restrictions it was not always possible to obtain permission for such a screen. The 1959 Act provided the owners of servient land (who wanted to prevent rights arising) with a system of notification which modifies section 3 of the 1832 Act.

The 1959 Act enables the owner of land, against which a right to light might be acquired, to apply to the local authority to register a notice in the local land charges register. The Act creates a legal fiction in that, in place of an actual screen, the notice (which must be in the form prescribed by the Act) describes a hypothetical screen, together with its dimensions, which would otherwise be erected. Before the application can be made, a certificate must be obtained from the Lands Tribunal that:

    (a) notice has been given to everyone who appears likely to be affected by the registration of such a notice; or

    (b) the case is exceptionally urgent.

The certificate must be lodged with the application.

Once the application is made, the local authority then registers the notice as a local land charge, and it expires one year later, so as to defeat any claim to a right of light. In other words, for a period of one year it has the effect of obstructing light, just as would the erection of the screen described in the notice. In a case of exceptional urgency, a temporary notice is issued, for such period as is specified in the Lands Tribunal's certificate. It is then the responsibility of the applicant to ensure that all those likely to be affected are notified, and to obtain from the Lands Tribunal a further certificate confirming this, so that the temporary notice can be extended for the full year.

For the forms of application for registration of a light obstruction notice, and for a certificate under section 2 of the 1959 Act, see page 204.

Anyone who claims that the erection of a structure infringes his right to light is entitled to apply to the court under section 3(5) of the Rights of Light Act 1959 for declaratory relief and an order cancelling the registration. The case of *Hawker v Tomalin* (1969) 20 P&CR 550 (CA) sets out the form of declaration that the court has the discretion to make. In that case, the defendant came into possession of a vacant site on the Isle of Wight, on which there had been a building, but it was destroyed by a bomb in 1942. The claimant acquired a building close to the defendant's site. The claimant built a new structure on his property, with a window in the same position as an old window in the previous building. Just before the twenty-year period expired the defendant registered a Rights of Light Act notice which stated:

"Registration of this notice is intended to be equivalent to the obstruction of the access of light to the said building across my land which would be caused by the erection of an opaque structure on all the boundaries of my land . . ."

and went on to give the dimensions of the hypothetical structure. Following the registration of the notice, the claimant was deemed to acquiesce in the obstruction. He therefore issued proceedings claiming a declaration that the defendant was not entitled to obstruct the light as set out in the notice, and an order that the notice be varied to permit the obstruction of the access of light to be no greater than would have been caused by the building that had stood on the site before it was obliterated by the bomb. The judge found for the claimant and ordered the entire notice to be vacated. The defendant appealed, and sought a variation of the notice.

The Court of Appeal was inclined to dismiss the appeal altogether. There were various arguments about the dimensions of the old building, but the parties eventually agreed that any structure that coincided with the defendant's evidence as to the size of the old building would not interfere with the claimant's right to light. The appeal judges found that the variation the defendant sought would be of no use, since all he had to do would be to register a new notice. However, the claimant had no objection to the variation of the order. The court therefore considered the appropriate form of declaration. Russell LJ's view was that:

> "it would be preferable that a declaration in such a case should be in a form indicating that part of an opaque structure of the dimensions and in the position indicated by the registered notice would cause an illegal obstruction of the plaintiff's right to light to his building."

He went on to specify the form of order, making a declaration as to the dimensions of a structure that would cause an interference, and ordered that the notice be varied to specify a structure that would not obstruct the right to light.

The owner of dominant land that becomes subject to a 1959 Act notice during the final year of the twenty-year period may treat his enjoyment of the right as having begun one year earlier than it did (section 3(4) of the Act). Otherwise, the owner of the prospective dominant tenement can do nothing during the twenty-year period to prevent a properly registered notice from becoming an interruption that will defeat a claim to a right to light. He could, however, seek to challenge the issue of the certificate by the Lands Tribunal.

Such a challenge was considered in the case of *Bowring Services Ltd v Scottish Widows' Fund & Life Assurance Society* [1995] 1 EGLR 158, [1998] 16 EG 206 (Ch D). A temporary certificate was issued with a time limit of four months, followed by a final certificate within that four-month period. The claimant issued a claim for a right to light pursuant to, *inter alia*, section 3 of the 1832 Act. The claim was issued within twelve months of the final certificate but beyond twelve months after the registration of the temporary certificate. On the question of whether the claimant had acquiesced in an interruption of his enjoyment of the right created by the registration of an obstruction notice, the judge had to decide whether the time limit ran from the lodging of the temporary certificate or the final certificate.

The judge found that under section 3(2) of the 1959 Act, time ran from first registration, that is, the lodging of the temporary certificate.

The claimant also complained that the certificate should not have been issued on the grounds that there was no exceptional urgency and that adequate notice had not been given. The judge found that since neither the issue of the Lands Tribunal certificate nor the registration of the obstruction notice infringed private rights, the claimant should have brought his challenge by way of judicial review rather than by means of a private claim.

9. Extinguishment

As with all other easements, it is always open to the owner of the dominant tenement to relinquish his right expressly by deed, and developers may negotiate the release of rights accordingly. See pages 72–73.

Release may be implied if the owner of the dominant tenement expressly or impliedly authorises something to be done on the servient tenement that will prevent his future enjoyment of the right. In *Armstrong v Sheppard & Short Ltd* [1959] 2 QB 384, [1959] 3 WLR 84, [1959] 2 All ER 651 (CA), the claimant raised no objection to the construction of a sewer under a pathway or to the construction of a manhole. At the time, however, he did not know that the piece of the pathway concerned belonged to him. When he discovered that, and on the defendant's refusal to remove the sewer and manhole at his request, he issued a claim for damages for trespass and for an injunction to restrain the further discharge of effluent through the sewer. He was awarded nominal damages (because the defendant had, technically, committed a trespass) but was refused the injunction. This was upheld on appeal on the basis that the claimant had not acquiesced in the interference with his legal right because he had not known that he owned the strip of land when he gave his consent. He was refused the injunction, however, because the damage was trivial. The defendant also cross-appealed that the action should have been dismissed because the claimant had given his consent. The Court of Appeal found that the consent was a defence to the trespass action but that because, *inter alia*, it was a gratuitous promise, it was revocable.

Otherwise, non-user is not by itself sufficient to extinguish the right unless there is evidence of actual intention to abandon the right.

This is true of all easements, but with light, where actual user is not a prerequisite to the acquisition of the right in the first place (*Courtauld v Legh*, above), evidence of intention is crucial. Such evidence would comprise, for example, the blocking up of windows. In the leading case of *Moore v Rawson* (1824) 3 B & C 332, the claimant demolished a wall containing some ancient windows and then erected a wall with no windows. Fourteen years afterwards the defendant constructed a building in front of the wall. Three years after that the claimant made a window in his wall in the place where one of the old windows had been and brought an action against the defendant for obstructing his new windows. The court held that the claimant had abandoned his right.

Nevertheless, non-use for a long period after a period of use raises a presumption of intention to abandon, so it is advisable for a claimant to ensure there is some evidence of an intention to preserve the right in order to rebut this presumption (*News of the World Ltd v Allen Fairhead & Sons Ltd* [1931] 2 Ch 402).

It may be argued against a claimant that he has lost the right to light by altering the premises. The leading case is *Tapling v Jones* (1865) 11 HL Cas 290. The claimant had a three-storey building with one ancient window in each storey. He altered the windows in the two lower storeys so that they occupied only part of the former openings. The third storey window was left unaltered. He then built two further storeys, each with a new window. The defendant built a wall that obstructed all the windows, as it was not possible to build the wall in such a way as to block only the new windows without also blocking the ancient ones. After the building had been erected, the claimant restored the altered windows to their original state and blocked up the new windows, and brought an action claiming obstruction of his ancient lights. It was held that enlarging the ancient window and opening a new window in a different position were not unlawful acts and could not extinguish the ancient lights. The defendant was entitled to obstruct the addition to the ancient window, or the new window, but he could not obstruct the old window.

Accordingly, the enlargement of a window is not evidence of an intention to abandon a right to light through the original aperture; it is rather an indication of the wish to retain it and to acquire something more. Although enlarging the size of an ancient window does not extend the right, it does preserve the existing right, and since the owner of the servient tenement is most unlikely to be able to obstruct the light through the enlarged part of the window without also obstructing the ancient light, in practice this might be thought to amount to a right to obtain more light through an aperture than the ancient window permitted. A claimant would, though, have to prove that there would still have been an actionable interference if the window had not been enlarged. The relevant measurement would therefore be the amount of light that the old window would have received. In *News of the World v Allen Fairhead & Sons Limited* (above), the claimant's premises were pulled down. A new building was constructed on the same site with a number of windows overlooking the defendant's building. Unfortunately, no thought was given to preserving any evidence of the position of the ancient windows. The defendant then demolished its building and started to erect new, taller buildings on its site. The claimant was concerned that its light would be obstructed, and brought proceedings. The defendant argued that the claimant had abandoned its ancient lights. Fairwell J stated:

> "If the plaintiff pulls down the building with ancient light windows and erects a new building totally different in every respect but having windows to some extent in the same position as the old windows, he cannot require the servient owners to do more than see that the ancient lights, if any, to which he is still entitled are not obstructed to the point of nuisance. He cannot require them not to obstruct non-ancient light merely because a portion of the window through which that non-ancient light enters his premises, also admits a pencil of ancient light. If the obstruction of the pencil itself causes a nuisance the plaintiff is entitled to relief, but if taking the building as it stands, the pencil obstruction causes no nuisance at all, the plaintiff is not entitled to relief."

In this case, because there was no evidence as to where the ancient windows had been and how they coincided with the new ones, no nuisance was proved.

10. Remedies

If a right to light is established and has not been extinguished, and if an obstruction is found to be a nuisance, the court goes on to consider whether an injunction or damages would be an adequate remedy. This was most recently considered in *Midtown Limited v City of London Real Property Company Limited* [2005] EWHC 33 (Ch). The claimant asserted that a proposed development by the defendant would substantially interfere with its prescriptive right to light. The claimant was the freehold owner of the dominant tenement which was let to Kendall Freeman, a firm of solicitors. The court found that the claimants (who included Kendall Freeman) had established rights of light and that the proposed development would affect those rights. The court applied the 50-50 rule and found that after the development all the rooms in the dominant tenement would be inadequately lit on that test.

The court went on to consider whether, in view of that, the light left after the development would be sufficient for normal purposes according to the ordinary notions of mankind having regard to the purposes for which the building was designed and the nature of that design (the *Colls v Home & Colonial Stores* test). As noted above, the argument that this was an office building which was always lit artificially, so the reduction of natural light was irrelevant, was rejected on the basis that there could never be a successful challenge to an infringement of light if the availability of artificial light was an answer. Accordingly the court found that the claimants would suffer a nuisance if the development proceeded.

Both claimants, Midtown and Kendall Freeman, sought an injunction, with damages in lieu if an injunction were refused. The court refused to grant Midtown an injunction for four reasons:

(a) Midtown was interested in the property only from the point of view of making money. If the value of the property were diminished this could be quantified and Midtown could be compensated accordingly.

(b) Because the property was let to Kendall Freeman there was no present loss because the lease would be unaffected by the infringement of light.

(c) Midtown had redevelopment proposals of its own which would render an injunction academic in any event.

(d) The defendant behaved reasonably and openly by drawing attention to the issue and suggesting meetings, only to be rebuffed by Midtown and Kendall, which the court found to be unreasonable.

Kendall Freeman was also refused an injunction partly as a matter of discretion, because they were also criticised for failing to respond to the defendant's open approach. Further, they had no capital interest that would be diminished in value and the proposed development would not affect their existing use of the property or any use to which they would put the property in view of the proposed development.

The court gave some consideration to the evidence of Kendall Freeman's partners and employees, but this was given fairly short shrift in line with the approach taken in *Carr-Saunders v Dick McNeil Associates Ltd* (above).

If damages are likely to be awarded, the question of quantifying them arises. In *Carr-Saunders v Dick McNeil Associates Ltd*, the court calculated the damages by reference to the defendant's bargaining position and how much the defendant ought to have paid to secure the claimant's consent to the obstruction. This is a matter for the discretion of the judge, taking account of all the evidence. A right to light surveyor can give precise calculations in respect of the loss of rental value, but such precision is likely to be of benefit only in commercial cases rather than cases concerning domestic premises where the prime consideration is usually the loss of amenity rather than the effect on the commercial letting value.

11. Checklists
Establishing the right
1. Identify any express grant or reservation in a lease or transfer, or restrictive covenant.
2. If there is none, establish whether there has been twenty years' use.
3. Ascertain the duration of any interruption(s).
4. Look for any evidence that the right has been extinguished.
5. Enquire whether an obstruction notice has been registered; if so, when.

Establishing an obstruction
1. The question is always the amount of light remaining, not the amount which has been taken away.
2. Consider whether the remaining light is sufficient for the ordinary purposes for which the building is used.

3. Obtain expert evidence from a right of light surveyor.
4. Obtain lay evidence and ensure the witnesses can give objective evidence of the amount of light required for the particular tasks they carry out in the property.

Injunction or damages
1. Identify any failure to engage in discussions with the developer/ neighbour.
2. Consider whether the effect complained of is a loss in capital value rather than the inability to use the building for the purposes for which it was designed.

Chapter 7

Nuisance

1. Introduction

Nuisance occurs where a landowner uses his land in a way which causes an unreasonable interference with the land of another – usually (but not essentially) an adjoining owner. The importance of the law of nuisance in regulating the conduct of neighbours is immediately apparent. A person whose neighbour makes life unbearable by constant noise, or by repeated bonfires, or by carrying out some noxious activity on his property may, if he achieves nothing by trying to reason with the neighbour, succeed in putting a stop to the unreasonable conduct by suing in the tort of nuisance and seeking an injunction within the proceedings. A nuisance may be a "public" or "private" nuisance. The former affects the public at large, as, for example, where there is interference with the use of a highway. This book, however, is concerned only with private nuisance, which occurs where only certain owners of land close to the problem are affected.

The right of action in nuisance is closely allied to other causes of action such as trespass, negligence and the so-called rule in *Rylands v Fletcher* (1868) LR 3 HL 330, which concerns a particular form of nuisance (see Chapter 9). The rule in *Rylands v Fletcher* may be invoked to formulate a cause of action where a person, for his own purposes, brings onto his land and keeps there anything likely to cause damage if it escapes. If it does escape, the owner is liable for all damage naturally flowing therefrom. It is quite likely, however, that the same conduct would equally give rise to an action in nuisance, although the reverse is not as often true. Where the defendant's negligence causes damage to his neighbour's property, it probably matters not whether the case is pleaded in negligence or nuisance.

Where the nuisance does not cause any actual physical damage, but affects a neighbour's enjoyment of his land, it is an actionable nuisance only if, when judged by the standards of the average person, it can be said to be a real interference with the comfort and convenience of living or using the land. The law does not come to the aid of someone who is abnormally sensitive to the conduct complained of. Further, the character of the neighbourhood is taken into account when a court considers whether or not there has been a real interference with the amenities of life for the ordinary person in that locality. Thus, certain activities which are carried out in premises in an industrial area are likely to be more acceptable than in a rural situation and, sometimes, *vice versa*.

Of course, there are circumstances in which the generation of noise, dust or fumes, for example, for a short period of time is necessary; and the length of time involved is a relevant factor for a court when deciding whether or not there has been an actionable nuisance. If, for example, a person needs to have noisy work done on his house, this may well not give rise to an actionable nuisance. Sometimes buildings need to be demolished or substantially renovated, entailing the use of sledgehammers and other heavy equipment. Provided that the owner of the building takes all reasonable steps to ensure that any inconvenience to the neighbourhood is kept to a minimum, and adopts the "best practices" available to the building industry to prevent harm, then he is not likely to be liable: *Andreae v Selfridge & Co* [1938] 1 Ch 1, [1937] 3 All ER 255. For example, noise should probably be restricted to the normal working day, avoiding Sundays. It is possible that planning permission to carry out work may be subject to conditions restricting the times during which work can be carried out so as to protect the interests of neighbouring residents.

By contrast, if the perpetrator of the act complained of is pursuing a course of conduct intentionally to annoy a neighbour, this would be one of the factors that the court would take into account when deciding whether or not there has been real interference with the neighbour's enjoyment of his land. An act which would not otherwise constitute an actionable nuisance may become nuisance by reason of this malicious intent (*Christie v Davey* [1893] 1 Ch 316). It may also cause the court to grant increased damages by reason of the aggravation by malice, or even to make an example of the wrongdoer.

In nuisances that cause damage to land, as opposed to interfering with the use and enjoyment of land, it is necessary to prove actual physical damage to establish the cause of action. Anticipated damage is insufficient, but if actual damage is imminent, an injunction may be obtained to prevent the damage from occurring. Where the nuisance consists of encroachment, such as overhanging tree branches, no actual damage is necessary. In such cases damage will be presumed by the law. In nuisance which affects the enjoyment of land, such as noise or smell, no actual damage to health need be proved. In such cases, damages are awarded to compensate for the discomfort which has been inflicted on the claimant.

2. The Claimant

A person who is in occupation of the land affected may sue in nuisance only if he has some proprietary interest in the land. Thus, for example, mere residents of properties who were not freehold or leasehold owners or tenants were not able to sue the owners of Canary Wharf for damages for nuisance arising out of the construction work being carried out in London's docklands (*Hunter v Canary Wharf Ltd* [1997] AC 655, [1997] 2 WLR 684, [1997] 2 All ER 426 (HL)). In *Pemberton v Southwark LBC* [2000] 1 WLR 1672, [2000] 3 All ER 924 (CA) it was held that a mere "tolerated trespasser" – in that case someone against whom a possession order had been made but suspended on condition that she paid rent arrears at a stated rate – did not have the necessary standing to sue in nuisance for damages for a cockroach infestation. It has been suggested, however, that the requirement for the claimant to have a proprietary interest in the affected land may not survive the Human Rights Act 1998; see *McKenna v British Aluminium Limited* [2002] Env LR 72, *The Times*, 25 April 2002 (Ch D), where Neuberger J nevertheless refused an application for summary judgment by claimants who had no proprietary interest.

If, however, the householder does have a right to sue, it does not matter that the nuisance began before he acquired his property provided, of course, that the nuisance is continuing (*GUS Property Management Ltd v Littlewoods Mail Order, The Times,* 21 June 1982 (HL)).

3. The Defendant

A person who creates a nuisance remains liable even after he has parted with possession of the premises upon which that nuisance was created. The person who acquires the land from the creator of the nuisance is also liable, as has been seen above, if he continues the nuisance. A person may be vicariously liable for the actions of his servants or agents. He is also, unusually, liable for the actions of an independent contractor, provided that it was reasonably foreseeable that the work the independent contractor was engaged to do was likely to cause a nuisance.

If a nuisance exists in premises which the owner subsequently lets, the owner remains liable even where, for example, the lease contains a covenant by the lessee to repair, providing that the owner knows or ought to have known of the nuisance at the date of the letting: *Bowen v Anderson* [1894] 1 QB 164. Where, however, the landlord retains a certain amount of control over the let premises, he may be liable in nuisance even though he is not aware of the nuisance at the date of the letting: *Smith v Scott* [1973] Ch 314, [1972] 3 All ER 645.

Where the landlord retains the obligation to repair, he is liable in nuisance resulting from the fact that the premises are in a state of disrepair, whether or not he was aware of the disrepair at the date of the letting; and he is under a duty to abate the nuisance as soon as he becomes aware of it. If he then fails to act to remedy the defect within a reasonable time, he is liable in nuisance for damage caused as a result of the disrepair, provided that this does not require him to improve the premises: *Southwark London Borough Council v Mills, sub nom Southwark LBC v Tanner; Baxter v Camden LBC (No. 2)* [2001] 1 AC 1, [1999] 3 WLR 939, [1994] 4 All ER 449 (HL).

A landlord is also liable for the acts of nuisance of his tenant if he lets the premises for a use that is inherently likely to cause a nuisance. In other words, the landlord in such circumstances is said to have authorised the nuisance. On the other hand, the creation of a nuisance by a tenant does not make the landlord liable if the tenant simply chooses to use the premises in such a way as to create a nuisance and the premises have not been let specifically for a particular use likely to cause an unreasonable disturbance to neighbours.

Furthermore, a landlord is not liable in nuisance to neighbours of his tenant where the tenant does nothing more than lead an ordinary existence. In the cases of *Southwark London Borough Council v Mills, Southwark LBC v Tanner* and *Baxter v Camden LBC (No. 2)* (above), the House of Lords held that the council landlord was not liable for noise nuisance in a situation where the tenants of flats in a particular block suffered intolerable noise nuisance from their neighbours, because the neighbours creating the noise were doing nothing more than going about their ordinary lives. The flats, although complying with the building regulations in force when they were built, transmitted the noise of every common domestic activity from one flat to another. The tenants would not have been liable to each other in nuisance because there had been no unusual or unreasonable use of their flats by them. The House of Lords held that the landlords were likewise not liable in nuisance.

4. Noise

Noise is probably the most common and least tolerable of the nuisances that neighbours can inflict upon each other. A study by MORI (Market and Opinion Research International) for the Department for the Environment, Food and Rural Affairs in 2003 found that one in three people in Britain says that noisy neighbours are a problem. One in seven people in densely populated urban areas claims that noisy neighbours affect quality of life; although forty per cent of these people have complained to their neighbours, the council or the police, the rest suffer in silence. Loud music, shouting and banging are the most common complaints. Allowing the constant barking of dogs without any attempt to control them may amount to a nuisance. Perhaps slightly more bizarre complaints have involved the crowing of cockerels in the countryside or the peeling of church bells on Sunday mornings.

Taking proceedings against the neighbour, seeking an injunction and perhaps damages in nuisance, is a draconian step. First, it can be expensive; secondly, there is always the risk that legal action may result in an escalation of the problem, given that the neighbours must continue to live in close proximity to each other. There is then the problem of establishing the evidence on which to base an action. The noise nuisance may not be regular, so that it is difficult to arrange for a recording of the noise level to be made. Specialist equipment may be required to monitor the decibel level. It is submitted that all these difficulties mean that court proceedings should be a last resort after all else has failed, and then only where the noise nuisance is intolerable.

Under the Environmental Protection Act 1990, local authority environmental health departments must take all reasonable steps to investigate complaints of noise nuisance. They use specialised equipment for measuring noise emissions in decibels. If noise nuisance is established, the local authority can issue a notice requiring the neighbour to stop causing the nuisance. If the neighbour fails, without reasonable excuse, to comply with the notice, he can be prosecuted and the local authority can confiscate the noise-making equipment.

Sometimes, however, notwithstanding the costs or the difficulties involved, civil proceedings are the only way forward, and the sums at stake may justify the claim. In *Dennis v Ministry of Defence* [2003] EWHC 793, [2003] Env LR 34, [2003] EHLR 17 (QBD), the claimants owned a Grade 1 listed mansion and an estate of 1,387 acres, situated two miles from an RAF base at Wittering. RAF Wittering is an operational and training base, where Harrier jump jets had been in use since 1969. Since 1989 the claimants had suffered noise and interference from aircraft flying "training circuits" overhead, such that conversation was temporarily impossible and children had been reduced to tears of fright. The claimants asserted that the value of the estate had been reduced by £7.1 million as a consequence; and that they had lost a further £2.3 million in revenue which they would have earned from shooting parties, conferences and film shoots which, because of the noise, they were unable to hold at the property.

The MOD's defence to the claim was on the following basis:

(a) the use of the land in the defence of the realm was a common and ordinary use and that the use of Harriers was reasonable;

(b) as this was a case involving detriment to the enjoyment of land, a balance had to be struck between the conflicting interests; and

(c) having referred to the public interest in defence of the realm, and as the RAF station was an established feature of the locality, no nuisance should be held to exist.

Buckley J found that the Harrier noise was a "very serious interference with the ordinary enjoyment of the property and it was a noise that no one should be forced to endure in any location". He held that the public interest in the RAF's being able to continue its training programme at RAF Wittering outweighed the individual private interests of the claimants, but that common fairness demanded that they be compensated for it. He took the view that the public interest element of the case should be considered at the stage of whether or not to grant the discretionary remedy, rather than at the initial stage of considering whether or not a nuisance existed at all. If it were considered at the initial stage, an injustice could be the result as selected individuals would suffer damage for the benefit of all without being able to obtain any compensation. He therefore refused an injunction to stop the Harriers from flying at the base, but the RAF could continue with its activities there only if the claimants were properly compensated.

As for the quantification of the damage, the claimants put forward a claim totalling £10 million, taking the past six years' losses, assessed at the rental value plus a figure for the diminution in capital value. The judge disagreed. The damages were banded into three parts:

(a) the loss of capital value;
(b) the past and future loss of amenity; and
(c) the past and future loss of use.

The judge found that the claimants had no intention of selling or letting the property, and, as the Harriers would be gone by 2012, the capital loss was not likely to be permanent. He assessed this at £300,000. Past and future loss of use was assessed at £600,000 and £50,000 was assessed for loss of amenity.

In the *Dennis* case, the claimants argued that there had been a breach of their human rights, specifically article 8 of, and article 1 of the First Protocol to, the European Convention on Human Rights. Article 8(1) states that everyone has the right to respect for his private and family life, his home and correspondence. Article 1 of the First Protocol provides that everyone is entitled to the peaceful enjoyment of their possessions. Although no separate damages in respect of human rights were awarded, the human rights jurisprudence was influential in the decision, particularly the decision to compensate the claimants even though the court found that the public interest outweighed that of the individual. It must be pointed out, however, that the judge in this case based his judgment in part on the decision in *Marcic v Thames Water Utilities* (see Chapter 9) which was subsequently overruled in the Court of Appeal.

5. Smoke

Smoke may constitute a nuisance at law when it emanates from neighbouring factories, from the burning of stubble by farmers, or the burning of bonfires by neighbours in their gardens. This sort of activity is largely controlled by statute.

It is a criminal offence to burn straw or stubble within fifty metres of buildings, and the burning of straw and stubble elsewhere is subject to time limits. This is provided by regulations made under the Environmental Protection Act 1990. The Clean Air Act 1993 has had a major beneficial effect in reducing smoke from factories.

It is now more likely for a houseowner to be affected by bonfires lit by a neighbour in his garden. Whether or not this constitutes a legal nuisance depends on the frequency of the bonfires; the length of time they are allowed to burn; the sort of material that is burnt; the time of day and the day of the week. What is and is not likely to be adjudged a nuisance by a court depends on all the circumstances. If a judge considers that the conduct complained of is sufficiently serious to amount to an unreasonable interference with enjoyment of the houseowner's land, then a nuisance is established. It is fair to say that successful cases, where the bonfire is essentially domestic, not commercial, are rare indeed. A potential claimant would need to have kept a diary of the times when bonfires were lit and the length of time that they were left to burn. Photographic or video evidence would also be likely to be useful.

6. Fumes and Smells

The emission of fumes and smells may constitute a nuisance if sufficiently strong, and either constant or of frequent occurrence. The problem with fumes or smells is that they cannot be seen and are difficult to record. It may be possible for an affected houseowner to enlist the assistance of the local authority's environmental protection department.

7. Defences

Act of trespasser
An owner or occupier of land is not liable for interference in his

neighbour's enjoyment of his land if that interference was caused by the acts of a trespasser committed without the owner's knowledge and consent, and where the owner has had insufficient time to "obviate [the] mischievous effects" of the nuisance (Lord Wright in *Sedleigh-Denfield v O'Callaghan* [1940] AC 880, [1940] 3 All ER 349).

This is the case even where it is known that a particular property is prone to illegal entry by trespassers who then carry out acts of vandalism, unless, perhaps, a claimant can show that the defendant had, but did not implement, effective means of control. A court will be slow to attribute liability in such circumstances. In *Maloco v Littlewoods Organisation Limited; Smith v Littlewoods Organisation Limited* [1987] AC 241, [1987] 2 WLR 480, [1987] 1 All ER 710, the House of Lords held that there was no duty of care on the owners of a cinema which was closed to the public and not in use, where vandals had entered the premises and lit a fire which spread to the claimant's property. The court indicated, however, that the result would have been different if the vandals had struck so many times before that the landowner should have been on notice that there was a problem with unauthorised access to the building.

Ignorance
As noted in Chapter 8, in the context of liability for damage caused by overhanging branches or encroaching tree roots, a landowner is not liable in nuisance if he is unaware of the nuisance and has not been given an opportunity to abate it. In *Ilford Urban District Council v Beal and Judd* [1925] 1 KB 671, the defendant built a wall on her own land but, unbeknown to her, over the route of a sewer which was eight to ten feet below the ground. The wall caused the sewer to crack. It was held that the defendant was not liable as she did not know, nor could she reasonably have been expected to know, that the sewer was there.

Contributory negligence
Contributory negligence may be a defence to an action in nuisance, but not where the defendant intended the consequences which actually occurred.

Prescription
It may be possible for a right to commit a nuisance to be acquired over

a period of time by prescription, but only where the right is capable of being an easement. A common example is where rainwater is allowed to run from the eaves of a property onto a neighbour's land.

There are limitations to the usefulness of the concept of prescription with regard to nuisance. The most important is that a right cannot be acquired by prescription against the world generally, and so the discharge of smoke from a factory or the emission into the atmosphere of fumes or smells cannot be established as a right by prescription. It has also been held that a houseowner cannot, by prescription, acquire the right to allow his trees to overhang his neighbour's boundary or for its roots to invade another's land. See *Morgan v Khyatt* [1964] 1 WLR 475. Further, it must be possible to measure and determine the extent of the user with some certainty for the right to be established. Where there is a constant change in the amount of inconvenience caused, it is difficult to see how this would ever result in the acquisition of a right. This would apply to noise, smoke, smells or vibration.

While a claimant may be prevented from recovering damages if he has acquiesced in the nuisance, this would not be binding on a successor in title.

See also Chapters 5 and 6 on prescription.

Statutory authority
Certain activities which would otherwise constitute a nuisance are specifically authorised by statute, and thus the relevant statute provides a defence to a claim.

In the case of *Allen v Gulf Oil Refining Ltd* [1981] AC 101, [1981] 2 WLR 188, [1981] 1 All ER 353 (HL), a private Act of Parliament authorised the defendant to acquire land for the construction of an oil refinery. Although the Act did not give any express power for the operation, as opposed to the construction, of the refinery, the House of Lords held that by implication the Act authorised this. As the defendants had statutory authority to operate the refinery, they could not be sued in nuisance for harm suffered by neighbouring properties, provided that the defendants could show that it was inevitable that, despite exercising every known precaution, the neighbouring properties would suffer the harm complained of.

In the Court of Appeal ([1980] QB 156 at page 168), Lord Denning had held that "in principle property should not be damaged compulsorily except on proper compensation being made for the damage done". This is echoed in Buckley J's approach to the public interest defence in *Dennis v Ministry of Defence*, above. In the House of Lords, in *Allen v Gulf Oil*, however, their Lordships in effect disagreed with Lord Denning. They said that Parliament had manifested an intention to take away the rights of the neighbours without providing compensation.

Perhaps the most controversial example of statutory authority for an activity which inevitably creates a nuisance concerns the operation of civil airports. It would be tempting for those opposed to the further expansion of civil airports to invoke the Human Rights Act 1998 as a basis for seeking compensation for those who would be adversely affected by the additional noise which would be generated. To succeed, however, *Allen v Gulf Oil* would have to be overruled, as would the more recent case of *Wildtree Hotels Ltd v Harrow LBC* [2001] 2 AC 1, [2000] 3 WLR 165, [2000] 3 All ER 289 (HL), where the principles set out in the *Allen* case were re-asserted.

Non-defences
Certain specific matters do not constitute a defence to a claim in nuisance. First, as Buckley J stated in *Dennis v Ministry of Defence* (above), public interest "is not in itself a defence, but a factor in assessing reasonableness of user". In that case, the public interest was served in maintaining the training flights, but the individual affected by the noise was compensated in damages.

Secondly, a defendant cannot escape liability for nuisance simply because the offending activity is being carried on in a fit or suitable location. As has already been observed, activities which might be considered acceptable in an industrial location may not be acceptable in a rural setting, but it does not necessarily follow that an activity can be carried on, even in an appropriate location, so as to cause injury or destruction to neighbouring property: *St Helen's Smelting Company v Tipping* (1865) 11 HL Cas 642.

Thirdly, it matters not that an activity which is in fact a nuisance is being carried on with all due care and skill in order to try to prevent neighbouring property being damaged (*Vanderpant v Mayfair Hotel Company* [1930] 1 Ch 138). As has been seen, however, in cases of nuisance caused by building works but not resulting in physical damage, carrying out the works in accordance with "best industry practice" is a defence: *Andreae v Selfridge & Co*, above.

Finally, it is no defence for a defendant to argue that the claimant became affected by the nuisance created by him only because he acquired his property after the nuisance had been established (*St Helen's Smelting Company v Tipping*, above). This must be considered, however, in the light of the proposition that, where an activity affects the comfort and enjoyment of land as opposed to causing physical damage, then the character of the locality is to be taken into account when assessing whether the activity can be said to interfere with comfort and convenience when judged by the standards of the average person. The denial of a defence that the claimant came to the nuisance may seem harsh. Why should an activity which has been carried on without complaint for a number of years be prevented because someone, quite possibly in full knowledge of the existence of that activity, chooses, say, to build a house so that it is affected by the activity? It may be argued that the complainant has himself to blame for being affected in those circumstances; he did not have to buy or build a house in that location. The law is, nevertheless, established, and a defendant may be driven to try to rely on a defence that the activity in question is not an unreasonable use of the land in that locality.

8. Remedies

Injunction

The main aim of a client who is suffering a nuisance caused by his neighbour is to bring the nuisance to an end. This means applying for an injunction and, if the nuisance is sufficiently serious, an interim injunction. The client would have to give an undertaking in damages, which is examined in greater depth in Chapter 4. An interim injunction would not be granted unless:

(a) the balance of convenience justifies it; and

(b) damages would not be an adequate remedy.

As has been seen from *Dennis v Ministry of Defence* (above), an injunction will not be granted if the court considers that it would be against the public interest to prevent the activity in question.

Damages

The general measure of damages for nuisance is the usual tortious measure, namely whatever loss is suffered by the claimant which flows naturally from the defendant's conduct. Damage is too remote if not foreseeable in respect of nuisance which requires negligence to establish liability. Where an injunction is sought, but refused, the court may choose to use another measure in damages "in lieu" of an injunction. This is considered further in Chapter 4.

Where nuisance causes damage to property, the measure of damages is the diminution in value of the property brought about by the nuisance, rather than the cost of rectifying the damage *(Moss v Christchurch Rural District Council* [1925] 2 KB 750).

It is a difficult task for a court to value the loss of enjoyment of property because this is not susceptible to valuation by expert evidence or by some mathematical or objective formula. The court in *Hunter v Canary Wharf Limited* (above, page 99) disapproved the use of the published guidelines used in personal injury cases. Predicting likely damages for loss of enjoyment of property is therefore elusive, making it difficult for a solicitor to calculate a cost-benefit analysis of instituting proceedings.

In *Milka v Chetwynd Animal By-Products LTL,* 7/8/2000, Carmarthen County Court, His Honour Judge Diehl QC awarded £3,000 for loss of amenity. This case concerned emissions of odours from the defendant's knackers' yard which interfered with the claimants' enjoyment of their adjoining caravan park business.

£10,000 was awarded by Mr Recorder C Morris-Cole in Haywards Heath County Court on 10 June 2002 in the case of *Fowler v Ellen Mary Jones* LTL 27/6/2002. This case involved allegations by the claimants that the defendant had caused smell, smoke and the unchecked barking of dogs to affect the enjoyment of their neighbouring property.

In *Dennis v Ministry of Defence* (above, page 102), Buckley J awarded global damages of £950,000 to reflect the loss of capital value to the claimant's property, the loss of amenity and loss of use. The judge took an "overview" and rejected an arithmetical calculation of damages, so we do not know how much he attributed to loss of amenity in this case.

For a specimen form of particulars of claim alleging nuisance, see page 205.

9. Checklist

1. Establish whether the client has a proprietary interest in the land affected.
2. If the neighbour's activity is not causing actual damage to the client's property but is affecting enjoyment, assess whether there has been real interference with the amenities of life as judged by the ordinary person in that locality.
3. Ascertain whether a nuisance which was merely temporary has been rectified.
4. Establish whether the neighbour's activity was intentional.
5. Ascertain whether the damage to the client's property was foreseeable by the neighbour.
6. Bring the nuisance to the neighbour's attention if that has not already been done, and ask him to abate the nuisance.
7. Establish what evidence is available. Diary entries, photographs, and noise readings or recordings may be needed.
8. Consider whether an interim injunction is necessary.
9. Consider whether the defendant is likely to have a defence.
10. Expert evidence as to diminution in value to the client's property as a result of the nuisance may be necessary.

Chapter 8

Trees and Hedges, Weeds and Pests

1. Introduction

There are probably no disputes which cause more hostility between neighbours than those concerning trees and hedges. Newspaper reports abound of litigation being pursued for years at enormous expense over the height of a neighbour's tree or *leylandii* hedge. It is not unknown for murders and suicides to be committed as a result of long-running battles. There is even a national lobby and support group called "Hedgeline" established for the victims of so-called "hedge bullying". Serious problems caused by the spread of weeds from neighbouring land or infestation by pests emanating from land belonging to others are less common, but they do occur and a landowner may need to know what he can do to remedy the situation.

In this chapter, the most common problems with trees, hedges, weeds and pests are identified, and the remedies available to neighbours who are affected are set out.

2. Trees and Hedges

Trees and hedges are, of course, highly beneficial if they are in the right place, properly maintained and kept in check. Unfortunately, they are sometimes planted in the wrong place, or neglected, such that their roots or branches cause damage to nearby property. Notoriously, a *leylandii* hedge left to grow unchecked can reach a height of up to thirty metres, overpowering a neighbour's garden, shutting out sunlight and spoiling the amenity.

Ownership

In dealing with a problem concerning a tree or hedge, it may be pertinent first to consider the rules governing ownership of the tree or hedge in question. If it is obviously on land within the client's ownership, he is likely to be free to do with it as he wishes, subject to certain restraints which are set out below. Where a tree or hedge is on or near a boundary between two properties, the position is less obvious and certain rules have built up over the years. Thus, a tree or hedge usually belongs to the owner of the land on which it was originally planted (*Masters v Pollie* (1620) 2 Roll Rep 141). Where, over time, a tree has grown and its roots and trunk have extended over the boundary into a neighbour's land, the tree is regarded as belonging to the owner of the land in which it was planted; see *Elliott v Islington London Borough Council* [1991] 10 EG 145, *The Times* 6 July 1990 (CA).

In respect of hedges, see also the "hedge and ditch presumption", and boundaries generally, in Chapter 2.

Tree preservation orders

The owner of a tree who wishes to reduce it in size, or otherwise carry out work to it, whether in response to a problem it has caused to a neighbour or otherwise, would be wise to make sure he has any necessary prior permission. In respect of a mature tree, the owner should ask the local authority, if he does not already know, whether a tree preservation order affects the tree.

In conservation areas, the owner must give the local planning authority six weeks' notice before cutting down or carrying out any work on any tree. This gives the authority time to consider whether or not to impose a tree preservation order. Notice need not, however, be given if the tree has a diameter of less than 7.5 cm, or 10 cm if it is to be felled as part of thinning operations.

The Town and Country Planning Act 1990 and the Town and Country Planning (Trees) Regulations 1999 (SI 1999 No. 1892) set out the requirements to be met before carrying out work to a tree subject to a tree preservation order, and the various exemptions from the need for consent. The sort of work prohibited by a tree preservation order is cutting down, uprooting, topping, lopping or wilfully damaging or destroying the tree without the local planning authority's consent. If work is carried out in contravention of a tree preservation order, the local authority may prosecute the landowner in the magistrates' court and a substantial fine (presently up to £20,000) may be imposed if a person cuts down, uproots or wilfully damages or destroys a tree in such a manner as to be likely to destroy it. Topping and lopping a tree can constitute such damage. In fixing the amount of a fine, the court takes into account any financial benefit that has accrued or is likely to accrue to a person convicted of the offence. This is aimed at deterring developers from cutting down trees subject to tree preservation orders to gain a financial benefit from being able to build on the land. Lesser contraventions of tree preservation orders attract a fine of up to £2,500.

A homeowner may object to the proposed felling or significant pruning of a tree in an adjoining or neighbouring garden. If permission for the proposed work has not been sought from the local authority, the objector may contact the local authority, asking that it take steps to prevent the proposed felling or pruning.

It is an offence to fell a tree without a licence from the Forestry Commission before a tree is felled. This requirement does not, however, apply to the felling of fruit trees, or of trees growing in a garden, orchard, churchyard or designated open space. If a garden becomes badly overgrown, however, it may no longer be regarded as a garden.

Overgrowing branches and encroaching roots
It is well known that at common law a landowner may lop the branches of his neighbour's tree if they grow over the boundary onto his land. The same principle applies to hedges. Strictly speaking, the person who lops his neighbour's branches should then return the lopped pieces of branch to his neighbour's land, although the neighbour would probably not thank him for doing so. The freedom to lop overhanging branches arises from the landowner's right at law to take reasonable steps to abate a nuisance; for further details, see Chapter 7.

Encroaching roots are treated in the same way as overhanging branches and so a landowner is entitled to cut encroaching roots. For a recent authority, see *Hurst v Hampshire County Council* [1997] 2 EGLR 164, [1997] 44 EG 206 (CA).

If the overgrowing branches are poisonous, the owner of the tree is liable in nuisance if his neighbour's cattle or horses eat the branches; see *Crowhurst v Amersham Burial Board* (1878) 4 Ex D 5 at 10. There is no liability, however, if the branches do not overhang the boundary and the animals reach over the boundary to eat the branches.

If a landowner is unable to lop his trees without causing the branches to fall onto his neighbour's land, he is entitled to carry out the lopping and allow the branches to fall. This does not carry with it a right to damage anything on the neighbour's land when a branch falls. If the tree is bearing fruit, then the tree owner is entitled to enter onto his neighbour's land to retrieve the fruit that has fallen with the lopped boughs (*Millen v Fandrye* (1626) Poph 161 at 163). Although this is the strict legal position, it is sensible, to avoid any difficulties, to discuss with the neighbour concerned facilities for both lopping the branches and recovering any fallen fruit.

Local authorities have statutory powers to order the lopping or pruning of trees or hedges which overhang the highway or any other road or footpath to which the public has access, where the passage of vehicles or pedestrians may be endangered or obstructed.

Damage caused by roots

Tree roots rarely cause damage by physically penetrating a building or its foundations. Damage is more likely to be the result of moisture being taken from the soil by tree roots during dry periods, causing foundations to move. This in turn may result in the walls of a building cracking by reason of subsidence. At other times of the year, the subsoil may recover and swell back up, causing what is known as "heave", as opposed to subsidence. A building so affected may require its foundations to be underpinned; it may also be necessary for the tree to be removed, although this may also cause extreme "heave" to take place.

Where actual damage is being caused to a neighbouring property by branches or roots encroaching from trees on the adjoining owner's property, an action in nuisance may be brought. Damages and an injunction may be sought, provided the tree owner has, or ought to have, knowledge of the problem and the consequent danger: *Smith v Giddy* [1904] 2 KB 448 and *Delaware Mansions Ltd v Westminster City Council* [2001] UKHL 55, [2002] 1 AC 321, [2001] 3 WLR 1007, [2001] 4 All ER 737. In the latter case, in the House of Lords, Lord Cooke (at paragraph 38) said that the law could be:

"summed up in the proposition that, where there is a continuing nuisance of which the defendant knew or ought to have known, reasonable remedial expenditure may be recovered by the owner who has had to incur it."

Again, where a tree is situated in the highway and the roots are causing damage to adjoining property, the owner of the property can sue the highway authority in nuisance, provided the damage was reasonably foreseeable and the highway authority has been given a reasonable opportunity to abate the nuisance – *Delaware Mansions Ltd v Westminster City Council*, above. In *LE Jones (Insurance Brokers) Limited v Portsmouth City Council* [2002] EWCA Civ 1723, [2003] 1 WLR 427, the city council had an agreement with the highway authority, Hampshire County Council, to supply services, including the control of tree roots. The city council tried to defend a claim that tree roots had caused damage to the claimant's property on the basis that the proper defendant should have been the county council. The defendant lost. Dyson LJ (at paragraph 11) held that:

"the basis for the liability of an occupier for a nuisance on his land is not his occupation as such. Rather, it is that, by virtue of his occupation, an occupier usually has it in his power to take the measures that are necessary to prevent or eliminate the nuisance."

Where the situation is less serious, for example, where the neighbour's virginia creeper spreads onto an adjoining owner's brickwork and causes damage to the brickwork, the affected owner would be in order to remove and cut back the plant to the boundary of the two houses. This is because the affected owner has a common law right to "abate the nuisance". There are, however, limits to self-help. In the case of *Dayani v Bromley London Borough Council (No 2)* [2001] BLR 503 (QBD), a developer bought a Victorian house that had been converted into flats. He renovated the house and built a block of flats in the grounds. He then let the property to the local authority, which owned the freehold of the children's home next door. Shortly after the lease was completed, one of the trees in the grounds of the Victorian house was blown over in a gale and ended up on the roof of the children's home, although it did not cause much damage. The local authority decided that the tree could not be saved, so they cut it back to the boundary of its land, leaving a stump approximately one metre high.

A few months later, cracks appeared in the developer's property which, it was claimed, were being caused by the swelling of the soil following the removal of the tree, resulting in "heave". The developer issued proceedings against the local authority alleging negligence and nuisance and, as the defendants were also his tenants, for breach of an implied covenant not to commit waste. The defendant's case was that it had done no more than it was entitled to do, namely, abate the nuisance. It was held, however, that the right to abate a nuisance was not unlimited. If a party has alternative ways of abating a nuisance, the less damaging method must be adopted.

This proposition has been criticised on the basis that it is unsupported by authority and, in any event, it was not relevant to the decision in the *Dayani* case because the judge there held that the decision to fell the tree was "reasonable and careful" in the circumstances, and the only practical option. It may be that one way of explaining the case is to say that, once the local authority had decided to remove the tree, it had a duty to do so in a way which would reduce or ameliorate the resulting heave.

Notice

The legal basis for liability for tree root damage is that a tree owner is under a duty of care to take reasonable steps to ensure that the activity of the tree is controlled, so as not to cause damage to a neighbour's property. This duty does not arise, however, until the landowner or authority with power to prevent or eliminate the nuisance has, or ought to have, knowledge of the nuisance and is given time to remedy or abate it. Any money a person spends to remedy damage caused by the roots of a tree belonging to his neighbour is not recoverable if expended before a reasonable time has elapsed after giving notice of the problem to the owner of the tree. This period varies according to the facts of the particular case. It is therefore important for the property owner who is affected to notify his neighbour, or the appropriate authority with responsibility for the care and maintenance of the tree in question, just as soon as a problem is discovered. In the case of *Delaware Mansions v Westminster City Council*, above, the defendant delayed dealing with the problem. If it had acted to remove the offending tree when first notified, it would have cost about £14,000. After the case had progressed through the courts to the House of Lords the cost came to over £1 million, including £570,000 for the cost of underpinning the building which had been damaged.

Damage caused by branches

If a tree becomes diseased or damaged, a branch or branches may fall from the tree and cause damage to a person passing underneath, or to a neighbour's property. Liability in this case is based in nuisance and negligence, which have already been discussed in Chapter 7. Both forms of liability depend on the landowner's being in some way culpable for the branch falling. So, if the tree has been regularly inspected by experts and their advice followed promptly, it is unlikely that the tree owner would be held liable for the resulting injury or damage. Failure to inspect could well prove costly. See *Chapman v Barking and Dagenham London Borough Council* [1997] 2 EGLR 141.

If a tree or a branch should fall, particularly onto the highway, the owner should clear it away promptly to avoid liability should someone collide with it.

Evidence

Before issuing any proceedings, it is important to ensure that there is evidence that it is the defendant's tree or trees that is causing the damage. For this purpose it may be necessary to commission an expert report from an arboriculturist. In *Siddiqui v Hillingdon London Borough Council* [2003] EWHC 726 (TCC), the claimants brought proceedings for damages in nuisance against the local authority which owned a large wood near to their homes. Their two houses had been built on land which had previously been a farm and apple orchard. The apple trees had been cleared from the site before the houses were built. The claimants' experts said that the cause of cracking and damage to the properties was subsidence resulting from the dehydration of the soil beneath the houses caused by the tree roots in the nearby wood. The defendant's expert maintained that the cause of the damage was the rehydration of the ground after the removal of the apple trees and their root systems from the ground. The judge preferred the defendant's expert's evidence. Important factors in reaching this conclusion were:

(a) the distance of the trees in the wood from the houses;

(b) the depth of the trees' root systems; and

(c) the fact that the level of one house had risen, indicating a continuous process of rehydration of the soil beneath that house.

Insurance

Most buildings insurance policies cover subsidence damage caused by the roots of a neighbour's tree. In such an event, it is probably preferable to claim on the policy and leave it to the insurance company to sue the neighbour if it considers it appropriate to do so, rather than for the client to incur the expense and the risk of taking proceedings himself.

3. High Hedges

Much that has been said about trees above applies equally to hedges. It is excessively high hedges which have become a significant problem in recent years. The main complaint is that they block out light to neighbouring properties. Where the hedge blocks light to a neighbour's window, the neighbour may have the right to take proceedings against the hedge owner for infringement of his right to light. This is not a straightforward cause of action, as it involves tricky calculations from experts in the field (see Chapter 6 for further details). In any event, such a cause of action is not available where it is the garden, rather than a window, which is suffering from the blocking of sunlight. The problem with high hedges seems to have been exacerbated by the increase in popularity of *cupressus leylandii*. While this plant can form an attractive hedge, it is fast-growing and needs frequent cutting. A problem quickly arises if these plants are neglected, since they can rapidly grow up to thirty metres high.

Before the Anti-Social Behaviour Act 2003, there was no remedy. Part 8 of the 2003 Act, however, establishes a procedure for making a complaint to a local authority concerning a high hedge. The affected owner or occupier of property can make a complaint on the ground that the reasonable enjoyment of his domestic property, or part of it, is being adversely affected by the height of his neighbour's hedge. The local authority may reject the complaint if it considers it to be frivolous or vexatious, or if reasonable steps have not been made to resolve the dispute amicably. For the provisions of the Act to apply, the hedge must:

    (a) consist wholly or predominantly of a line of two or more evergreen or semi-evergreen shrubs;

    (b) be more than two metres in height;

    (c) act, to some degree, as a barrier to light or access; and

(d) by virtue of its height, be adversely affecting the complainant's reasonable enjoyment of his domestic property. This includes his garden.

The local authority must then decide what action needs to be taken to remedy the matter and to prevent its recurrence. All relevant factors have to be taken into account, including the views of the hedge owner and the effect of the hedge on the wider amenity of the area. The local authority may then issue a remedial notice. Failure to comply with such a notice constitutes an offence, and the offender is liable, on conviction in a magistrates' court, to a fine of up to £1,000. Further, the court may issue an order requiring the hedge owner to carry out the required work within a prescribed time. If the hedge owner fails to do so, the local authority may itself carry out the work and recover the cost from the owner. The Act includes provisions for the hedge owner to appeal against the decision of the local authority. A local land charge can be registered in respect of any unpaid expenses, and so bind any future owner of the land.

The 2003 Act applies only to evergreen hedges of two or more trees; it does not assist the homeowner who is affected adversely by, say, a single massive evergreen or a line of deciduous trees. One other shortcoming in the legislation is that it provides no deadline by which a local authority must make a decision, or a timetable for action to be taken. On the other hand, local authorities have a general duty to act reasonably in all the circumstances, which may act as a spur, but there is still the risk that an adversely affected homeowner may be left frustrated for a considerable length of time by a dilatory local authority.

Hedgerows

As far as hedgerows are concerned, the Hedgerows Regulations 1997 (SI 1997 No. 1160) require notice to be given to the local authority of proposed works. If the authority considers the hedgerow to be "important" it issues a "retention notice". It is a criminal offence not to comply with these regulations and notices.

4. Checklist: Trees and Hedges

1. The owner of the tree or hedge must first be identified.
2. Branches or encroaching roots can be lopped without notice.

3. If damage is being caused, notice must be given to the owner or responsible authority, to allow the opportunity to abate the nuisance.
4. Establish whether the owner or responsible authority has failed to remedy the problem within a reasonable time.
5. If notice has been given and the nuisance has not been abated, proceedings for damages and an injunction may be commenced, but it must be possible to prove that the damage is indeed caused by the tree in question; expert evidence may be necessary.
6. Consider whether there is buildings insurance cover rendering it unnecessary for the client to issue proceedings.
7. A complaint to the local authority may be made if an evergreen hedge over two metres high is adversely affecting the client's enjoyment of his property, but only after trying to resolve the problem amicably.

5. Weeds

The Weeds Act 1959 makes it an offence to allow certain types of weed to spread from a piece of land, if the Department for Environment, Food and Rural Affairs or the local authority, acting on behalf of the Minister, has served a notice requiring the recipient to prevent the weeds from spreading. The weeds concerned are "injurious weeds". Section 1(2) of the 1959 Act specifies spear thistle, creeping or field thistle, curled dock, broadleaved dock and ragwort as the prescribed weeds.

An adjoining owner may bring an action in nuisance and/or negligence against the offending neighbour, provided he can prove that he has suffered damage as a result of the spread of injurious weeds from his neighbour's property. This is the logical conclusion from the case of *Leakey v National Trust* [1980] QB 485, [1980] 2 WLR 65, [1980] 1 All ER 17 (QBD), where a landowner was held liable for the fall of earth due to natural causes from a steep bank causing damage on his neighbour's land. Presumably liability does not lie until the offending landowner has notice of the damage being caused by the spread of weeds from his land, and has been given the opportunity to remedy the situation.

In the New Zealand case of *French v Auckland City Council* [1974] 1 NZLR 340, the defendant was found liable for damage caused by thistles growing from seed which had blown from neighbouring land. All the circumstances had to be taken into account, the court said, including:

(a) the extent of the spread of the weeds;

(b) the damage likely to be caused;

(c) the location of the properties; and

(d) the cost and practicality of preventing the spread.

It was suggested that the parties' circumstances could be taken into account. Thus a poor defendant might not have to do what a rich defendant might be expected to do.

As in the case of the spraying of pesticides (see page 125) the landowner must take reasonable care when spraying herbicides not to cause damage to a neighbour's property.

Japanese knotweed

The spread of Japanese knotweed *(fallopia japonica)* is an increasing problem. It was introduced into the United Kingdom as an ornamental plant, but spreads aggressively and is extremely difficult to eradicate. It grows in dense clumps up to three metres high and is often found alongside railway lines, roads, derelict sites and riverbanks. While it is not toxic to animals or humans, it destroys other plants under its dense canopy of leaves and can undermine the foundations of buildings. It spreads when its root system is cut and the cuttings are carried elsewhere by people or by water. This is not a plant which is covered by the provisions of the Weeds Act 1959, but the Wildlife and Countryside Act 1981 makes it an offence to "plant or otherwise encourage" the growth of Japanese knotweed, and so cutting the plant or roots or disturbing the soil where it is growing could constitute an offence if not carried out correctly.

Japanese knotweed plants, and the soil in which they have grown, are classified as "controlled waste", and a landowner who seeks to dispose of any such plants or polluted soil must complete waste transfer documentation as required by the Landfill (England and Wales) Regulations 2002 (SI 2002 No. 1559). A number of companies specialise in the eradication of Japanese knotweed.

All that has been said above about weeds in general applies equally to Japanese knotweed.

6.   Pests

There are two aspects to how pests may affect neighbours. The first is that a person may be harbouring pests on his land and the pests may escape and cause damage to crops or buildings on another person's land, or even cause illness or disease. The culprits may be rats, rabbits, deer or foxes. The other aspect is the damage that may be caused by the use of pesticides and insecticides and their spread to neighbouring land. Both aspects are regulated extensively by statute.

Starting, however, with the common law, there is a distinction between the person who actively encourages animals onto his land which then cause problems for his neighbours, and those who remain passive. In *Farrer v Nelson* (1885) 15 QBD 258, the defendant was the lessee of certain shooting and sporting rights over an estate, part of which was a farm leased to the claimant. About 450 pheasants were reared all over the estate and released into a coppice adjoining the farm. As many as 100 pheasants at a time were seen running in Farrer's adjoining field, when his grain and other crops were ripening. The court found that Farrer was entitled to recover the amount of the damage so occasioned.

By contrast, *Seligman v Docker* [1949] Ch 53, [1948] 2 All ER 887, concerned wild pheasants. Docker owned or had shooting rights over land, part of which was let to Seligman. During the season 1947–1948, Docker's coverts were filled with an inordinate number of wild pheasants, which, in their search for food, gravely damaged Seligman's crops. Seligman sued for an injunction to prevent Docker allowing or encouraging "unreasonable quantities of pheasants" from occupying the land so as to injure him, and an injunction restraining him from unreasonable or excessive user of the sporting rights or the right of preserving game. Romer J held that the presence of the large number of pheasants was due not to any "unreasonable action" by Docker, but to the exceptional weather conditions prevailing in the summer of 1947. Secondly, he held that Docker was not under any legal obligation to Seligman to reduce or disperse the pheasants when it became known that the number was so considerable. They were wild animals, or *feræ naturæ*, and the fact that Seligman had no right to shoot them did not impose on Docker any duty in law to shoot them himself.

The authority of *Seligman's* case is now doubtful. It is more likely than not that the law now takes the view that, if a landowner or occupier fails to take reasonable steps to prevent or minimise the risk of harm by a hazard caused by nature to neighbouring landowners, which he knew or ought to have known would cause such harm, then the offending landowner may be liable to his neighbour in negligence or nuisance. In *Holbeck Hall Hotel Ltd v Scarborough Borough Council* [2000] QB 836, [2000] 2 WLR 1396, [2000] 2 All ER 705 (CA), it was suggested that the duty owed may depend on the individual circumstances of the parties, so that a poor landowner may not be expected to do as much as a wealthier landowner. The case concerned the erosion of soil from the defendant's land, causing land beneath a neighbouring hotel to collapse due to lack of support. Although it does not concern weeds or pests specifically, the principles are probably the same. When a case specifically on the point comes before the courts, *Holbeck Hall,* rather than *Seligman* is likely to be followed.

Under section 98 of the Agriculture Act 1947 and under the Pests Act 1954, a landowner or occupier can be required to take action to control pests on his land. Section 1 of the 1954 Act designates the whole of England and Wales (apart from the City of London, the Scilly Isles and Skomer Island) as a rabbit clearance area, requiring landowners to take or kill any wild rabbits living on or resorting to their land unless they can show that it is not reasonably practical to do so. If it is not practical to kill the rabbits, the landowner or occupier is obliged to prevent them from causing damage to other land by, for example, erecting rabbit-proof fences.

Where there is a serious infestation of rabbits or other pests on his land, a neighbour who has suffered damage as a consequence may make a complaint to the Department for the Environment, Food and Rural Affairs. The damage must be to his crops, livestock, foodstuff, trees, hedges, banks or works on land. The landowner or occupier from whose land the pests have migrated is given a reasonable time to remedy the situation. If he fails to do so within the timescale specified in the notice served on him, the notice is confirmed by a second notice served on the occupier of the land and (if the land is let out) on any landlord. If he still fails to take action, the occupier may be summonsed to appear before a magistrates' court. On summary conviction, a fine not exceeding £500 may be imposed. Alternatively, the Minister can arrange for a third party to carry out the work at the expense of the occupier of the land.

Where a landowner incurs expense which was reasonably necessary to comply with the statutory requirements he may apply to the county court for an order that the expense should be borne wholly or partly by someone else who had an interest in the land in question (section 100(5) of the Agriculture Act 1947).

Section 98 of the 1947 Act applies not only to rabbits, but also to hares, rodents, deer, foxes, moles and wild birds other than those protected under the Protection of Birds Act 1954. The Department for the Environment, Food and Rural Affairs publishes useful advisory leaflets on the subject.

7. Domestic Animals

The keeper of an animal which does not belong to a "dangerous species" as defined in section 6(2) of the Animals Act 1971 is liable for damage caused by the animal if:

    (a) the damage is of a kind which the animal, unless restrained, was likely to cause, or which, if caused by the animal, was likely to be severe; and

    (b) the likelihood of the damage or its being severe was due to the characteristics of the animal, not normally found in animals of the same species or not normally found except at particular times or in particular circumstances; and

    (c) those characteristics were known to the keeper

(section 2(2), Animals Act 1971).

A person is the "keeper" of an animal if:

    (a) he owns the animal or has it in his possession; or

    (b) he is the head of a household of which a member under the age of sixteen owns the animal or has it in his possession.

Furthermore, once a person is an animal's keeper, he remains its keeper until someone else satisfies the definition of "keeper". At common law, cats do not come within these provisions (*Buckle v Holmes* [1926] 2 KB 125).

It is a defence for the keeper to prove one of the following:

    (a) that the damage is due wholly to the fault of the person suffering the damage;

    (b) that the injured person accepted the risk;

    (c) that the person injured was a trespasser, provided that either the animal was not kept in the place where the damage was

> inflicted for the protection of people or property or, if it was
> kept there for that purpose, that it was not unreasonable to do
> so

(section 5, Animals Act 1971).

Thus, before liability can be established, a claimant would have to prove that the animal's keeper had knowledge of the animal's characteristics and its propensity to cause damage. This is reflected in the popular saying, that every dog is allowed one bite, meaning that unless and until a dog has bitten once, it cannot be shown that its keeper knew of its propensity to bite.

On dogs, see also the Clean Neighbourhoods and Environment Act 2005 (page 147); and, in respect of certain breeds of dog, the Dangerous Dogs Act 1991.

8. Pesticides

Turning to the damage caused by the negligent spraying of crops with pesticides, this too may found a claim for damages. In the case of *Tutton v A D Walter* [1986] QB 61, [1986] 3 WLR 797, [1985] 3 All ER 757 (QBD), a farmer, Mr Walter, was found liable in negligence for the death of the claimant's bees caused by pesticide sprayed onto Mr Walter's crop of oil seed rape. The court held that the owner of land, who knew that bees were kept within foraging range of his land, owed a duty to the beekeeper not negligently to carry out on his land activities which, although wholly carried out on his land and otherwise lawful, he knew or ought reasonably to have foreseen would be harmful to the bees. It was found that spraying pesticide on the crop, while it was in full flower, was likely to injure the bees. The defendant knew this, and knew that the claimant had hives in the area; he therefore owed the claimant a duty of care. By failing to heed warnings about the time to spray, the defendant was held to have breached his duty of care.

This case extends a landowner's duty of care so that it applies even to things on a neighbour's property (in this case, bees) which had strayed by foraging onto the defendant's own land. Indeed, counsel for Mr Walter argued that the bees were in effect trespassers on Mr Walter's land and, as Lord Reid said in *British Railways Board v Herrington* [1972] AC 877, [1972] 2 WLR 537, [1972] 1 All ER 749 (HL):

"An occupier does not voluntarily assume a relationship with trespassers. By trespassing they force a "neighbour" relationship on him. When they do so he must act in a humane manner – that is not asking too much of him – but I do not see why he should be required to do more".

The judge in *Tutton v Walter*, however, found it difficult to "accept the concept that bees may be invitees, licensees or trespassers"; bees could not be categorised as wrongdoers; they benefit farmers by pollinating their crops; and their keepers cannot control where they forage.

9. Checklist: Weeds, Pests and Domestic Animals

1. Complain to the local authority and ask it to take action against the neighbour if the weeds causing injury to the client's land are covered by the Weeds Act 1959.

2. Complain to the Department for Environment, Food and Rural Affairs if pests to which the Agriculture Act 1947 applies are causing damage to the client's land.

3. Consider an action in negligence and for nuisance if there is sufficient evidence to prove, on a balance of probabilities, that it is the neighbour's weeds or pests, emanating from the neighbour's land, which are causing the problem. The damage would have to be reasonably significant to justify the issue of proceedings.

4. In the case of a domestic animal, ascertain whether the animal in question has previously caused damage of a similar nature such that the neighbour, as keeper of the animal, must have known of its nature and propensity to act in the way complained of.

Chapter 9

Water, Waste Water and Drainage

1. Introduction

Most problems with regard to water, waste water and drainage arise when land is flooded. Flooding may be caused by the natural seepage of water from higher to lower ground after heavy rainfall; by rivers bursting their banks, again usually following severe weather; by defects in the public drainage system, or by the inadequacy of the system to cope with the demands placed upon it. Flats may be affected by water escaping from other flats in the building. In this chapter, typical problems, and the steps which may be taken to ameliorate them, are looked at.

2. Natural Flow or Escape of Water

As a general rule, at common law, a landowner has no legal responsibility for damage caused by water escaping naturally from his land, in the course of the ordinary and proper use of that land. Thus, where someone's property suffers flooding from storm water which pours off a neighbour's land which is at a higher level, the person whose property is damaged cannot sue his neighbour for compensation. This is so provided that the owner of the higher land has not accumulated water there unnaturally, or been guilty of misuse of his land, or been guilty of negligence, or caused the water to flow on to the lower land in a more concentrated form (*Home Brewery Co v William Davis & Co (Leicester)* [1987] QB 339, [1987] 2 WLR 117, [1987] 1 All ER 637 (QBD)).

Just as the owner of the land at the lower level cannot complain about the natural flow or percolation of water through the soil onto his land from the higher level, the owner of the lower land is not obliged to take the water. It is permissible for him to erect barriers to prevent such water flowing onto his land, even if this causes damage to the higher land. The lower owner is not liable for his actions, provided he has acted with reasonable care and skill and does no more than he needs to protect his own land.

The position is different where a "watercourse" is concerned. A "watercourse" was defined in the Australian case of *Lyons v Winter* (1899) 25 VLR 464 as:

> "a stream of water flowing in a defined channel or between something in the nature of banks. The stream may be very small and need not always run, nor need the banks be clearly or sharply defined, but there must be a course, marked on the earth by visible signs, along which water flows."

A watercourse may be natural, such as a stream or river, or artificial, such as a drainage ditch or aqueduct, but does not include tidal waters. The owner of a stream or river does not necessarily own the banks. If the banks are in different ownership, each owner owns the bed of the stream or river up to the mid-point. The owner of a bank (known as a riparian owner) has the right to:

(a) have a natural stream or river come to him in its natural state in flow, quantity and quality and to go from him without obstruction; and

(b) the ordinary use of the water.

This is subject to every other riparian owner's rights along the length of the watercourse. Thus, an owner higher up a stream may use the water for domestic use and may water his cattle, but he may not dam the water for this purpose. Ordinary use must be reasonable and must not interfere with the quantity or quality of the stream for owners lower down the watercourse.

3. Non-natural Use: Rylands v Fletcher

In the landmark case of *Rylands v Fletcher* (1868) LR 3 HL 330, a landowner built a reservoir on his land. This was obviously a "non-natural" use of the land. The reservoir burst, causing the water in it to escape and flood a neighbouring mine. The owner of the reservoir was found liable to the affected mineowner. This case established a new form of liability, known simply as the rule in *Rylands v Fletcher*. It may be summarised thus: a person is liable to compensate his neighbour if he brings onto his land and keeps there some inherently dangerous substance or thing, which then "escapes" from his land and causes damage to a neighbour's property. The substance or thing need not necessarily be a large volume of water. It may be gas, fire, explosives, electricity, poison or, as in one case, a fairground attraction called a "chair-o-plane".

To succeed in obtaining compensation, the neighbour must prove that it was this escape of water which caused his loss (which should not be difficult), and that it was foreseeable that the damage would be caused if the water escaped. The rule in *Rylands v Fletcher* may therefore be regarded as an extension of the law of nuisance to cases of isolated escapes and, indeed, this was the view of the House of Lords in the case of *Cambridge Water Co Ltd v Eastern Counties Leather plc* [1994] 2 AC 264, [1994] 2 WLR 53, [1994] 1 All ER 53 (HL). In that case the defendant was a leather manufacturer, which used a solvent in the tanning process. There were regular spillages of small amounts of this solvent onto the concrete floor of the factory. Unbeknown to the defendant, this solvent seeped through the floor into the sub-strata of the soil and percolated through to contaminate the water in a bore-hole from which the claimant extracted water to supply to the public. The bore-hole was 1.3 miles away from the defendant's works, and it was calculated that it would take about nine months for solvent to travel that distance through the soil.

The water company sued the leather manufacturer in negligence, nuisance and under the rule in *Rylands v Fletcher*. The claims in negligence and nuisance were dismissed because it was held that the defendant could not reasonably have foreseen that the repeated small spillages of solvent would enter the underground strata or that detectable quantities would be found in the claimant's bore-hole.

At first instance, the judge held that, as far as the claim under *Rylands v Fletcher* was concerned, the use of solvent in the tanning business was a natural use of that land, as it was a leather factory. The Court of Appeal, however, held the defendant strictly liable for the contamination and awarded damages in excess of £1 million. The House of Lords overruled the Court of Appeal. Their Lordships held that, under *Rylands v Fletcher*, foreseeability of damage of the type suffered if the hazardous thing escaped from the defendant's land was a prerequisite of liability. It arose only if the defendant knew or ought reasonably to have foreseen that the hazardous thing would cause damage. *Rylands v Fletcher* established "strict liability" in the sense that, where an escape occurs in the course of a non-natural use of land, it is no defence for the defendant to show that he had exercised all due care to prevent the escape.

The *Cambridge Water* decision was considered in the case of *Transco plc v Stockport Metropolitan Borough Council* [2003] UKHL 61; [2004] 2 AC 1, [2003] 3 WLR 1467, [2004] 1 All ER 589. Here, the defendant owned a block of flats. The water supply to the flats was stored in tanks in the basement. The pipe along which the water flowed into the tanks failed and water escaped. The leak was not discovered for some time, resulting in a considerable amount of water percolating to an embankment which supported the claimant's gas main. The embankment collapsed, leaving the gas main exposed and unsupported. The claimant repaired the embankment and claimed the cost from the defendant.

There had been no negligence on the part of the defendant, and so the claimant sued under the rule in *Rylands v Fletcher,* arguing that the defendant was liable without proof of negligence under the rule. The claimant won at first instance, but the Court of Appeal reversed the decision. This time the House of Lords agreed, and held that the rule in *Rylands v Fletcher* was not to be abrogated or absolved by the principles of negligence. In this case, however, the supply of water through the pipe was not an unnatural user of the land. It created no greater risk than was normally associated with domestic plumbing. The case therefore did not come within *Rylands v Fletcher* and the appeal was dismissed.

It is a defence for the owner of the land from which a non-natural accumulation of water (or any other substance or thing that may fall within the rule in *Rylands v Fletcher*) has escaped to prove:

   (a) that the escape or the damage caused thereby was due to an act of God; or

   (b) that the escape or the consequent damage was caused by a third party over whom he had no control, and it was not something that he should have foreseen and guarded against; or

   (c) that it was the claimant himself who caused the damage; or

   (d) that the water was accumulated on the defendant's land by and for the benefit of a third party; or

(e) that the water was collected with the consent of the claimant and for his benefit; or

(f) in certain cases, that the act was done with statutory authority, unless there was negligence.

An act of God has been described as an operation of natural forces "which no human foresight can provide against, and of which human pretence is not bound to recognise the possibility": *Greenock Corporation v Caledonian Railway* [1917] AC 556, 576. It must be impossible to provide against. This in effect means that it is only the most extreme of circumstances that qualify as acts of God, such as earthquakes or exceptional tidal waves. It is perhaps strange that an act of God should constitute a defence to a claim based on the principle that he who brings onto his land a potentially dangerous substance, does so at his peril. He is fixed with liability because he has placed his neighbours at risk and it is immaterial that he was not at fault if the dangerous substance escapes. It is curious that he should, then, escape liability if the reason the substance escapes is an occurrence of nature as opposed to any other cause.

If a householder or owner or occupier of a building causes water to fall from his eaves and gutters onto his neighbour's land, thereby causing damage, this may amount to an actionable nuisance. If, however, roof water is collected in a tank and it is caused to escape by the actions of a third party over whom the owner of the building where the tank is situated has no control, then the building owner is not liable: *Carstairs v Taylor* [1871] LR 6 Ex 217. Nor is the owner of a building liable if his neighbour has consented to the arrangement for the discharge of the roof water.

4. Burst River Banks and Leaking Watercourses

Increasing demand for housing has resulted in planning permission being granted for houses to be built on flood plains, thus exposing them to flooding if the river bursts its banks. Such development can also affect the natural drainage of storm water into rivers. The problem is exacerbated by the fact that the building of roads to service housing developments may cause water to run off the land more quickly than it would have done had the rainwater been able to drain into the soil naturally. According to the Environment Agency, five million people, in two million properties, live in areas where there is a risk of flooding. Questions of liability where damage is caused by a river flooding its banks or drainage schemes being inadequate are likely to arise ever more frequently.

By virtue of the Environment Act 1995, the Environment Agency has overall responsibility for, among other things, the control and management of main rivers in England and Wales; and it has inherited the function of the National Rivers Authority in respect of flood defences. Its functions in this regard are exercised through flood defence committees. The Agency may raise drainage charges or authorise borrowing for flood defence purposes.

The Water Resources Act 1991, as amended by the Water Act 2003, deals with the Environment Agency's functions in respect of flood defences and the raising of revenue in connection with them. The powers given by the Act are permissive only, so there is no obligation on the Environment Agency to carry out maintenance or new works on main rivers, and the Agency has no liability for damage caused by the flooding of main rivers. Ordinary watercourses which are not main rivers are the concern of internal drainage boards and local authorities. The primary obligation to drain and protect land from flooding, however, rests with the landowner. The legislation supplements the common law by giving additional powers to the relevant statutory bodies, and generally confers powers, rather than imposes duties, on those bodies.

Statutory undertakers are not immune from liability if they have been negligent. In the case of *Geddis v Proprietors of Bann Reservoir* (1878) 3 App Cas 430, the defendants failed to clean and widen a river bed, which caused the river to overflow and damage the neighbouring owners' property. The reservoir owners were held liable.

Moreover, section 209 of the Water Industry Act 1991 provides that "where an escape of water, however caused, from a pipe vested in a water undertaker causes loss or damage", the undertaker is strictly liable. In this instance, an act of God, or an act of a third party, is no defence.

In respect of watercourses which are not main rivers, the starting point when considering who may be liable for flooding has been held to be that the owner of the bed of a natural watercourse or an artificial channel is not liable if the stream or piped ditch overflows due to the natural silting up of the watercourse or channel, or due to the growth of weeds: *Normile v Luddle* (1912) 47 ILT 179. This old case is unlikely to be followed in the future, as a result of the decision in *Leakey v National Trust* (above, page 120). This was not a case on water, but concerned a natural hill which slipped, causing damage to neighbouring land. The defendant argued that this was an accident of nature for which there could be no liability in nuisance without negligence. Following a decision of the Judicial Committee of the Privy Council in *Goldman v Hargrave* [1967] 1 AC 645, [1966] 3 WLR 513, [1966] 2 All ER 989, the Court of Appeal found the defendant liable in nuisance. As Lord Wilberforce said in *Goldman v Hargrave*:

> "it is only in comparatively recent times that the law has recognised an occupier's duty as one of a more positive character than merely to abstain from creating, or adding to, a source of damage or annoyance".

Further, under section 24 of the Land Drainage Act 1991, where there is an artificial watercourse, such as a piped culvert, which has become obstructed, the local authority or other drainage authority may serve a notice, on the person who has allowed it to become obstructed and who has power to remove the obstruction, to remove it. Failure to do so could result in prosecution and a fine of up to £5,000. The drainage authority may carry out the work and charge the cost to the person in default.

By section 25 of the 1991 Land Drainage Act, similar provisions apply to ordinary watercourses, although the maximum fine is £2,500. The person served with the notice can apply to the magistrates' court that some other person ought to have been served with the notice, or ought to contribute towards the cost of the works specified in the notice.

A person who alters the course of a natural stream is liable for damage caused by the escape or overflow of water, should it prove that the new channel is inadequate for the purpose or has been constructed defectively: *Menzies v Earl of Breadalbane* (1828) 3 Bligh NS PC 414. A local highway authority may be liable in private nuisance to a landowner whose land is flooded because a culvert constructed by the highway authority is inadequate to cope with the quantity of water naturally flowing through a stream over which the highway is built: *Bybrook Barn Garden Centre Ltd v Kent County Council* [2001] BLR 55, [2001] Env LR 30, (2001) LGLR 27 (CA).

As mentioned above, several very old cases establish the principle that a landowner is entitled to protect his land from flooding, and may construct an embankment for that purpose even if it means that the amount of water flowing over neighbouring land in time of flood is increased. Where flood water has already collected on land, however, the owner of the land is liable for damage caused by the escape of that water if the escape is brought about by a wilful act on his part which is not within the ordinary or natural use of the land.

The owner of a riverbank is entitled to raise the banks of the river to confine flood water within the banks and to prevent it overflowing onto his own land, provided that in doing so he does not cause damage to another's land or property.

5. Inadequate Public Drainage

Before 1 September 1989, water and sewerage services were supplied by water authorities. The functions of the water authorities were privatised on that date and are now exercised by water or sewerage undertakers. The Secretary of State for Trade and Industry has a duty to ensure that companies appointed to be water and sewerage undertakers cover every area of England and Wales. Sewerage undertakers have a general duty to provide public sewers in their areas so that those areas continue to be effectively drained, and to empty those sewers and to deal with their contents: section 94(1), Water Industry Act 1991. A local authority may act as an agent of a sewerage undertaker in certain circumstances. Owners of domestic premises have a statutory right to connect to a public sewer provided notice is given to the statutory undertaker. The undertaker has twenty-one days in which to object to the connection on certain specified grounds – for example, if it considers that the construction or condition of the sewer or drain is sub-standard: Water Industry Act, section 106.

By section 199 of the Water Industry Act 1991, sewerage undertakers have a duty to keep records of every public sewer vested in them, but are not required to keep records of a sewer laid before 1 September 1989 if they do not know of the sewer or have reasonable grounds for suspecting its existence.

It occasionally happens that the public drainage system is inadequate to cope with the demand placed upon it. This can cause flooding during downpours of rain because the drainage system cannot carry away the volume of surface water fast enough. Whether a householder affected by such a problem may seek compensation from the sewerage undertaker was considered by the House of Lords in the case of *Marcic v Thames Water Utilities Limited* [2003] UKHL 66, [2004] 2 AC 42, [2003] 3 WLR 1603, [2004] 1 All ER 135 (HL). Mr Marcic owned a house in the London Borough of Harrow. Thames Water was the water and sewerage undertaker for that area. The sewers serving Mr Marcic's house had been laid down in the 1930s. There had subsequently been considerable housing development in the area and the sewerage system was under increasing pressure. From June 1992, Mr Marcic's house was regularly and seriously affected by flooding from both surface and foul water from the overloaded sewers. As noted above, there is a statutory right for domestic premises to connect to and use the public sewers, and Thames Water could do nothing to prevent the new houses that were being built from discharging into the old system. Thames Water could have enlarged the existing sewers or built new ones, but it had done neither.

Mr Marcic issued proceedings against Thames Water claiming that:

(a) they were in breach of statutory duty;

(b) they had been negligent;

(c) they had committed nuisance;

(d) they were in breach of article 8 of, and article 1 of the first protocol to, the European Convention on Human Rights incorporated into English Law by the Human Rights Act 1998; and

(e) they were liable under the rule in *Rylands v Fletcher*.

The statutory duty, breach of which was alleged, was to ensure that its area was properly drained by an adequate sewerage system: section 94(1)(a) of the Water Industry Act 1991. If a sewerage undertaker is in breach of this duty, section 18 of that Act enables the Secretary of State, or the Director General of Water Services, to make an enforcement order requiring the undertaker to comply with its duty. Section 18(8) of the Act (now substituted by schedule 8, paragraph 4, Water Act 2003) limits the remedies available for acts or omissions by a sewerage undertaker. The only remedy is the power under section 18 to make an enforcement order. That was of no use to Mr Marcic in his attempt to obtain compensation from Thames Water.

In the High Court, Mr Marcic lost his claims under common law.

The court held that the defendant had not been negligent, had not committed a nuisance and was not liable under *Rylands v Fletcher*. The judge did find, however, that the defendant had breached Mr Marcic's human rights. The right under article 8 is the right to respect for private and family life and the home. Article 1 of the first protocol contains the right to peaceful enjoyment of possessions – in other words, the protection of property. It was held that the exemption in article 8(2) that a public authority may interfere with the exercise of the right under article 8 "as is necessary in the interests of the economic well-being of the country", did not apply to these circumstances. The defendant was also found to have acted incompatibly with article 1 of the first protocol.

The case went to the Court of Appeal, which agreed with the High Court on the human rights position, and that there had been no breach of statutory duty, but it did find that Thames Water was liable in nuisance. It considered that the distinction between nuisance and negligence was of academic interest only, and therefore discussed in detail nuisance only, although the reasoning could apply to both. The Court of Appeal also considered that it was unnecessary to consider the rule in *Rylands v Fletcher*, in view of its finding on nuisance.

The Court of Appeal considered four old cases, the latest of which was decided in 1924, in which it had been consistently held that failure to construct new sewers did not constitute a nuisance. It then considered three later cases, where it had been found that there was a duty on the occupiers of land to prevent nuisance occurring where they had previously allowed a nuisance to continue and had thereby adopted it. The court considered that the principle in these three later cases should now be applied to the four sewer cases. The inadequate sewers constituted a nuisance and Thames Water had failed to take reasonable steps to remedy the situation in circumstances where it knew, or should have known, what was happening and the damage that was being caused.

On further appeal, the House of Lords evidently took a clear decision that, as a matter of policy, it should not allow individual householders to institute proceedings against sewerage undertakers for failure to build sufficient sewers. Their Lordships held that this would be inconsistent with the statutory scheme and allow individual householders to by-pass the statutory scheme irrespective of whether or not the Director General of Water Services had taken steps to obtain an enforcement order. It was for the Director General to decide whether or not a sewerage undertaker had failed in its duty and whether or not an enforcement order should be made.

Their Lordships also disagreed with the Court of Appeal's analysis of the law of nuisance. The four sewer cases should not be brought within the principles laid down in the three later cases, namely that a landowner has a duty to take reasonable steps to prevent a nuisance arising from a known source of hazard, even though the landowner did not himself create the hazard. This principle involved weighing up what it would be reasonable to expect a landowner to do to prevent his land becoming a source of injury to his neighbours. However, a sewerage undertaker was no ordinary landowner because statute prevented the sewerage undertaker from denying new connections being made to the system. Weighing up what would be reasonable for a sewerage undertaker to do would involve considering questions of capital expenditure, the ability to raise finance, charges to consumers and the apportionment of resources to customers in different regions to ensure that they received the same level of services. These were not matters for the court to decide but, as Parliament had decreed by section 18 of the Water Industry Act 1991, for the Director General of Water Services.

Finally, the House of Lords considered the human rights arguments but found that the Court of Appeal had failed to take account of the statutory scheme which was compliant with the Human Rights Act 1998. Following the 2003 decision of the European Court of Human Rights in *Hatton v United Kingdom* (2003) 37 EHRR 28, a fair balance had to be struck between the interests of the individual and the community as a whole. For Parliament to have acted fairly it had to provide a scheme which balanced the interests of the customers whose properties were prone to flooding, with the interests of other customers of the sewerage undertaker. By imposing a drainage obligation on undertakers and entrusting enforcement to the independent Director General, the statutory scheme gave Mr Marcic a remedy by way of judicial review of the decision of the Director General if he decided not to take enforcement action.

Mr Marcic therefore made legal history, but lost his case and had to endure ten years of flooding by surface and foul water; it was not until 2002 that Thames Water began to carry out the necessary remedial work. It is also clear that a decision of the Director General not to take enforcement action is subject to judicial review, and, with hindsight, it was probably a mistake for Mr Marcic not to have taken that route.

A modest statutory compensation scheme exists for internal flooding, but on average the compensation paid has been only £125 per incident, and it does not cover external flooding. Some sewerage undertakers make a voluntary payment for external flooding, however, and all voluntarily provide a free clean-up, disinfecting and effluent removal service.

6. Failure of Private Sewer Pipes

Sometimes a householder suffers a backing-up of effluent that floods into the house caused by blocked pipes. The problem may be cured by rodding the sewer pipes. If this is unsuccessful, it may be that the sewer pipe has collapsed. It is then a matter of ascertaining where the collapse has occurred. A failure in the smaller bore private pipes which connect the dwelling to the main sewer is more likely than a collapse of the larger bore main sewer itself. If it is a public sewer which is in disrepair, then it is the sewerage undertaker who is liable to repair the pipe. Where the problem is somewhere along the route of a private pipe, then the householder who owns the pipe where the collapse has occurred is liable to remedy the problem. A local authority has power under section 17 of the Public Health Act 1961 to require the owner of a house with a blocked sewer to clear it. Under section 35 of the Local Government (Miscellaneous Provisions) Act 1976, the local authority has power to repair the pipe, but must give notice to the owner and occupier of the land before exercising the power. The cost of the works is recoverable from the owner of the pipe, and the owners of other land served by the pipe in question can be required to contribute towards the cost. A person who is required to make a payment may appeal to the county court, within six weeks, on the ground that someone else should be required to pay some or all of the cost.

The owner of a sewer or drain has a duty to ensure that the effluent does not escape and cause damage to other people's property. If he is in breach of that duty, he is liable under the rule in *Rylands v Fletcher*. Even if he has a right to drain through a neighbour's land this right permits him to do so only through a sewer pipe. Liability arises even though the owner of the pipe was unaware of its condition: *Humphries v Cousins* (1877) 2 CPD 239. The damage must be foreseeable: *Cambridge Water Co Ltd v Eastern Counties Leather plc* (above, page 129).

7. Escape from Internal Water Supply Systems

A series of nineteenth century cases established that, where water has been brought into a building for the use of the occupants and that water escapes, the person who has possession and control of the water, or the apparatus from which it escapes, is not liable for damage caused to the property of other occupiers of the building unless he, or his employee for whom he is vicariously liable, was negligent. The only exception is where the damage is caused by the escape of water from a pipe which is vested in a water undertaker or the Environment Agency. As noted above, by section 209 of the Water Industry Act 1991 and section 108 of the Water Resources Act 1991, an undertaker or the Environment Agency is liable for loss or damage caused by water from such a pipe no matter how the escape happened. There is no liability, however, where the escape of water was caused wholly by the person who sustained the loss.

A landlord of residential premises which are flooded by the escape of water from the internal water supply may well be in breach of express or implied obligations to the tenant to repair certain installations in the premises. If express, the obligation is set out in the tenancy agreement. If there is no written agreement, or if the agreement is silent as to the landlord's repairing obligation, section 11(1) of the Landlord and Tenant Act 1985 applies. It implies into a lease of a dwelling-house, for a term of less than seven years, the following term:

"… a covenant by the lessor:

(a) to keep in repair the structure and exterior of the dwelling-house (including drains, gutters and external pipes),

(b) to keep in repair and proper working order the installations in the dwelling-house for the supply of water, gas and electricity and for sanitation (including basins, sinks, baths and sanitary conveniences, but not other fixtures, fittings and appliances for making use of the supply of water, gas or electricity), and

(c) to keep in repair and proper working order the installations in the dwelling-house for space heating and heating water."

If the landlord is in breach of an express or implied covenant to repair, and this has led to an escape of water which has caused damage to the tenant, the landlord is liable to the tenant, but only if he has had notice of the disrepair and has failed to remedy it. Further, the landlord is liable to the owner or occupier of premises other than those of his tenants affected by the escape of water only if he was negligent.

In the case of *Wadsworth v Nagle* [2005] EWHC 26 (QB), a landlord of two flats in a block was sued by the tenant of the lower flat when the failure of sealant round the bath in the upper flat caused water to penetrate and cause dampness in the flat below. The claim was brought under section 4 of the Defective Premises Act 1972. This section imposes a statutory duty of care on landlords in respect of defects occurring in leased premises, and it arises as soon as the landlord has notice of the defect. His duty is to take such care as is reasonable in all the circumstances to see that those likely to be affected by the defect are reasonably safe. Those likely to be affected include the tenant, neighbours and users of the adjacent highway. It was held in *Wadsworth v Nagle* that the claim could succeed only if the landlord had an express or implied right to enter the upper flat to re-seal the bath. As this flat was let on a long lease and the obligation for internal repair was on the tenant, and no right for the landlord to enter and repair in default had been reserved, there was no liability on the landlord's part for the damage to the lower flat.

A tenant of, say, a flat in a block of flats is liable to other tenants in the block if, due to his negligence, he causes water to escape from his flat and damage properties below, for example, where a bath is left running so that it overflows and pours through the floor into the flat below, causing damage to carpets, furniture and decorations. There must, however, be negligence in order for there to be liability in such circumstances. Where a lavatory in an upper flat flooded the flat below, the tenant of the upper flat was held not to be liable as he had not been negligent in causing the defect to occur (*Ross v Fedden* (1872) LR 7 QB 661). The same logic applies where pipes burst causing water damage to flats on lower floors.

8. Checklist

1. If there has been an escape of water collected on someone's land

as a non-natural user of the land, which has caused damage to neighbouring property, the rule in *Rylands v Fletcher* may be invoked to establish liability, subject to defences.

2. Where flooding has been caused by the natural drainage of water from a higher to a lower level, there is no liability.

3. If damage has been caused by the discharge of rainwater from the eaves of a neighbouring property, this may be a nuisance. The offending owner should be notified of the problem and given the opportunity to remedy it.

4. Where flooding has been caused by a blocked stream or piped ditch on a neighbour's land, a complaint should be made to the neighbour, then to the local authority and/or drainage authority, with a request to the authority to take action.

5. If flooding has been caused because a neighbour has altered the course of a natural stream, the neighbour is liable for the damage caused.

6. Where flooding has been caused by a highway being built over a culvert, the highway authority may be liable.

7. Where the public storm or foul sewers are inadequate for the purpose, a complaint to the sewerage undertaker may be made. If this is ineffective, a complaint to the Director General of Water Services is appropriate, with a request for an enforcement order to be made. If no enforcement order is made, it may be appropriate to seek judicial review.

8. If there is a problem with a blocked private sewer pipe, the owner of the pipe is liable to repair the pipe. The sewerage undertaker can do the work and recover the cost from the owner.

9. Where water damage has occurred due to the failure of an installation in a dwelling-house let for less than seven years, the landlord may be liable if he has had notice of the problem.

10. If damage has been caused by the negligence of the owner of a flat which causes water to go through the floor into the flat below, the owner of the upper flat is liable to compensate the owner of the lower flat for the damage.

Chapter 10

Anti-Social Behaviour

1. Introduction

The various causes of action available at law to those suffering adversely from the conduct of their neighbours are described elsewhere in this book. But most ordinary people, whose income or capital is nevertheless over the limits for public funding, are inhibited by the likely cost of seeking the court's assistance. It has already been seen that local authorities have power to intervene in some specific matters; for example, to abate noise nuisance or to require high hedges to be reduced in size. Depending on the nature of the behaviour complained of, it may also be possible for a householder to ask the local authority, the police or a registered social landlord to take action to obtain an anti-social behaviour order (ASBO) against an individual or individuals of the age of ten years and above. The cost of any such proceedings is borne by the authority which takes the action. This power, along with that under the Housing Act 1996 to seek an injunction to curb unacceptable behaviour, are discussed in this chapter, as are local mediation schemes set up to resolve disputes.

Finally, a number of less serious but nevertheless annoying acts of anti-social behaviour have been made criminal offences by the Clean Neighbourhoods and Environment Act 2003. The provisions of this Act are being brought into force in stages and at the time of writing this book, not all sections are yet effective. The Act does not enable a householder to take direct action to prevent his neighbour from engaging in the type of anti-social behaviour covered by the Act, but it does allow the police or local authority to take proceedings to prevent the behaviour from recurring. The type of anti-social behaviour covered by the Act is set out below; see page 147.

2. Anti-Social Behaviour Orders

ASBOs were introduced by the Crime and Disorder Act 1998 and were designed to tackle loutish behaviour in public places, usually committed by young people, and often fuelled by drink and/or drugs. In the event, however, ASBOs have not been confined to such groups. For example, in 2004, a Norfolk farmer was made subject to an ASBO for allowing his pigs to wander onto his neighbours' land causing damage to gardens and crops. The neighbours could no doubt have taken their own proceedings in the county court seeking damages and an injunction, but they did not need to do so. It may not have been Parliament's original intention that ASBOs should be used in this way, but if the local authority is prepared to invoke the legislation in circumstances such as these, then the individual(s) affected would be well advised to pursue this course, particularly if the main aim is to put a stop to the behaviour, rather than to seek damages. The individual(s) affected must, of course, first persuade a relevant authority (the local authority, chief of police or registered social landlord) to bring the proceedings.

The authorities were at first slow to invoke the new procedure. In the eight months following the introduction of ASBOs, only 104 orders were made throughout the country; in 2001, 322 orders were made. But between November 2003 and the end of 2004, 2,600 orders were issued. At the same time, there seems to be little consistency between the various authorities, Greater Manchester accounting for one-fifth of all orders made, while some other authorities have made no applications at all.

The definition of anti-social behaviour
Section 1(1) of the Crime and Disorder Act 1998, as amended, states that an order can be applied for:
   (a) where a person has acted "in an anti-social manner, that is to say, in a manner that caused or was likely to cause harassment, alarm or distress to one or more persons not of the same household as himself; and
   (b) that such an order is necessary to protect relevant persons from further anti-social acts by him".
The term "anti-social behaviour" covers a wide range of conduct and includes behaviour that causes a nuisance or annoyance to another. The behaviour does not have to affect the community generally. The

type of behaviour contemplated under the legislation could include loud parties, rowdy or drunken behaviour, leaving rubbish or abandoning cars, harassment or intimidating behaviour.

It has been said that "harassment is well understood but hard to define" (P Infield and G Platford, *The Law of Harassment and Stalking,* LexisNexis, 2000). It is the effect on the victim, not the conduct itself, which determines whether or not an act constitutes harassment. The legislation is intended to protect injuries to feelings and self-esteem. Thus, any form of behaviour which annoys another could technically amount to harassment.

Furthermore, to fall within section 1(1) of the Act it is not necessary for it to be proved that anyone was actually harassed, alarmed or distressed; it is sufficient to show that the conduct *was likely* to cause harassment, alarm or distress. This is an "evaluative exercise" which the judge has to carry out: Auld LJ in *Chief Constable of Lancashire v Potter* [2003] EWHC 2272 (Admin), *The Times*, 10 November 2003.

Even if the requirements of section 1(1)(a) are met, an ASBO will not be granted unless section 1(1)(b) is also satisfied, namely that an ASBO is "necessary to protect relevant persons from further anti-social acts by" the defendant. This is a further "evaluative exercise" undertaken by the judge. There must be a risk that the defendant will commit further anti-social acts. Thus, if the conduct complained of was out of character or an isolated incident, the court may not be satisfied that there is any need for an order. Similarly, the court may decide not to grant an order where the defendant convinces the court that he regrets his behaviour and will not repeat it.

The procedure

The relevant authority may make an application for an ASBO, to the magistrates' court. The magistrates' court deals with the matter under its civil jurisdiction. Civil rules of evidence apply, so hearsay evidence may be adduced. This is of particular importance in cases where witnesses are too concerned for their own safety to give evidence themselves, freely and openly. But where it is alleged that the defendant has actually carried out acts of an anti-social nature, the criminal standard of proof must be satisfied: *R (on the application of McCann) v Manchester Crown Court* [2002] UKHL 39, [2003] 1 AC 787, [2002] 3 WLR 1313, [2002] 4 All ER 593.

The application must be made within six months from the date of the behaviour concerned, although previous incidents may be referred to in evidence to demonstrate a pattern of behaviour.

The effects of the order
If an order is granted, it prohibits the defendant from doing certain acts. For example, the defendant may be ordered not to go to a particular place. The prohibitions must be clear and specific in time and place so that the defendant can be under no misapprehension as to what he is forbidden to do. The minimum duration of an order is two years.

If an ASBO is breached, the defendant commits a criminal offence and is liable to a term of imprisonment of up to five years.

Interim ASBOs
An application for an interim ASBO may be made, in a similar way to an application for an interim injunction in civil proceedings generally, but requires the permission of the justices' clerk, who must be satisfied that an interim order is necessary. An applicant for an interim order must be careful to ensure that the case is truly urgent; only in the most extreme cases is it likely that the application will be allowed to be made without notice.

An interim order takes effect as soon as it is served on the defendant. If it is not served within seven days of being made, it is of no effect. An interim order lapses if the application for the ASBO is withdrawn or refused.

3. Injunction under the Housing Act 1996
A useful provision, of assistance to those living in the neighbourhood of tenants of local authorities, registered social landlords and housing action trusts, is section 13 of the Anti-Social Behaviour Act 2003. This section has replaced sections 152 and 153 of the Housing Act 1996 and added new sections 153A to E. Under these new sections the relevant landlord may apply to the county court for an injunction to prohibit anti-social behaviour which "directly or indirectly relates to or affects the housing management functions of a relevant landlord". This conduct does not need actually to cause nuisance or annoyance to a particular individual; it is sufficient that it is *capable* of causing

nuisance or annoyance to people in the neighbourhood. Where that conduct includes the use or threat of violence, or there is a significant risk of harm, the court may attach a power of arrest and exclude the defendant from his home under an ouster order, and from a particular area under an exclusion order. Such draconian orders should be sought only in serious cases.

In *Moat Housing Group South Ltd v Harris and Another* [2005] EWCA Civ 287, [2005] 3 WLR 691 (CA), the claimant applied for an injunction without notice under sections 153A, 153C and 153D of the Housing Act 1993 as amended by the Anti-Social Behaviour Act 2003, the injunction to include an ouster order. The claimant was a registered social landlord of a fairly new estate in Hampshire. Mr Harris and Ms Hartless were former co-habitees. Ms Hartless lived in one of the claimant's houses as tenant, together with her four children, aged between six and fourteen years. The residents on the estate complained that the defendants and their children, together with another family, had committed anti-social behaviour. It was also alleged that the children bullied other children on the estate and that Ms Hartless encouraged them in this behaviour. She and Mr Harris were also accused of threatening residents.

The district judge decided, at a hearing without notice, that the defendants' appalling behaviour justified an ouster order requiring Ms Hartless to leave her home, and an exclusion order preventing the defendants from entering a large part of the area where they lived. A power of arrest was also granted. Without any prior notice or warning, Ms Hartless was then visited, at 9 p.m., by her landlord's representatives and the police, attempting to evict her and the children. The police were evidently uneasy about evicting a single mother and four children at that time of night and suggested to Ms Hartless that she telephone a solicitor. The solicitor obtained an order from a High Court judge staying the ouster and exclusion orders. When the matter came before the court it was made clear that "no order should be made in civil or family proceedings without notice to the other side unless there is a very good reason for departing from the general rule that notice must be given". The court should act without notice only in cases of emergency where the interests of justice or the protection of the applicant or a child demands immediate intervention. Such cases are rare. In *Moat Housing* the judge added that a "without notice" order should be proportionate to the mischief it is designed to prevent.

Further, it would have been appropriate simply to have made an order restraining the defendants from contacting witnesses, prohibiting them from causing nuisance or annoyance, and directing them to exercise reasonable parental control over their children.

4.   The Clean Neighbourhoods and Environment Act 2005

As mentioned in the introduction to this chapter, certain forms of anti-social behaviour are targeted in the Clean Neighbourhoods and Environment Act 2005.

The Act makes it an offence for anyone engaged in the business of selling motor vehicles to leave two or more vehicles within 500 metres of each other on a road or roads where they are exposed or advertised for sale. The Act also make it an offence to carry out works of repair, maintenance, servicing, improvement or dismantling of a motor vehicle on a road, unless the work is being carried out as a consequence of an accident or breakdown occurring within the previous 72 hours, or a local authority has authorised such work to be carried out after that period.

There are provisions in the Act relating to the clearance of litter and refuse, the prevention of fly-posting and keeping dogs under control.

Noise nuisance created by intruder alarms being left to ring is catered for, local authorities being empowered to designate "alarm notification areas". A "responsible person" can then be required to nominate a key-holder in respect of alarmed premises, who is able to silence the alarm. Where the alarm has been sounding continuously for more than twenty minutes, or intermittently for more than one hour, and the noise is likely to give those living or working in the area reasonable cause for annoyance, then an authorised officer of the local authority has power to gain entry to the premises to silence the alarm if the nominated key-holder cannot be brought to do it.

5.   Mediation Schemes

Many local authorities have anti-social behaviour teams, including anti-social behaviour co-ordinators. They may attempt to resolve problems by way of community mediation. Mediation can help to deal with unacceptable behaviour, such as the inconsiderate parking of cars, children playing in the street, and noise nuisance, for example by barking dogs.

Local authorities which do not have community mediation schemes, and even those which do, may refer a matter to a mediation organisation such as Mediation UK or, in the North of England, UNITE. These are both voluntary organisations. Their websites are www.mediationuk.org.uk and www.unite-mediation.org respectively.

The mediator's role is to help the parties themselves to come to a solution which is acceptable to both sides. This is useful in cases concerning anti-social behaviour of the types discussed in this chapter, where litigation is not the ideal way of resolving the situation. Apart from the expense of taking the matter to court, both parties have to continue living as neighbours and the antagonism which can be generated by litigation is not conducive to good neighbourly relations once a case is over.

Mediation, through the auspices of the local authority, is often a sensible option, and a solicitor who has the client's best interests at heart should canvas this course of action and, in appropriate circumstances, recommend it. Not all clients are, of course, amenable to this kind of process and may be determined to have their day in court. Furthermore, the perpetrator of the anti-social behaviour may not co-operate, perhaps denying that his behaviour is having a deleterious effect, and/or refusing even to discuss modifying his behaviour. In such circumstances, the neighbour who is the victim may have to try to persuade the relevant authority to apply for an ASBO, or prove, with a view to court action, that the offending behaviour constitutes a tort or perhaps even a criminal offence.

6. Checklist

1. Is the client suffering from harassment, alarm or distress caused by the actions of neighbours or their children?
2. If so, are the neighbours tenants of a local authority, registered social landlord or housing action trust?
3. If the answers to 1 and 2 are yes, it may be appropriate to complain to the landlord asking for action under sections 135A to E of the Housing Act 1996 to be taken.
4. If the answer to 1 is yes, but the answer to 2 is no, a complaint to the local authority or the police, depending on the nature of the

conduct in question, may be appropriate, with a view to their seeking an ASBO or referring the matter to community mediation.

5. Minor types of anti-social behaviour may come within the Clean Neighbourhoods and Environment Act.

Chapter 11

Covenants

1. Introduction

A client may complain that his neighbour is doing something on his land which the client does not care for. The neighbour may, for example, be planning to build another house on the land, or operate a taxi business from home. The client may say that the neighbour cannot do what he is proposing to do; that there is something in the deeds to prevent it. If there is, it is probably a restrictive covenant. If the client's complaint is that the neighbour is not complying with an obligation contained in his deeds to do something, such as maintain a fence, for the benefit of the client's property, then this could mean that the neighbour is in breach of a positive covenant.

The first part of this chapter is devoted to restrictive covenants; whether or not they are enforceable, and if so, how; and how they may be modified or extinguished. After a brief reference to positive covenants, the second part of the chapter concerns covenants in leases of houses and flats, and how they regulate the behaviour of the landlord and tenant.

2. Restrictive Covenants

A restrictive covenant is a promise contained in a deed not to do something on or concerning the covenantor's land, which promise exists for the benefit of the covenantee's land. Such covenants are usually imposed to regulate the use of land being sold, for the protection and benefit of land being retained. The most common examples of restrictive covenants are those which limit the number of buildings which may be erected on the land sold, or the use to which those buildings may be put. The exact meaning of a particular covenant is, as will be seen, a matter of construction of the words used.

To establish whether or not the client has the benefit of a restrictive covenant preventing his neighbour from doing the thing to which the client objects, the title deeds must be consulted to ascertain whether, at some time in the past, the owner of the neighbour's land entered into a covenant not to do the act complained of.

There is no particular form of wording that has to be adopted in order to create a restrictive covenant (*Mackenzie v Childers* (1890) LR 43 ChD 265), provided that the words used show that the parties intended that there should be an agreement between them that one of them would refrain from doing the act in question. On the other hand, the covenant must not be so vaguely worded as to be void for uncertainty: *National Trust v Midlands Electricity Board* [1952] Ch 380, [1952] 1 All ER 298.

Obviously, one party to the deed containing the covenant has, on the face of it, the benefit, and the other has the burden of it. In addition, since the introduction of the Contracts (Rights of Third Parties) Act 1999, a third party may have the right to enforce any term of the contract if the requirements of the Act are satisfied. This is so if the contract containing the covenant says that the third party may enforce it, or the contract purports to confer a benefit on him in addition to or instead of another party. The third party must be identified in the contract, either personally, or as a member of a class of a particular description.

Registration

To be valid against successors in title to the original covenantor, a restrictive covenant created after 1 January 1926 must be registered. In the case of unregistered land, a restrictive covenant is registrable as a land charge of class D(ii), and the covenant is void against a purchaser for value of the legal estate unless it is so registered (Land Charges Act 1972, section 4(6)). Registration as a class D(ii) land charge constitutes actual notice of the covenant to all persons for all purposes, so long as the registration continues in force (Law of Property Act 1925, section 198(1), as amended by the Land Charges Act 1972).

Where registered land is concerned, the position before the coming into force of the Land Registration Act 2002 was that a restrictive covenant would be protected by way of a notice in the charges register. If the covenant was not so noted, then the land vested in the registered proprietor free of the restrictive covenant, and any purchaser of the legal estate would take free of it, even if he actually knew that the covenant existed,

Since 13 October 2003, when the 2002 Act came into force, a restrictive covenant must be protected by the entry of an agreed or unilateral notice in the register of the title to the land affected (section 32(1), Land Registration Act 2002). If the restrictive covenant was already noted on the register before that date, it remains valid.

Enforcement by and against successors in title
The original party to the deed who has the benefit of the covenant can enforce it against the other contracting party who has given the promise. In practice, the more usual situations concern successors in title of the original parties, and questions of enforceability between them. The original covenantor remains liable under the covenant even after disposing of the land; in the event of enforcement proceedings against him, he would usually wish to bring into the proceedings his successor in title – the person who has breached the covenant – as an additional defendant under Part 20 of the Civil Procedure Rules, and seek an indemnity from him.

The Court of Appeal, in *Smith and Snipes Hall Farm v River Douglas Catchment Board* [1949] 2 KB 500, [1949] 2 All ER 179 (CA), stated that, at common law, the benefit of restrictive covenants passes to successors in title if:

  (a) the covenant shows that the parties intended this to happen;
  (b) the covenantee holds an interest in the land to be benefited;
  (c) the land to be benefited is described so as to be ascertainable accurately (with the aid, if necessary, of extrinsic evidence); and
  (d) the covenant "touches and concerns the land".

Evidence of intention is usually derived from the wording of the covenant itself. A standard clause would be "The covenantor covenants with the covenantee, his successors in title, and those deriving title under him". Even if these words are not included, they are deemed to be included by virtue of section 78(1) of the Law of Property Act 1925.

The requirement that the covenant must "touch and concern" the land means that the covenant must have been intended to benefit the land itself, as opposed to benefiting the covenantee personally: *Morrells of Oxford Ltd v Oxford United Football Club Ltd* [2001] Ch 459, [2001] 2 WLR 128 (CA). The covenant must affect the nature, quality, mode of use or value of the benefited land: *P & A Swift Investments v Combined English Stores Group* [1989] AC 632, [1988] 3 WLR 313, [1988] 2 All ER 885 (HL).

At common law, the burden of restrictive covenants could not pass to successors in title. Thus, to be enforceable at common law, it must be shown not only that the person seeking to enforce has the benefit of the covenant, but also that the person against whom enforcement is sought is bound by the covenant; as has been seen, the burden of a restrictive covenant does not pass to successors in title at law. Consequently, for all practical purposes, where neither party is the original contracting party, proceedings at common law can be ruled out; the claim must be pursued in equity.

The equitable rules
For the equitable rules to be relied upon to enforce a restrictive covenant against a successor to the original covenantor, the claimant must show that the benefit of the covenant has passed to him in equity. He must therefore show that:
  (a) he has retained land capable of being benefited by the covenant;
  (b) that land is ascertainable with reasonable certainty;
  (c) the covenant touches and concerns the land; and
  (d) the benefit of the covenant has been assigned to the purchaser or annexed to land acquired by him.
The benefit of a covenant can be assigned just like the benefit of any other contract. It is necessary to show that every time the land was transferred, an assignment was effected, so that the person seeking to enforce the covenant can demonstrate an unbroken chain of assignments back to the original covenantee. The assignments must also take place simultaneously with the transfers of the land: a subsequent assignment is not sufficient, because the benefit of a covenant cannot exist separated from the land to which it appertains: *Re Union of London & Smith's Bank Ltd's Conveyance* [1933] Ch 611.

It is much easier if the benefit of the covenant is attached to the land by annexation, as the benefit then passes automatically on every subsequent transfer of the land. There is usually an express annexation of the covenant when granted. The usual form of wording is that the covenant is made "for the benefit of" the specified land. Another form of annexation is to state that X covenants with Y "the owner for the time being of" the specified land. The annexure has to be to the land. It is not sufficient to state that the covenant is "made with Y, his heirs, successors, executors, administrators and assigns" because these people are not linked with the benefited land: *Renals v Cowlishaw* (1878) 9 Ch D 125.

In *Crest Nicholson Residential (South) Ltd v McAllister* [2004] EWCA Civ 410, [2004] 1 WLR 2409, [2004] 2 All ER 991 (CA), the court applied certain *obiter dicta* in the Court of Appeal case of *Federated Homes Ltd v Mill Lodge Properties Ltd* [1980] 1 WLR 594, [1980] 1 All ER 371, that, provided the land to be benefited is clearly identified, section 78(1) of the Law of Property Act 1925 provides a statutory annexation of the covenant to the land. This section states:

"A covenant relating to any land of the covenantee shall be deemed to be made with the covenantee and his successors in title and the persons deriving title under him or them, and shall have effect as if such successors and other persons were expressed."

If this is correct, then it is not necessary for the person seeking to enforce the covenant to show that the covenant was properly annexed to the land or assigned.

There is a potential problem where a covenantor gives a covenant for the benefit of a large area of land. It might be the case that not all the land is capable of being benefited by the covenant and, if so, the covenant will not be binding on a purchaser of part of the land which was not capable of benefiting from the covenant, unless the covenant is expressed to be "for the whole or any part of" the land in question. The burden of a restrictive covenant may run with the land in equity so that the covenant can be enforced against a successor in title of the original covenantor. This was established in the case of *Tulk v Moxhay* (1848) 18 LJ Ch 83. A restrictive covenant is thus an "equitable burden on the land", which is unenforceable against a *bona fide* purchaser of the legal estate in the burdened land who does not have notice of the covenant.

Building schemes

Where a new estate of houses is being planned, the developer/vendor often lays out the land in plots, and imposes similar restrictive covenants on each property, intending that each purchaser will have the right to enforce the covenants against any other purchaser of the properties in the scheme. This is known as a building scheme. Where such a scheme exists, even though the developer/vendor sells off all the plots so that he no longer retains an interest in any land in the scheme, the covenants remain enforceable. The idea is that all the owners of properties within the scheme are under the same obligations, which are also for their mutual benefit. It forms a kind of "local law" on the estate. The most common covenants in a building scheme are designed to retain the appearance of the area in a particular way, for example, by requiring all front gardens to be kept "open plan". It would defeat the whole idea of the scheme, which all the purchasers buy into, if the covenants were to become unenforceable once the developer/vendor had sold the last plot.

To ascertain whether or not a building scheme is in existence the question is whether the covenants were intended to be for the benefit of the various purchasers, or for the benefit of the vendor's remaining property. In the case of *Elliston v Reacher* [1908] 2 Ch 374, the Court of Appeal approved four requirements for a building scheme where the claimant is suing for breach of covenant. The requirements are that:

(a) all material parties derived their title from a common vendor;
(b) before selling the plots to the claimant and defendant, or their respective predecessors in title, the vendor laid out the estate, or a definite part of it, including the parties' land, for sale in lots subject to restrictions which (though they might vary in some particular) were consistent only with a general scheme of development;
(c) these restrictions were (and were intended to be by the vendor) for the benefit of all the lots, whether or not it was also intended and did benefit the vendor's land; and
(d) the parties, or their predecessors in title, bought their land on the footing that the restrictions were intended to inure for the benefit of the other lots in the scheme.

In subsequent cases it has been held that the above four tests are to be used as a guide only: the important question is whether the parties intended to create a building scheme.

For a purchaser to take subject to the covenants under the building scheme, the developer/vendor must register the covenants in respect of each plot against the first purchasers in the same way that restrictive covenants generally must be registered if they are to be enforceable against purchasers of the legal estate (see above, page 151).

Construction of restrictive covenants

As stated above, the precise meaning of a particular restrictive covenant is a matter of construction in every case.

A covenant to use premises as a private dwelling house only is broken if the nature of the use of the premises changes so that the character is no longer that of a dwelling house. So, the covenant is broken if the covenantee uses the premises as a school (*Wickenden v Webster* (1856) 25 LJ QB 264), or as a boarding house (*Hobson v Tulloch* [1898] 1 Ch 424), but not if the premises are let to four students with separate study bedrooms but sharing a lounge, kitchen and bathroom (*Roberts v Howlett* [2002] 1 P&CR 234).

The recent case of *Martin v David Wilson Homes Ltd* [2004] EWCA Civ 1027, [2004] 3 EGLR 77 (CA) concerned a covenant "not to use or permit or suffer any buildings to be erected thereon or on any part thereof to be used for any purpose other than as a private dwelling house". It was held that the use of the word "a" did not mean that only one dwelling house could be erected.

Remedies for breach

Restrictive covenants are enforced and breaches remedied by means of court action for damages for breach of contract and, usually, for an injunction to prevent the continuation or recurrence of the breach. In certain circumstances, however, an action may fail, or the result may differ from that which was sought. These circumstances are as follows:

(a) the character of the area where the land is situated may have changed significantly, or there may have been other changes of circumstances which render the covenant worthless to protect the land which benefits from the covenant;

(b) the covenantee may have acted in such a way as to acquiesce in the breach. The acquiescence must be of such a nature as to amount to its being unconscionable for the covenant to be enforced: *Shaw v Applegate* [1977] 1 WLR 970, [1978] 1 All ER 123 (CA). Where a covenant has been broken for over twenty years continuously, it may well be taken to have been released;

(c) an injunction to prevent the breach of covenant or positively to remedy the breach will not necessarily be granted. An injunction is a discretionary remedy and is not granted where damages are an adequate remedy.

In the case of *Wrotham Park Estate Co Ltd v Parkside Homes Ltd* [1974] 1 WLR 798, [1974] 2 All ER 321, the defendant developers had built a number of houses in breach of a covenant not to develop except in strict accordance with an approved layout plan. The covenant had been registered. The breach was deliberate. The judge found the defendant liable, but refused to grant an injunction which would have required the houses to have been pulled down. Although the claimants had not suffered any loss as there was no diminution in the value of the land they retained, the judge did not merely award nominal damages. Instead, he awarded the claimants damages equivalent to five per cent of the defendant's profit, estimating it to be the sum that a covenantor would be prepared to pay for the release of the covenant.

In this and other cases where buildings have been erected in breach of covenant, the courts have not been prepared to grant injunctions where the claimants have stood by and watched the buildings being built without applying for an interim injunction.

The *Wrotham Park* case has been followed in *Jaggard v Sawyer* [1995] 1 WLR 269, [1995] 2 All ER 189 (CA) and *Gafford v Graham* (1999) 77 P&CR 73, [1999] 3 EGLR 75 (CA);

(d) if the land with the benefit of the covenant comes under the same ownership as the land subject to the covenant, then the covenant disappears and does not reappear if one of the pieces of land is sold again.

As a breach of covenant is a breach of contract, the usual rules relating to damages for breach of contract apply. The purpose of damages is to place the injured party, so far as money can do it, in the same position as he would have been in had the covenant been complied with. The contractual rules with regard to remoteness of damage also apply. The person in breach is liable to compensate the other party for such damage as may fairly and reasonably be considered as arising naturally from the breach.

Injunctions are dealt with elsewhere in this book.

The modification of restrictive covenants

Under section 84 of the Law of Property Act 1925 an interested person may apply to the Lands Tribunal wholly or partially to discharge or modify a restrictive covenant affecting freehold land. Before discharging or modifying a covenant, the tribunal must be satisfied that:

(a) due to changes in the character of the property or the neighbourhood or other circumstances, the covenant is obsolete (section 84(1)(a)); or

(b) the continued existence of the covenant would impede some reasonable user of the land for public or private purposes (section 84(1)(aa)); or

(c) those having the benefit of the restriction, being of full age and capacity, have agreed, expressly or by implication, by their acts or omissions, to the covenants being discharged or modified (section 84(1)(b)); or

(d) the proposed discharge or modification will not injure those who have the benefit of the covenant (section 84(1)(c)).

If the covenant is discharged or modified, the Lands Tribunal has power to order compensation to be paid to the covenantee. The basis of this compensation is either the loss suffered by the covenantee as a result of the discharge or modification, or to reflect the lower price that the covenantor paid for the land as a result of its being subject to the covenant.

Where a covenant was imposed as part of a building scheme it may be more difficult for an applicant to succeed in having it removed. Similarly, where the applicant was an original contracting party, it is difficult for that party to obtain a release.

Although the jurisdiction of the Lands Tribunal to modify or discharge a restrictive covenant is discretionary, an order ought to be made under section 84 if the case comes within the provisions of that section, unless there is a good reason for an order not to be made (*Re*

University of Westminster's Application [1998] 3 All ER 1014, (1999) 78 P&CR 82 (CA).

Where there are objectors to the discharge or modification of the covenant, and those objectors have themselves benefited from a breach of the covenant in question, then any compensation that the Lands Tribunal is empowered to order may be reduced or denied altogether. In the case of *Re Kennet Properties Ltd's Application* (1996) 72 P&CR 353, [1996] 2 EGLR 163 (Lands Tribunal), some of the objectors, in breach of the covenant, had had houses built on the land which was the subject of the covenant; others had built beyond a stated line in breach of the covenant. The former were denied compensation and the latter had their compensation reduced.

Grounds: When considering the grounds upon which to make an application under section 84 it is worth remembering that the Lands Tribunal disapproves of applications in which all the grounds in section 84 are pleaded in the alternative. The tribunal expects the applicant to choose the ground appropriate to the case.

Ground (a) above is applicable where the covenant is "obsolete", that is, the covenant can no longer serve its original purpose. So, for example, a covenant restricting building on a piece of land to the erection of a single dwelling house will not protect that land if, since the covenant was imposed, all the land around and about it has been developed by the building of blocks of flats. It does not follow that the covenant is obsolete if only some development has taken place in breach of covenant, but it may well be obsolete if the character of the whole neighbourhood has changed as a result of such development. It does not follow that, simply because planning permission has been granted for a particular development which would be prevented if the covenant against such development were effective, the Lands Tribunal would take the view that the covenant is obsolete, or that the covenant is impeding a reasonable user of the land. The planning permission is *prima facie* evidence that the proposed use of the land is a reasonable use of the land, but there may be other reasonable uses for the land which do not require the release or modification of the covenant. See *Re Azfar's Application* [2002] 1 P&CR 17 LT.

In the case of *Re Bass Ltd's Application* (1973) 26 P&CR 156, [1973] JPL 378 (Lands Tribunal), it was stated that, in considering a section 84(1)(aa) ground (impeding reasonable user), the tribunal

should pose the following questions:
1. is the proposed user reasonable?
2. do the covenants impede that user?
3. does impeding the user secure practical benefits to the objectors?
4. if yes, are those benefits of substantial value or advantage?
5. if no, would money be adequate compensation?

Section 84(1)(aa) is subject to a limitation imposed by section 84 (1A), which was inserted into the 1925 Act by the Law of Property Act 1969. A modification or discharge under subsection (1)(aa) is available only if the restriction:

"(a) does not secure to persons entitled to the benefit of it any practical benefits of substantial value or advantage to them; or

(b) is contrary to the public interest;

and that money will be an adequate compensation for the loss or disadvantage (if any) which any such person will suffer from the discharge or modification".

Section 84(1B), also inserted by the 1969 Act, goes on to state:

"In determining whether a case is one falling within subsection (1A) above, and in determining whether (in any such case or otherwise) a restriction ought to be discharged or modified, the Lands Tribunal shall take into account the development plan and declared or ascertainable pattern for the grant or refusal of planning permissions in the relevant areas, as well as the period at which and the context in which the restriction was created or imposed and any other material circumstances."

Subsection (1C) of section 84 of the Act enables the Lands Tribunal to add provisions restricting the user of, or building on, land if the tribunal considers it reasonable to do so and the applicant agrees. The tribunal may refuse to modify a restriction without those additional provisions.

Procedure: The procedure in the Lands Tribunal is governed by the Lands Tribunal Rules 1996 (SI 1996 No. 1022) and a practice direction issued by the tribunal. Once the application to modify or discharge a covenant has been lodged with the Lands Tribunal, the tribunal issues directions. The tribunal requires the applicant to draft a publicity notice for approval by the tribunal; it may supply a precedent for this purpose. The tribunal then either approves the notice, or approves it subject to specified amendments. The directions also state upon whom the notice of the application should be served and how public notice of the application should be effected. This is usually by placing the notice in local newspapers and at the site of the land which is the subject of the application. The directions also state the period within which objections to the application are to be received by the registrar of the Lands Tribunal. This is twenty-eight days from the date of the notice, and the date must be included in the notice. The notice also states that:

(a) those who lodge objections become parties to the proceedings;

(b) objectors may appear at the hearing, if there is one; and

(c) the tribunal may make an award of costs against an unsuccessful party.

When the period for objections has elapsed, the applicant must file with the tribunal a certificate of compliance with the directions, listing all the persons served with the notice and attaching a page of the newspaper in which the notice was published. Once this has been done the tribunal may be prepared to deal with the application on the basis of the paperwork supplied if there are no objectors, or it may proceed to a hearing. The tribunal can refuse to exercise its discretion in an applicant's favour, even if no one objects to the modification or discharge of the covenant: *Re University of Westminster's Application* [1998] 3 All ER 1014, (1999) 78 P&CR 82 (CA).

Where the tribunal orders the discharge or modification of a restriction subject to the payment of compensation, the discharge or modification does not take effect until the registrar has endorsed on the order that the compensation has been paid. The tribunal may order that the compensation be paid within a specified time, failing which the order will cease to have effect.

An appeal from a decision of the Lands Tribunal may be made on a point of law only, by way of case stated, to the Court of Appeal. Any appeal must be made within twenty-eight days of the tribunal's decision.

Other methods of releasing covenants
A covenant may be released by agreement between the party who has the benefit of the covenant and the party who has the burden. The

party with the benefit of the covenant may seek payment for the release of the covenant. How much can be exacted depends on how important it is to the covenantor to be released, and the extent to which the covenant actually benefits the covenantee. If the parties agree to release the covenant, their agreement should be evidenced by entering into a deed of release.

A covenant is also released where the land with the benefit of the covenant and the land with the burden of it come into the same ownership: *Re Tiltwood, Sussex* [1978] Ch 269, [1978] 3 WLR 474, [1978] 2 All ER 1091 (Ch D). There is one exception to this rule: building schemes. In such cases, the covenant springs back into existence once two plots which came under common ownership are restored to separate ownership: *Texaco Antilles Ltd v Kernochan* [1973] AC 609, [1973] 2 WLR 381, [1973] 2 All ER 118 (PC).

3. Positive Covenants

More usually, a client seeks to prevent an activity by enforcing a restrictive covenant, but occasionally there may be a positive covenant in existence which the client wishes to enforce. The rules relating to positive covenants, which require action on the part of the covenantor, are different from those which govern restrictive covenants.

If, for example, A sells part of his land to B who is required by covenant to construct and keep maintained a roadway which is a shared accessway to A's and B's land, does the benefit and burden of such a covenant pass to successors in title? First, the original covenantor remains liable under the covenant even if he parts with the land. It is important, therefore, that if B sells his land, he obtains a covenant of indemnity from his purchaser, because the burden of the covenant does not pass to successors in title.

The general rule is that neither the benefit nor the burden of positive covenants runs with the land, so that once either piece of land changes hands, the covenant cannot be enforced either by a successor to the covenantee or against a successor to the covenantor. This is unsatisfactory in cases such as that in the example above concerning the maintenance of the roadway.

This problem may be overcome by the doctrine that a person cannot take a benefit under a deed without taking on the obligations attached. In *Halsall v Brizell* [1957] Ch 169, [1957] 2 WLR 123,

[1957] 1 All ER 371, land was sold off in building plots and the vendor retained the roads and sewers. It was held that the house owners had no right to use the roads and sewers without contributing to their upkeep. Although the positive covenant under the transfer deed to maintain the road could not be enforced under the rules relating to the enforcement of covenants against the successors in title to the original covenantors, the effect was the same. It is, however, fair to note that the rule in *Halsall* is invoked rather more often than it actually succeeds.

4. Covenants Between Landlord and Tenant

The law relating to landlord and tenant is extensive and often complex. It is beyond the scope of this book to do more than point out some general principles relating to covenants in leases; beyond that, readers are advised to consult the specialist works on the subject.

A lease contains provisions setting out the rights and obligations of both the landlord and the tenant. The covenants on the part of the landlord are likely to be fewer than those of the tenant. They usually set out the extent of the landlord's repairing and insuring obligations (if any) and provide for the landlord to grant the tenant "quiet enjoyment" of the demised premises, but probably little else. Quiet enjoyment is the right to enjoy the premises without interruption or interference from the landlord.

Implied covenants

Even if there is no express covenant on the part of the landlord to repair the property, this may be implied. Section 11 of the Landlord and Tenant Act 1985 states that in a letting of residential premises for less than seven years there is implied a covenant that the landlord will keep in repair the structure and exterior of the property, and the installations for the supply of water, gas and electricity and for space and water heating.

Other implied covenants on the part of the landlord are to allow the tenant quiet enjoyment of the property and not to derogate from his grant. The latter overlaps the former; the landlord must not take away with one hand what he gives with the other. Thus, where there was a clause in a lease that the premises were to be used for the business of a timber merchant and the demised premises included a wood-drying shed which required the free flow of air, the tenant was able to prevent the landlord building on nearby land which would have prevented the free flow of air to the timber drying shed, as this would have derogated from the grant of the lease of the premises made by the landlord: *Aldin v Latimer Clark, Muirhead & Co* [1894] 2 Ch 437.

The covenants on the part of the tenant are usually much more extensive, enabling the landlord to regulate the tenant's use of the property; they may deal, for example, with whether or not the tenant can keep an animal on the premises, hang out washing, or have an exposed television aerial.

Enforcement

The landlord may, of course, seek to enforce a covenant in a lease to which his tenant is subject if the tenant breaches that covenant. Very often, however, it is not the landlord who is affected by the tenant's behaviour but some third party, such as a neighbour of the tenant, who is perhaps another tenant of the same landlord. Usually, the neighbour cannot directly enforce the covenant and require the wrongdoing tenant to comply with his covenants, because the neighbour is not a party to the contract (that is, the lease or tenancy agreement between the landlord and tenant). On the other hand, the leases of individual flats in a block often contain a covenant by the landlord to enforce the covenants against one tenant at the request of another tenant. It is usually a precondition that the aggrieved tenant pays the landlord's costs of taking the action. In this way, indirectly, an affected tenant can force another tenant to comply with his covenants. Otherwise, the flat owner has to rely on the general law, such as that of nuisance or negligence, to control the activities of neighbouring flat owners.

The question whether covenants in leases may be enforced by or against successors in title to the original tenant has been greatly simplified by the Landlord and Tenant (Covenants) Act 1995, which provides that the benefit and burden of all landlords' covenants and tenants' covenants pass on an assignment of the whole or any part of the premises, or of the reversion in them (section 3). The Act applies to all leases entered into after 1 January 1996. For older leases, the law which applied prior to this Act continues to apply. This is not dealt with in detail here, but for all practical purposes, it may be said that the successors in title to the original tenants are subject to the covenants contained in their leases and are liable to the landlord should they be in breach.

Perhaps the most significant change to the law which the 1995 Act brought about was to introduce some relief for an original tenant after the lease had been assigned. Under the law in force before 1 January 1996, as for covenants in respect of freehold land, the original parties remained liable even after an assignment. Thus, an original tenant under a lease for, say, ninety-nine years remained liable under the covenants contained in the lease for many years after he had assigned the lease. He could find that some tenant to whom the lease had been assigned after several intervening assignments might fail to pay the rent, and the landlord could look to the original tenant to pay the arrears. In a time of rising rents this did not matter too much because the landlord could always forfeit the lease and re-let at a higher rent. In the recession of the 1990s, however, rents fell dramatically and original tenants found that landlords were demanding what were often considerable sums, on the default of a subsequent tenant of whom the original tenant may have had no knowledge.

This problem was addressed in the 1995 Act. In respect of leases created before 1 January 1996, section 19 provides that an original tenant cannot be required to pay rent or a fixed charge owed by the current tenant unless he had been served with a notice by the landlord in a prescribed form. That notice cannot claim for more than six months' rent, although the landlord can serve a series of notices. Second, an original tenant who pays up under such a notice can require the landlord to grant him an overriding lease. This makes him the landlord of the recalcitrant tenant and puts him in control, so that if the current tenant defaults again, the original tenant can forfeit the lease and re-let to a more reliable tenant.

For leases entered into after 1 January 1996 ("new leases"), the original covenantor is released from his covenants once the lease is assigned. Without more, this would have seriously affected the landlord, who would no longer be able to enforce the lease covenants against the original covenantor. Subsequent tenants are also released on assignment. To counteract this, the 1995 Act assists landlords by enabling them to require the tenant to enter into an authorised guarantee agreement so that the tenant has to guarantee his own assignee's performance of the lease covenants. The 1995 Act also provides that the parties may agree in advance the circumstances in which the landlord may refuse consent to an assignment, and the conditions which the landlord may impose for granting consent to an assignment.

Forfeiture

There is, of course, one additional remedy available to a landlord of leasehold premises where his tenant is in breach of covenant, and that is that he may be able to forfeit the lease. Where the breach is non-payment of rent, no notice has to be given to the tenant before the landlord can take steps to forfeit. For any other breach, the landlord must serve a notice on the tenant under section 146 of the Law of Property Act 1925. This notice must specify the breach and, where the breach is capable of remedy, require it to be remedied within a reasonable time. If the tenant does not remedy the breach, then the landlord can proceed to forfeit. By section 168 of the Commonhold and Leasehold Reform Act 2002, a landlord must obtain a determination that the tenant of residential premises is in breach of covenant before he can serve a section 146 notice and then forfeit the lease.

The only way that a landlord of *residential* premises may forfeit his tenant's lease is by court action for an order for possession. The forfeiture is effected as soon as the proceedings are issued and served, but the landlord is not entitled to possession until the court orders it.

A landlord can lose the right of forfeiture if he waives it by doing some act, in the knowledge of the breach, which signifies that he is treating the lease as continuing. The usual way in which a landlord waives his right to forfeit is by demanding or accepting payment of rent.

A tenant may ask the court for relief from forfeiture. This is usually given if the tenant remedies or promises to remedy the breach within a reasonable time and pays the landlord's costs.

Assured and assured shorthold tenancies

If the residential tenant has an assured or an assured shorthold tenancy, the landlord cannot forfeit, as section 5 abrogates the common law of forfeiture. The procedure here for obtaining possession would be for the landlord to serve a notice under section 8 or 21 of the Housing Act 1988, and commence proceedings for possession once the notice period has expired. Section 8 is applicable where the tenant is in breach of one of the terms of the tenancy where only two weeks' notice, expiring at the end of a period of the tenancy, need be given.

The procedure under section 21 is longer in that the notice period is two months, but no proof of fault or breach is required. Section 21 is used where the landlord seeks possession at or after the end of the fixed term of the tenancy. If the landlord carries out the correct procedure under section 21, the court has no discretion and must grant the landlord a possession order. Under section 8, the nature of the breach is determinative of whether a possession order is mandatory or discretionary. For example, if the tenant is two months or more in arrears of rent as at the date of the notice and the date of the hearing, the court has no discretion but to make a possession order. If the rent is less than two months in arrears at either date, then the court has a discretion whether or not to make an order. In such circumstances it usually makes a possession order suspended on terms as to the repayment of the arrears.

5. Checklist

1. If the original parties to the covenant still own their respective land, both positive and negative (i.e., restrictive) covenants can be enforced.
2. To be valid against non-original parties, a restrictive covenant must be registered.
3. The benefit of restrictive covenants may be enforced in law and equity by successors to the covenantee, subject to conditions.
4. The burden of a restrictive covenant does not in law pass to successors in title to the covenantor, but may pass in equity.
5. If the covenant is part of a building scheme, those owning plots forming part of the scheme are able to enforce, but are also subject to the covenants.
6. It may be possible to apply to the Lands Tribunal for a restrictive covenant to be released or modified.
7. It may be possible to enforce a positive covenant against successors in title by virtue of the principle that he who takes the benefit must also bear the burden.
8. An injunction will not necessarily be granted; damages may be an adequate remedy. Acquiescence in the breach is also relevant.
9. In respect of covenants contained in a lease, there may be a

provision whereby a tenant can require the landlord to enforce covenants against a tenant neighbour.

Chapter 12

The Resolution of Disputes

1. Introduction

Before embarking on litigation with a neighbour, it is advisable to consider the following hitherto unwritten principles, distilled from long experience in this field:

    (a) both parties will be convinced that they are right, that their opponent is on the verge of insanity, evil or both, and that they cannot possibly lose;

    (b) both parties will tell their advisers that they do not care how much it costs; they are fighting over an important principle, the importance of which will diminish as the costs mount;

    (c) an offer, which is rejected out of hand at the start of a dispute, will start to look very attractive after £25,000 has been spent;

    (d) as costs mount, the dispute stops being about the substance of the argument and focuses instead on costs;

    (e) neither party will come out of the dispute feeling satisfied with the outcome and will invariably maintain that the law is an ass and the only winners are the lawyers.

If these fundamental principles could be grasped at the outset, then warring neighbours would probably resolve their differences much sooner and without recourse to law.

At all times during a dispute, therefore, the parties and their advisers should be thinking not about pursuing each step of the process relentlessly, but about how the dispute can be settled in a way which is acceptable to both parties, and which avoids expending vast sums of money in legal costs. Contrary to popular opinion, lawyers do not view neighbour disputes as a licence to print money. Lawyers have a duty to manage cases in a sensible and cost-effective manner and to search for viable solutions and alternatives to trial, more so now than ever before.

Since the advent of the Civil Procedure Rules in 1998, courts have an overriding objective to deal with cases justly. This principle pervades the whole of the rules, so that when applying the rules, judges must seek to give effect to it. Rule 1.1(2) defines dealing with the case justly as including, so far as is practicable:

"(a) ensuring that the parties are on an equal footing;

(b) saving expense;

(c) dealing with the case in ways which are proportionate:

    (i) to the amount of money involved,

    (ii) to the importance of the case,

    (iii) to the complexity of the issues,

    (iv) to the financial position of each party;

(d) ensuring that it is dealt with expeditiously and fairly; and

(e) allotting to it an appropriate share of the court's resources, while taking into account the need to allot resources to other cases."

Accordingly, strict adherence to the letter of the rules is no longer as important as managing the case in a way that fulfils the overriding objective. Under rule 1.3, the parties are required to help the court to further the overriding objective, and under rule 1.4 the court must further the overriding objective by actively managing cases.

The overriding objective is of fundamental importance in neighbour disputes, which can be difficult to keep under control. It is very easy for the parties, who are close to the dispute, to lose all sense of objectivity. A large part of the lawyer's job is to help them to see the dispute in the wider context.

Much of this work can be done at the outset, when the party first consults a solicitor. The prospective litigant needs to understand the merits of his case, that is, how likely he is to win or lose; how much it is likely to cost; whether he is likely to recover any of his legal costs; and the consequences if he loses. He also needs to view the case in the context of his continuing relationship with his neighbour, and the effect that the existence of the dispute is likely to have on the future saleability of his property.

2. Costs

In any litigation, but particularly in neighbour disputes that are often fought between people with modest means, it is vital that the litigant understands the potential financial consequences of the course upon which he is about to embark. Nothing disrupts the solicitor-client relationship more frequently than misunderstandings about costs. If costs are not kept tightly under control, the solicitor is likely to encounter difficulties in recovering fees. Common complaints are that little or no information was given about costs at the outset; that the estimate was exceeded; and that the solicitor failed to keep the client informed of rising costs.

Disputes between a solicitor and a client over costs can be harmful and interfere with the main objective, which is to resolve the dispute. If the solicitor and client maintain a constant dialogue about costs throughout the case, then such problems are less likely to occur.

Information about costs

At the first meeting with the client, the solicitor should give the client an idea of the likely costs. If the first meeting is arranged over the telephone, the solicitor should ensure the client understands that there will be a charge for the first meeting if that is what the solicitor intends. If the costs are calculated on the basis of an hourly rate, then the solicitor should ensure the client is given the hourly rates of all those who may be called upon to work on the case.

If it is likely that more than one legal professional will work on the case, then the client must understand this and be given full information about the identities of those people and their hourly rates. Sometimes it is necessary for another lawyer to deal with a matter which arises in the absence of the solicitor with conduct of the case. If it is likely that a more senior lawyer, with a higher hourly rate, will be involved, the client must be told at the outset. If the solicitor tells a client that the hourly rate is £140, and in fact a partner does some work on the case at £250 an hour, the client is unlikely to pay the extra cost, unless he has been told in advance that this may happen.

The Solicitors' Costs Information and Client Care Code 1999 (as amended, 9 March 2004) (the "Costs Code") sets out the information about costs that must be given to a client at the outset of a case, and which must be recorded in writing. This should be discussed at the first meeting, and the best place to record it is in the letter setting out the terms of the solicitor/client retainer (for an example of such a letter, see page 206). As well as providing an estimate of the costs of the first stage of the work, the solicitor must give the best estimate that it is possible to give of the likely cost of bringing the matter to a conclusion, assuming it proceeds to a full trial. In doing so, the solicitor needs to think about every eventuality, including the need for expert evidence; the number of witnesses; how long the trial will last; and whether counsel will be retained, and, if so, at what level and for what tasks.

The client should be warned that predicting legal fees is a very inexact science and that any estimates given will need to be refined and updated as the case proceeds. It is good practice to review costs at least every six months, but if the case is moving very rapidly, then more frequent reviews may be advisable.

Cost-benefit and risk analysis
The client also needs to assess whether the cost of the litigation is really worth the benefit to be gained. This is usually the most difficult area to control because it requires a degree of emotional detachment that the client may not have. Paying £50,000 to secure an area of land scarcely large enough to erect a greenhouse would be considered by most to be a bad investment. Nevertheless, litigants frequently expend sums of this magnitude pursuing litigation, usually because their relationships with their neighbours are so poor that they are prepared to spend such sums to inflict what they perceive to be a defeat.

The reality is that a complete victory is very rarely achieved and therefore there is little point pursuing a personal vendetta with the aim of winning at all costs. If this point can be appreciated, then the cost-benefit analysis will be of real value.

As well as considering whether the issues that are in dispute and the desired outcome justify the amount of costs likely to be incurred in pursuing them, the solicitor must analyse the risks and set out very clearly the possible consequences of losing the case. If a litigant loses his case, then he will have to pay not only his own solicitor's costs, but the costs of his opponent as well. This is an extremely important consideration and may affect the decision whether or not to pursue the case. For example, the argument may be over a strip of land which is the only means of access to a house. It is vital for the house owner to establish that he has a right of way over that land. He might consider it worth spending £25,000 to secure that right. However, if his solicitor advises him that he has only a 50 per cent chance of success, this may put a rather different gloss on it. Although he has a 50 per cent chance of winning and recovering his costs, he has an equal chance of losing and doubling the amount of money he spends. In those circumstances, he may be better off purchasing a right of way from his opponent for the best price he is able to negotiate.

Analysis of risk is not an exact science, but clients often like to have their chances of success expressed in percentage terms. To do this with any degree of accuracy, it is necessary to break the case down into its component parts. For example, if the issue is "has the defendant trespassed on the claimant's land?" then that can usually be answered "yes" or "no" and it is usually possible to offer a percentage chance of establishing a trespass. The matter will be complicated, however, if the defence is that the land has been acquired by adverse possession. To succeed, the claimant has to prove, first, that the building in question indeed straddles the legal boundary; and, secondly, that the defendant has not acquired the land by adverse possession. If the assessment on risk were 70 per cent of succeeding on trespass and 60 per cent of succeeding in defending the adverse possession claim, then, without further thought, it might be said there is a 65 per cent chance of success overall. However, applying the correct mathematical calculation to the chances of winning on each issue (70 per cent x 60 per cent), which is necessary because the case will be lost unless the claimant succeeds on both issues, the chances of succeeding are only 42 per cent. This may cause the claimant to think more carefully about whether to embark on the litigation.

The *Costs Code* requires the solicitor to provide a written risk and cost-benefit analysis at the commencement of the case. Again, this should be recorded in the retainer letter. It is well worth investing time at the beginning of the case to think through all these issues carefully. The client who has received a comprehensive risk and cost-benefit analysis from his solicitor may well decide to resolve the dispute outside the court system rather than rush headlong into court proceedings.

Decision tree analysis
Some solicitors have started using "decision tree analysis" to help their clients reach decisions. A decision tree is a statistical tool used to

assess the potential outcome of a number of different alternatives. There are two types of decision tree. The first is quantitative. It ascribes a value to each potential outcome, and multiplies that by the chance that that outcome will occur. This is particularly useful in disputes that have a monetary value.

However, the second type of decision tree, a qualitative decision tree, is more suited to neighbour disputes, which are frequently about something other than money. The best way to illustrate the function of a qualitative decision tree is by way of example. Suppose a purchaser buys a house on a large plot of land and intends to extend his house. Unfortunately, when he applies for planning permission, his neighbours object and during the course of the objection, the buyer discovers that the neighbours contend that the boundary is in such a position as to make his proposed extension impossible. In addition, the neighbours have erected a fence along the line where they say the boundary is. It is not obvious from the deeds who is right.

The buyer has a number of alternative courses of action that he wants to consider with his solicitor, as follows:

(a) to remove the fence, erect a structure along the line where he believes the boundary to be, and start to build once planning permission comes through;

(b) to issue proceedings immediately for trespass, including an application for an interim injunction requiring the removal of the fence and a declaration as to the true location of the boundary;

(c) to employ a surveyor to visit the site and prepare a report giving his opinion as to the true location of the boundary, with a view to sending it to the neighbours and issuing a claim based on it if they do not accept it;

(d) to invite the neighbour jointly to appoint a surveyor to prepare a report and plan and to agree that both parties will be bound by the surveyor's findings.

The solicitor prepares a decision tree as set out on page 175. This is a convenient way of mapping out the alternatives, and it facilitates a comprehensive evaluation of the alternative courses of action and the likely outcomes. Having worked through the tree, the best alternative becomes very clear; that is, the buyer should retain his own surveyor because a favourable survey will mean he can litigate from a position of strength. Conversely, an inconclusive or unfavourable survey will give him a chance to re-think before involving the neighbours at all.

Decision Tree 1

Options   *Outcomes*

1. Direct action → litigate → win: 50% / lose: 50%
   neighbour litigates (likely)
   remove fence and build → neighbour accepts (unlikely)

2. Purchaser retains own surveyor
   - favourable → litigate from strength → win (likely) / lose (unlikely)
   - build → neighbour litigates (less likely than before report) / neighbour accepts (more likely than before report)
   - inconclusive → reconsider project
   - unfavourable → abandon project

3. Appoint joint expert
   - favourable → proceed with certainty
   - unfavourable → abandon project

An expert determination at this stage may be cost-effective, but if it is unfavourable, the project must be abandoned. Alternatively, the self-help remedy looks risky if the buyer thinks his neighbour will litigate as a result. The chances of succeeding by means of self-help improve after obtaining a favourable surveyor's report. Finally, it is clear that litigating without first obtaining any kind of expert evidence is nothing more than a lottery.

The decision tree can be made more sophisticated by attributing percentage chances to each outcome, which, when worked through, can identify an outcome that, statistically, has the best chance of success. This can be particularly useful when formulating settlement offers or deciding whether to accept an offer; these matters are considered further later in this chapter.

Recovery of costs from the opponent

One topic to be thoroughly explained is the recovery of costs. A common misconception among litigants is that if they win the case, the opponent will have to pay all the costs. The general rule, of course, is that costs follow the event, the loser paying the winner's costs. Litigants must be warned, however, that this does not amount to a 100 per cent indemnity. There is no guarantee that the court will order that the loser should pay the whole of the winner's costs. This is particularly relevant to neighbour disputes, where judges are often reluctant to exacerbate what is already a deteriorating relationship by making a costs order against one party. Judges are often tempted to make no order for costs. Offers to settle can also have a significant effect on costs awards. A party who has been successful may find that his award for costs is decreased if he has not accepted a reasonable offer, particularly one which would have put him in as favourable a position as the judgment in his favour. This is considered further later in this chapter.

The assessment of costs

Even if the court orders the loser to pay his opponent's costs in full, those costs may be subject to detailed assessment if they are not agreed. If neighbour disputes themselves are acrimonious, then the satellite litigation that can ensue over costs can be even more so. Litigants need to be told, at the outset, about the assessment procedure so that it does not come as a surprise at the end of the case. The cost of the assessment procedure, including the fees of the costs draftsman and the court fee, has to be met.

If detailed assessment is ordered, then a costs draftsman must be retained to draw up a detailed bill of costs. The solicitor's files are submitted to the costs draftsman who prepares a detailed breakdown of all the work that has been done on the case. Although this is referred to as a "bill", the client should not confuse it with the bills rendered by a solicitor to the client. The bill is then served on the paying party's solicitors with supporting invoices and fee notes evidencing the solicitor's out-of-pocket expenses, such as counsel's fees and expert's fees. The bill is served with a "notice of commencement of assessment". This must be served within three months of the order for costs. If it is not served within this time, then the receiving party is still able to assess the costs, but is likely to be deprived of the interest on costs to which he would otherwise have been entitled.

The paying party has twenty-one days to serve any points of dispute, which can be prepared by the party's solicitor or a costs draftsman. If, for example, it appears that excessive time was spent on a particular item, then the paying party should set out in the points of dispute how much time he thinks should have been spent. If the costs judge agrees, then the amount the paying party has to pay will be limited to that amount.

The receiving party has the right to reply to the points of dispute. If agreement cannot be reached, the receiving party should apply to the court for an assessment hearing. The application must be made within three months of the expiry of the three-month period within which the assessment procedure must be commenced.

At the hearing, the costs judge (who may be a district judge in the county court, or, in the High Court, a judge who deals exclusively with legal costs) considers the points of dispute and makes a decision on each one. It is then the responsibility of the parties and their representatives to calculate the amount of costs for which the paying party is responsible. The judge also decides who should bear the costs of the assessment, which he summarily assesses.

It is often wise to seek to truncate this process by making an offer on costs, as it will have the same effect as offers made in the substantive dispute. Offers are made under rule 47.19 of the Civil Procedure Rules and should be expressed as being "without prejudice as to the costs of the detailed assessment proceedings". Neither the existence nor the substance of the offer can be communicated to the court until the question of the costs of the detailed assessment proceedings is decided. At that point, the court takes the offer into account in deciding who should pay the costs of those proceedings. Such an offer is equivalent to a *Calderbank* offer in the substantive proceedings (see page 183).

The receiving party then lodges the bill with the court and applies for a costs certificate. Once this is issued by the court, it must be paid within fourteen days. If not, the receiving party is entitled to interest, at the judgment rate, on the sum ordered to be paid.

Standard and indemnity bases for assessing costs

The difference between the standard and indemnity bases for assessing costs needs to be explained to clients. The usual order is for costs to be assessed on the standard basis. If there is any doubt about the reasonableness of the costs incurred, then the benefit of the doubt is given to the paying party. If the costs are being assessed on the indemnity basis, the benefit of the doubt is given to the receiving party.

It is wise to warn the client that if the costs are assessed on the standard basis then he should expect to recover no more than 65 to 80 per cent of the money he spends on legal fees. It is important that the client understands this at the outset. If not, and there is then a reduction on detailed assessment, the client will legitimately ask why he should pay his solicitor any more than his opponent has been ordered to pay.

If the matter is allocated to the fast track, then the court should assess the costs, although the judge may be tempted to order detailed assessment. To avoid the time and costs of a detailed assessment, and if it is unlikely that costs will be agreed, summary assessment is preferable.

The client should also be warned that the costs order and the assessment might not be the end of the matter. If the costs are not paid, the client will have to expend further legal costs enforcing the order. Enquiries should be made of the client before any litigation is commenced to ensure that if a costs order is secured, the opponent has the means to pay.

Continuing review

Costs estimates and the cost-benefit and risk analyses should be revisited regularly as the case progresses so that the client is not taken by surprise by a sudden increase in costs, or by a bill that exceeds an estimate. Apart from issues of compliance with the *Costs Code* and best practice, a client who is surprised by a bill is less likely to pay it than one who has been kept abreast of the costs situation, particularly if the outcome is not entirely what the client would have wished.

Budgeting

The solicitor should sit down with the client and try to work out a budget. Even if the client wins the case and is able to recover some or all of his costs, he will be primarily responsible for paying his legal fees, and will have to pay his lawyers as he goes along. It is therefore important that the solicitor and client agree the best way to manage the funding, dealing with matters such as the frequency of billing, the timing of updates on progress, and the setting of a costs limit which cannot be exceeded without the client's authority. The solicitor needs to understand the best time to render a bill. Most solicitors bill regularly, as often as once a month. There may be certain times that suit the client better than others and this should be canvassed in advance. If the case is likely to go on for several months, it may be appropriate for the client to set up a monthly standing order for an agreed sum in favour of the solicitor. The solicitor can then invoice at the end of the month. Any surplus on the solicitor's client account should be returned to the client, with interest if appropriate. Conversely, if there is a shortfall at the end of the month, the standing order can be increased for a month or two to clear it.

It can be beneficial to prepare a detailed budget for the case, particularly if it is complex. By looking ahead and identifying the steps that will need to be taken from beginning to end, the solicitor and client can work out a proposed timetable, and calculate the expenditure that is likely to be required each month. This will allow the client to budget for the case, and manage his cash flow, knowing in advance the months during which expenditure is likely to be particularly heavy. It also allows both solicitor and client to see the case as a whole. Frequent review and updating of the budget helps keep the costs under control.

Alternative forms of funding: insurance
A solicitor should always advise a potential litigant to check any insurance policies he may hold to see whether they include legal expenses insurance. It is potentially negligent not to give this advice. If the litigant does have cover, the terms of the policy should be checked carefully. If the claim is accepted, the insurer usually covers only costs incurred once it has accepted the claim. The litigant must pay any costs incurred before the inception of cover and this needs to be explained clearly at the first meeting. If the insurer accepts the claim, it often insists on instructing a solicitor on its own panel. Although this appears to frustrate the principle that a client must be free to choose his lawyer (principle 11.01 of The Law Society's *Guide*

to the Professional Conduct of Solicitors), an exception is made for legal expenses insurers. The Insurance Companies (Legal Expenses Insurance) Regulations 1990 (SI 1990 No. 1159) provide that the client's freedom of choice may be restricted, except that:

> "(a) where there is a conflict of interest between the insurer and the insured, the insured has a free choice of solicitor;
> (b) where, under legal expenses insurance, the insured has recourse to a lawyer to defend, represent or serve his or her interest in any enquiry or proceedings."

(Principle 6.01 of the *Guide to Professional Conduct*, at paragraph 3.)

It is, nevertheless, possible to persuade an insurer to use the solicitor who has advised previously, particularly if that solicitor has a relationship with the insurer (known in the industry as "freedom of choice" cases).

"After the event" legal expenses insurance is available, but is rarely offered for boundary disputes unless backed by a conditional fee ("no win, no fee") agreement, which solicitors are unlikely to offer for such a case, as the outcome is rarely sufficiently certain.

3. Using the Court Process to Best Effect

As well as undertaking a detailed consideration of the merits of the claim, the risks and the cost-benefit, it is advisable to spend some time preparing a case plan. A claimant has the luxury of being able to take the time he needs for the planning stage, whereas a defendant is bound by the court timetable. Nevertheless, for both parties, it is vital that the objectives are identified and that a plan for achieving those objectives is prepared. This can be done in conjunction with the budget.

Case plan

The case plan should set out what the client ideally wants to achieve and how much the client is prepared to spend to attain that objective. It should detail what evidence will be required to prove each issue in the case. This can be updated as the case proceeds and the issues are crystallised. The client can start to identify and produce to the solicitor documents in his possession that are relevant to the case. This will allow the solicitor to plead the case to best effect, and save time and costs when the disclosure stage is reached. Potential witnesses should also be identified. If expert evidence is likely to be required, the case plan should take into account the type of expert who will be needed and include a budget for expert's fees.

It is also wise to identify the client's "bottom line" that is, what the client will settle for if the ideal objective cannot be achieved, or proves too expensive to achieve. Another point to be addressed in this context is whether, if the client's position deteriorates as the case proceeds (because, for example, evidence comes to light which proves some part of the opponent's case), the client would be prepared to discontinue. The client should be warned of the consequences of discontinuance, namely that he will have to pay his opponent's costs up to the date of discontinuance, to be subject to detailed assessment if not agreed.

Pleadings

Lack of clarity in pleadings can be addressed by the use of requests for further information and clarification under part 18 of the Civil Procedure Rules. Such requests are made in writing and must be clearly marked as being made under part 18. They can be made in the form of a letter, but if they are long, it is preferable to include them in a separate document under the full case heading. If a case has been poorly pleaded, a part 18 request, if well drafted, can exploit the weaknesses in an opponent's case and possibly force the opponent into making admissions. The request must set out the time within which a response must be made, usually fourteen days. If no response is received, the maker of the request can apply to the court for an order that the reply is served. An order is usually accompanied by an order for the cost of the application to be paid by the defaulting party. Failure to comply with the order is another opportunity to apply for an unless order.

Unless orders

A well thought-out case plan puts a party firmly in the driving seat and allows him to be proactive rather than reactive. The solicitor should aim always to be one step ahead of the opponent. The case plan should help identify milestones, allowing the solicitor to plan ahead so that court directions can be complied with in a timely fashion. If the steps in the proceedings are completed on time, or within the time available, this will pressurise the opponent. If the timetable is allowed to slip, this signifies a loss of control and creates a risk of being put on the wrong foot. Further, the party in default risks attracting the wrath of the judge. Judges are increasingly active in case management and do not hesitate to make orders of their own motion. These can be quite draconian and may even include striking out a claim. Although such orders may be set aside, the cost of applying to do so would be an unnecessary expense. Equally, delay by the opponent should not be tolerated. While it is usual to agree short extensions of time, particularly for filing and serving pleadings, any more than one extension should be avoided, and any delay by the opponent should, if possible, be turned to advantage. "Unless" orders can be used to good effect. An unless order is an order that, unless a party takes a step within a specified time, his claim will be struck out, or he will be debarred from further defending the claim. Although an application for an unless order rarely has such an extreme result, it will pressurize the opponent, and may mean that the evidence is poorly prepared because of the time pressure.

Summary judgment

The solicitor should be constantly on the lookout for opportunities to strike out the whole or part of the claim or defence and to apply for summary judgment under part 24 of the Civil Procedure Rules. Opportunities include inadvertent admissions being made in the pleadings or in documents, inadequate pleadings or failure to disclose any cause of action or defence. Care is necessary, however, since such an application gives the opponent an opportunity to get his house in order by amending the case. It may be preferable to leave the opponent's case as it is and increase the chances of winning at trial. On the other hand, the opponent would probably have to pay the costs of the application, and would be responsible for any costs that arise from the amendment, whether he wins or loses the action.

4. Settlement

As the costs of a neighbour dispute can be high, it is sensible to think about settling the case out of court even before proceedings are issued. An offer made at the outset may be very similar to what is achieved at the end of court proceedings. The only difference may be the price tag. As noted elsewhere in this book, judges are often tempted to find a middle way and make no order for costs, resulting in an unsatisfactory outcome and a large legal bill.

If the litigant and his solicitor start thinking creatively, from the outset, about how a dispute might best be resolved, they are much more likely to hit upon a workable solution than if they focus entirely on winning at all costs. Even if the offers that are made are not accepted, they have a function – that of maximising the litigant's position on costs.

Most offers are made "without prejudice". Anything said in a without prejudice letter or conversation cannot be referred to in the court proceedings. Accordingly, the parties are able to speak much more freely about the issues in the case and make concessions that will not be made in the proceedings themselves. The court is not privy to any without prejudice correspondence.

Calderbank offers
Offers made "without prejudice save as to costs" have two functions. The first is to explore settlement, just like an ordinary "without prejudice" offer. However, although the court does not see the offer during the trial, once the judge has made his decision, it can be shown to the judge and may influence his thinking when he is deciding who should pay what costs. The principle was formulated in *Calderbank v Calderbank* [1976] Fam 93, [1975] 3 WLR 586, [1975] 3 All ER 333 (CA). A "Calderbank letter" is labelled "without prejudice save as to costs" and ends with words to the effect: "Although this letter is marked 'without prejudice' we reserve the right to show its contents to the judge at the trial of this action when the question of costs falls to be decided". The judge then has a discretion to take the offer into consideration when making orders for costs at the end of the case. This type of offer is particularly appropriate for neighbour disputes where a number of different issues need to be resolved, but where neither party is looking for monetary compensation. For example, a dispute may concern:

Issue A: the location of a boundary,
Issue B: the ownership of a strip of land,
Issue C: the existence of a right of way.

Suppose the defendant makes an offer conceding issues A and C, in return for issue B being resolved in his favour. If the judge finds for the claimant on issues A and C but for the defendant on issue B, then this will be no better a result for the claimant than if he had accepted the defendant's offer. Without the offer, the judge may have awarded the claimant two thirds of his costs. Once the judge knows about the offer, he may well exercise his discretion in the defendant's favour, and reduce the award of costs. The effect of these offers should not be under-estimated.

Part 36 offers

The Civil Procedure Rules introduced a more formal regime with a view to enshrining the *Calderbank* principles into a rule. Offers made under part 36 of the Civil Procedure Rules have a very clear set of consequences. Although the judge retains discretion as to costs, part 36 sets out the powers of the judge if he decides that the offer should be taken into account.

To attract part 36 consequences, an offer must comply with the requirements set out in part 36. It must state whether it is intended to deal with the whole or part of the claim and/or the whole or part of any counterclaim. If it includes an offer to pay money, it must state whether or not it includes interest; the money must be paid into court (a "part 36 payment") if proceedings are under way, or, if the offer is made before proceedings, once those proceedings are issued. It must state that the offeree has twenty-one days from the date of receipt of the offer to accept it. Finally, it must state that after the twenty-one days have expired, the offer may be accepted only with the permission of the court, or if the parties agree liability for costs.

If a defendant makes an offer which is more advantageous than the result the claimant achieves at trial, then the claimant may be penalised in costs, even if he wins at trial. The court may order that he can recover his costs only up to the date the offer was made. It can also order the claimant to pay the defendant's costs from the latest date the offer was capable of acceptance. Conversely, a claimant who makes a generous offer and still wins may be awarded costs on the indemnity basis rather than the standard basis, and interest on the costs at up to 10 per cent above base rate for some or all of the period starting with the latest date on which the defendant could have accepted the offer without needing the permission of the court.

The disadvantage of a part 36 offer is that if it is accepted, the offeror must pay the offeree's costs up to the date of acceptance. If the case has a monetary value then this may be a sensible commercial decision – that is, it is better to pay £50,000 of a £100,000 claim and

£5,000 in costs than to proceed to trial and be ordered to pay £100,000 plus £50,000 costs. Neighbour disputes often have little or no monetary objective so that the commercial incentive is not as compelling. If an offer is made that includes "no order for costs" then it does not comply with part 36 and is better made as a "without prejudice save as to costs" offer. The cost consequences of part 36 will not follow, but the court can exercise its discretion to apportion costs as it sees fit, which may include depriving a party of costs to which he would, but for the offer, have been entitled and *vice versa*.

Open offers
If a party is particularly confident of his claim, or if he is prepared to make an offer that the judge will see, the offer can be made in open correspondence. Open offers can be extremely effective, particularly if they make worthwhile concessions. They put maximum pressure on the opponent, who knows that the offer will be contained in the trial bundle and that the judge will read it. If a judge sees a reasonable offer, it may inform his thinking about the entire case, and influence his final decision. Indeed, he may use that offer as the basis for his decision. While an open offer does not technically attract part 36 consequences, it is extremely likely that the judge will use part 36 as a guide when deciding what effect on costs a good open offer should have.

Any offer, including a part 36 offer, can be made before proceedings begin. Under rule 36.10, the court takes such offers into account. If the offer includes a payment of money, that payment must be made into court within fourteen days of service of the claim form.

Decision tree analysis
Decision tree analysis can be helpful in deciding how to pitch an offer, and whether or not to accept an offer. A probability tree can be prepared, in which the possible outcomes at trial are each allocated a chance of success. The principle is straightforward. If all outcomes that are mutually exclusive but collectively exhausted are listed, one of them must happen (a 100 per cent chance), so 100 has to be divided between them.

For example, in a trespass action where damages are likely to be awarded in lieu of an injunction, the defendant may make a monetary offer to dispose of the claim. The claimant may be advised that he has a 60 per cent chance of winning, and therefore a 40 per cent chance of losing. The lawyer may consider that, having won (60 per cent), there is a 70 per cent chance of beating the offer. The chance of winning *and* beating the offer is 60 per cent x 70 per cent = 42 per cent. The chance of winning on liability but not beating the offer is 60 per cent x 30 per cent = 18 per cent. It is easy to see this in a probability tree. Note that at each stage the total chance of all outcomes adds up to 100 per cent.

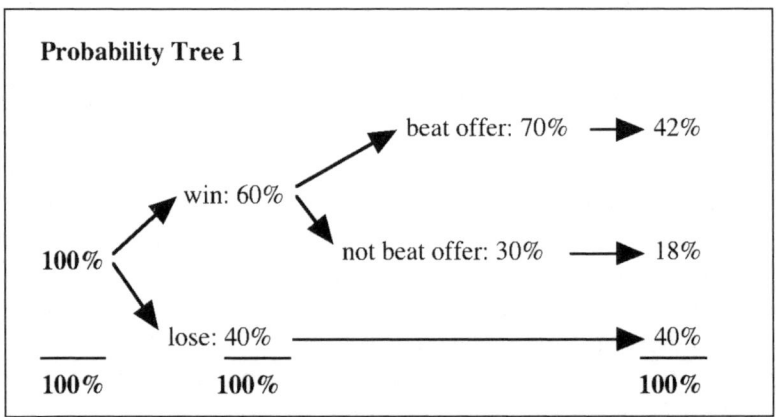

Probability Tree 1

beat offer: 70% → 42%

win: 60%

100%

not beat offer: 30% → 18%

lose: 40% → 40%

100%   100%   100%

This tree shows clearly that the chance of a satisfactory outcome is 42 per cent. The chance of an unsatisfactory outcome is 18 per cent + 40 per cent = 58 per cent.

This analysis can be employed to good effect where the issues are simple matters of liability and damages, but it can also be applied to disputes where damages are not necessarily an issue, for example, boundary disputes. In a typical boundary dispute there are usually several possible outcomes, for example:

    (a) the boundary is exactly where the claimant says it is;

    (b) the boundary is exactly where the defendant says it is;

    (c) the boundary is in another position but is closer to the claimant's line than to the defendant's line;

    (d) the boundary is in another position but is closer to the defendant's line than to the claimant's line.

The following percentage chances may be attributed to the four possible outcomes:

    (a) the court upholds the claimant's case as to the location of the boundary (10 per cent);

(b) the court upholds the defendant's view as to the location of the boundary (10 per cent);

(c) the court finds that the boundary is on neither line but is closer to the claimant's line than the defendant's line (50 per cent);

(d) the court finds that the boundary is on neither line but is closer to the defendant's line than the claimant's line (30 per cent).

On this basis, the claimant's case looks reasonably good with a 60 per cent chance of success (outcomes (a) + (b)).

If the defendant makes an offer to split the difference and to agree a boundary line that is roughly between the two alternative positions argued on behalf of the two parties, then the claimant will have to consider:

(a) whether the court is likely to agree with him as to the position of the boundary; and

(b) even if it does not, whether he can do better than the offer that is made (that is, the boundary is neither where the claimant nor the defendant says it is, but is not far enough in the defendant's favour to match the defendant's offer).

The probability tree would look like this:

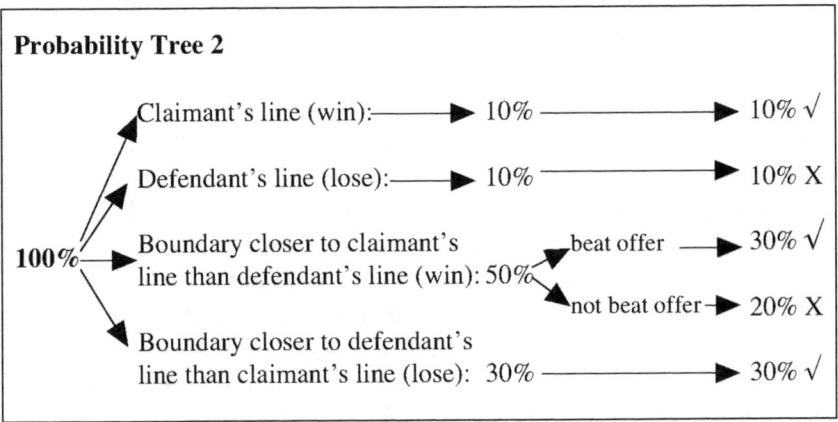

Probability Tree 2

Claimant's line (win): ——▶ 10% ————————▶ 10% √

Defendant's line (lose): ——▶ 10% ————————▶ 10% X

100% ——▶ Boundary closer to claimant's line than defendant's line (win): 50% — beat offer ——▶ 30% √ — not beat offer ——▶ 20% X

Boundary closer to defendant's line than claimant's line (lose): 30% ————————▶ 30% √

Outcomes are marked as satisfactory (√) or unsatisfactory (X). In this situation there is a 30 per cent chance of beating the offer and a 20 per cent chance of not beating the offer, which makes the decision very close to call. When the chances of beating the offer are added to the chances of an outright win (and therefore also beating the offer) the percentage improves to 40 per cent, but this is lower than the chances of winning before the offer was made (60 per cent) and may therefore lead the claimant to consider the offer very carefully, perhaps more carefully than he would have done had the exercise not been carried out.

5. Mediation

Mediation is a process in which an independent person, a mediator, assists the parties to come to an agreement outside the formal court process. A mediator does not have the power to decide the case in favour of one party or the other. His role is to facilitate an agreement. A skilled mediator can often broker a deal even when the parties appear to have reached an impasse and the relationship between them has broken down entirely. Mediators almost always have a legal background, either as a solicitor or barrister, and are usually still in practice. It is advisable to appoint a mediator accredited by one of the recognised organisations, such as the Centre for Effective Dispute Resolution or the Alternative Dispute Resolution Group.

Consequences of refusing mediation
The Civil Procedure Rules provide that courts should actively encourage mediation. Rule 1.4(1) requires them to further the overriding objective of enabling the court to deal with cases justly by actively managing cases. Rule 1.4(2)(e) defines "active case management" as including "encouraging parties to use an alternative dispute resolution procedure if the court considers that appropriate and facilitating the use of such procedure". The standard allocation questionnaire gives the parties an opportunity to ask for the proceedings to be stayed while they try to settle the case by alternative dispute resolution. Case law has expanded the notion of "active case management" and "encouraging parties" to use mediation by seeking to penalise parties who refuse to engage in mediation, even where those parties are ultimately successful in the litigation. There has been a number of recent decisions in which such draconian measures were applied to successful parties; these include *Dunnett v Railtrack plc* [2002] EWCA Civ 303, [2002] 1 WLR 2434, [2002] 2 All ER 850. In *Halsey v Milton Keynes NHS Trust* [2004] EWCA Civ 576, [2004] 1

WLR 3002, [2004] 4 All ER 920, the Court of Appeal reviewed some of these decisions and discussed the role of the court in encouraging parties to engage in mediation. It was held that the court should continue to do so, but should not force the parties to mediate. In particular, any exercise of the court's discretion on costs to deprive a successful party of some or all of his costs on the grounds of refusal to participate in mediation should be exceptional, and the unsuccessful party must satisfy the court that the winner acted unreasonably in refusing to mediate.

The court has resisted a recent attempt to extend this decision. In *Reed Executive plc v Reed Business Information Ltd (Costs: Alternative Dispute Resolution)* [2004] EWCA Civ 887, [2004] 1 WLR 3026, [2004] 4 All ER 942 (CA), although the defendant succeeded on appeal, the claimant applied for 70 per cent of its costs of the trial, and all of its costs of the appeal, on the grounds that the defendant had acted unreasonably in refusing mediation. In support of its application, the claimant sought permission to rely on "without prejudice" correspondence. The court dismissed the application, stating that it had no power to order disclosure of without prejudice correspondence in order to decide the question of costs.

Halsey appeared to ameliorate the effect of *Dunnett*, but in *Burchell v Bullard and Others* [2005] EWCA Civ 358, the Court of Appeal reinforced the message that parties have to be very careful when deciding whether or not to accept an invitation to mediate. In this case the defendant refused mediation before proceedings were issued. In applying the principles set out in *Halsey,* the court found that the claimant had discharged the burden of proof in establishing that the defendant's refusal to mediate was unreasonable. However, the refusal pre-dated *Dunnett* and *Halsey*, so the Court of Appeal did not impose any additional costs sanction. Nevertheless, Lord Justice Ward reinforced the message that the "the profession can no longer with impunity shrug aside reasonable requests to mediate", and went on to say that "The parties cannot ignore a proper request to mediate simply because it was made before the claim was issued. With court fees escalating it may be folly to do so."

Thus it is still necessary to proceed with caution; a party who refuses even to consider whether a case is suitable for mediation is at risk of an adverse costs order, especially if the court has made an order requiring the parties to consider alternative dispute resolution.

An effective strategy is to invite the opposing party to agree mediation in open correspondence. The invitation should ask the opponent to say whether he will agree to mediation and if not, why not. If such a request is met with refusal, a litigant can gain the advantage on the question of costs by setting out, again in open correspondence as far as it is possible to do so, the reasons why such refusal is unreasonable. A trail of such correspondence can be relied on when the question of costs falls to be decided by the trial judge.

The advantages

Apart from the potential adverse costs consequences of refusing to mediate, mediation may lead to savings in relation to the parties' own costs. If mediation is attempted at an early stage, the parties may make a considerable saving if the dispute is resolved.

There are also good practical reasons why mediation should be considered. There is a limit to how far a court can resolve disputes over rights of way or boundaries. Often there is a black and white answer, but it may not completely suit either party. For instance, in a dispute of which the authors have knowledge, the claimants had a right of way over their neighbours' land from which they could gain access to the main highway. They could also get to the highway from the front of their property, but when their neighbours increased the height of their fence, they found their view of the road from the front of their property was impeded, making it difficult to use that way onto the road. They therefore wished to use their right of way and brought proceedings seeking the removal of a gate, which obstructed it. The defendants did not want the claimants to use the right of way, but the claimants did not particularly want to use it either. What they wanted was to be able to see their way onto the road from the front. Eventually the parties agreed that the defendants would pay a sum of money to the claimants to relinquish the right of way and the defendants agreed to keep their fence at a certain height. This is not a resolution that could have been achieved in court.

Procedure

If the parties do agree to mediate, then both parties should go into the mediation with an open mind, for it to stand the greatest chance of success. It is sometimes sought to limit the scope of the mediation or to make a party's participation in the process conditional upon the other party's agreeing to, or doing, something first. Adopting at the outset a position from which a party cannot deviate is likely severely to limit the chances of a successful mediation process. All the issues, including the question of costs, need to be available for discussion if an overall settlement is to be achieved.

The appointed mediator directs the process. He needs information on the background to the case, all relevant documents and, if proceedings have been issued, the pleadings and all the evidence that has been exchanged. If proceedings have not been issued, or if they are at the pre-disclosure stage, then the parties need to be careful that all the evidence on which they will rely at the mediation is provided to their opponents before the mediation takes place. If the parties have complied with the pre-action protocol(s) then the evidence should have been disclosed at the outset. It is not helpful for a party to be surprised, at the mediation, by documents he has not previously seen, particularly documents that may change his position. It is submitted that in such circumstances it would not be unreasonable to adjourn the mediation to allow time to consider the documentation and its effect on the receiving party's case. If to do so would mean sending everyone away to re-convene on another day, then serious consideration is clearly called for, but if a party cannot continue without prejudicing his position, then there will be no alternative.

The parties should attempt to agree the contents of the pack of documents to go before the mediator, including an agreed chronology and statement of issues. The parties may be invited by the mediator to put forward a "position statement" setting out their positions at the commencement of the mediation. If so, each party is given an opportunity to present this orally at the outset.

Finalising an agreement
If agreement is reached, it is important to finalise it before the mediation meeting breaks up. Mediations can often take several hours, and the parties and their representatives, having reached an agreement in principle, may be tempted to leave matters there, with a view to drawing up the agreement at a later date. The advantages of doing so are obvious – the participants may be tired and more liable to make errors or omissions than if they approach the matter afresh the next day. But this can be a double-edged sword if, next day, the parties think of something else they want to put into the agreement, or decide

they want to change something, or worse, renege on the position reached the day before. In the authors' experience, it is always preferable to draw up the agreement at the end of the day and for everyone to sign it.

Costs

Finally, if mediation is an option to be pursued, the solicitor should include the likely cost in his initial estimate to the client, including the costs of the mediator himself, but in doing so should not assume that the mediation will be the end of the matter.

Other forms of alternative dispute resolution

Other forms of alternative dispute resolution include:

(a) "without prejudice" meetings between lawyers, with or without the parties present;

(b) expert determination, where both parties agree a suitable expert (an independent solicitor or a surveyor, perhaps) to read the written submissions of both parties, and then make a decision, both parties agreeing to be bound by that decision;

(c) early neutral evaluation, where both parties jointly submit the case to a barrister for an opinion as to the likely outcome. This can be binding or non-binding.

6. Settlement at Trial

If one party refuses to engage in mediation, reasonably or unreasonably, or if mediation fails, the parties may have no choice but to continue with, or proceed to, litigation.

Civil trials are often settled at the door of the court and neighbour disputes are no exception. Solicitors must take care when recording the terms of such a settlement, particularly where there are time pressures. The most common way of bringing such a dispute to an end is by the parties entering into a "Tomlin Order" (for a template for such an order, see page 201). The proceedings are stayed pending compliance with the terms of the agreement reached between the parties. These terms are recorded in a schedule attached to the order and the parties have permission to apply to the court to enforce the terms of the schedule if they are not complied with. The schedule may require the parties to execute further documents, for example, a deed of compromise, particularly if it is intended to fix legal boundaries or transfer parcels of land. The same principles apply to an agreement reached following mediation, particularly if proceedings have already been issued and it is necessary to draw up an order that records the terms of the agreement.

7. Preparation for Trial

If all else fails and the matter proceeds to a full trial, then thorough preparation is the key to a successful outcome. It is outside the ambit of this work to examine in detail the step-by-step procedure leading to trial and the trial itself, but there are some elements of the preparation process that are particularly important in neighbour disputes.

If witnesses are to be called to give oral evidence, it is advisable to issue witness summonses, even where the client's instructions are that the witness concerned will attend the trial. An important witness may unexpectedly go away on a business trip or holiday, saying he or she is no longer able to attend the trial. If a witness summons has not been issued and served, then the witness cannot be compelled to attend. This could seriously prejudice the outcome. The purpose of the witness summons should therefore be clearly explained to the client.

The trial bundles should be diligently prepared, preferably by agreement with the opposing solicitors, to ensure that all attending the trial can find their way around the bundles as quickly and easily as possible. If the witness statements refer to documents, they should be cross-referenced so that it is easy for the advocates, witnesses and judge to refer to them as they are considered in the oral evidence. If there has been a number of witness statements (for example, if there have been interim applications) then, to avoid duplication, the exhibits should not be attached if they appear elsewhere in the bundle in the form of documents. The witness statements can instead be cross-referenced to the page number of the documents concerned in the bundles. Finally, bundles must be carefully paginated so that the page number is easily discernible and in the same place on every page.

If plans are included in the evidence then they should be coloured, preferably using a colour photocopier rather than colouring them by hand. If photographs are to be included, then the best available copies should be used. Copies of copies are insufficient; everything should be copied from a master original.

If video evidence is to be used, the solicitor should ensure that the court has the necessary equipment to view it, and try to establish that it is in working order in advance of the trial. It is useful to arrive early on the first day to make sure everything is in place; that the video is wound back or forward to the right point; and that it is ready to start.

8. Checklists

Costs/cost-benefit and risk

1. Ensure that the client has the fullest possible information about costs at the outset:
   - explain the hourly rates,
   - give accurate and comprehensive estimates,
   - undertake regular reviews,
   - prepare a budget,
   - discuss alternative forms of funding,
   - explain the summary and detailed assessment procedures.
2. Prepare a full cost-benefit and risk analysis at the outset and re-visit as the case progresses.
3. Consider using decision tress to assess possible outcomes.

The court process

1. Prepare a case plan.
2. Use part 18 requests if the pleading is not clear.
3. Consider strike-out and summary judgment.
4. Use applications for "unless" orders to keep the case on track.

Offers and settlement

1. Think about settlement at an early stage.
2. Consider making part 36 offers both before and after proceedings are issued.
3. Consider making open offers.
4. Consider using decision trees to assess offers.
5. Offer mediation or other forms of alternative dispute resolution.

Preparation for trial

1. Issue and serve witness summons(es).
2. Agree contents of bundle if possible.
3. Cross-reference witness statements with documents.
4. Always use colour plans and colour photocopies of photographs.
5. Ensure equipment is available and working.

Appendix: Forms

Specimen Particulars of Claim: Misrepresentation
(See Chapter 1.)

IN THE [. . . .] COUNTY COURT   Claim No:

BETWEEN:

[names]		Claimants
– and –		
[names]		Defendants

PARTICULARS OF CLAIM

1.   The Claimants purchased the freehold property known as [name and address] ("the Property") from the Defendants on [date].

2.   The Defendants had been freehold owners of the Property since [date]. The Property is and at all material times was registered at HM Land Registry under title [. . . .]. A copy of the Land Registry office copies relating to the title is attached as Exhibit "A".

3.   On [date] the Defendants signed a Seller's Property Information Form ("SPIF") in readiness for the sale of the Property to the Claimants. A copy of the SPIF is attached at Exhibit "B".

4.   At section 2 of the SPIF the Defendants gave answers in the negative to the standard questions about their knowledge about disputes relating to the Property or any neighbouring properties and about having ever received complaints about anything they had or had not done as owners of the Property.

5.   Further, on or around [date] the Defendants showed the Claimants round the Property and the second Defendant expressly told the Claimants that the neighbours in the locality were good and friendly.

6.   Further, in reply number [. . . .] of their replies to requisitions on title the Defendants responded to a requisition asking them to confirm the written information given by them to the Claimants prior to exchange of contracts, including in the SPIF, was true and accurate by confirming that to their knowledge it was true and accurate, save as varied in subsequent communication. There had been no such communication varying the Defendants' answers in the SPIF or varying what they had told the Claimants when they viewed the Property. Accordingly, by virtue of their reply to

requisition [. . . .] the Defendants represented to the Claimants that to their knowledge the information given by them to the Claimants in the SPIF and orally was complete and accurate.

7.   In the premises the Defendants represented both orally and in writing that:

    i.   to their knowledge there were no disputes about the Property or any neighbouring properties and that there had been no such disputes in the past;

    ii. they had never received any complaints about anything they had or had not done as owners of the Property;

    iii. the neighbours in the locality were good and friendly; and/or

    iv. each of these representations was complete and accurate.

As such the Defendants misrepresented the facts to the Claimants. It is averred that the Defendants knew the Claimants would act in reliance on the said misrepresentations and that the said misrepresentations either alone or together with other representations would be an inducement to the Claimants to enter into a contract of purchase of the Property.

8.   The Defendants at all relevant times knew or ought to have known that:

    i.   it was very important that their answers in the SPIF were correct, complete and accurate because the Claimants would rely upon them when deciding whether or not to proceed with their purchase of the Property: a warning note to this effect was expressly given to the Defendants on the first page of the SPIF;

    ii. incorrect, incomplete or inaccurate information given by them to the Claimants or mentioned by them in conversation with the Claimants might mean the Claimants could claim compensation from them or even refuse to complete the purchase: a warning note to this effect was also expressly given to the Defendants on the first page of the SPIF.

9.   In reliance on the said representations the Claimants entered into a contract to purchase the Property on [date] and completed the transaction on [date]. A copy of the said contract is attached at Exhibit "C".

10.   The said representations made by the Defendants were false and were made fraudulently in that the Defendants well knew or recklessly failed to inform the Claimants, not caring whether the information they provided was true, accurate and complete, that there had been numerous disputes between themselves and the owners of [name of neighbouring property], Mr and Mrs [. . . .] ("the Neighbours"), in particular, [details]. Alternatively such misrepresentations were made negligently or innocently.

11.   The said representations were false and made fraudulently in that the Defendants well knew or recklessly failed to inform the Claimants, not caring whether the information they provided was true, accurate and complete, that

there had been numerous disputes between themselves and the Neighbours. Alternatively such misrepresentations were made negligently or innocently.

PARTICULARS

1. [Give full details of the disputes that have been concealed.]
2. The Neighbours were not good and friendly neighbours.
3. Such disputes and/or complaints are ongoing and have not been resolved.
4. If the Defendants had informed the Claimants of the true, complete and accurate facts they would not have proceeded to purchase the Property. Further, a hypothetical purchaser with knowledge of the true, complete and accurate facts would either not have proceeded with the purchase or would have paid much less for the Property.
5. By reason of the Defendants' said fraudulent, negligent and/or innocent misrepresentations the Claimants have suffered loss and damage.

PARTICULARS OF LOSS AND DAMAGE

1. Damages for diminution in value of the Property resulting from the existence of the said disputes and/or complaints and their effect on the market value of the Property such damage to be determined by expert surveyor's evidence to be adduced at trial.
2. Damages for distress and inconvenience suffered by the Claimants to be assessed.
3. Damages to cover the legal and other costs incurred by the Claimants in dealing with subsequent and ongoing disputes and/or complaints that have arisen between themselves and the Neighbours.
4. Further pursuant to Section 69 of the County Courts Act 1984 the Claimants are entitled to recover interest on the amount found to be due at such rate and for such period as the Court shall think fit.

AND THE CLAIMANTS CLAIMS

i.   Damages
ii.   Interest
iii. Further and other relief
iv.   Costs

[Statement of Truth, etc.]

Specimen Particulars of Claim: Obstruction of Right of Way and Trespass over Boundary
(See Chapters 2, 4 and 5.)

IN THE [. . . .] COUNTY COURT   Claim No:
BETWEEN:

<table>
<tr><td></td><td>[name]</td><td>Claimant</td></tr>
<tr><td></td><td>– and –</td><td></td></tr>
<tr><td></td><td>[name]</td><td>Defendant</td></tr>
</table>

PARTICULARS OF CLAIM

Introduction:
1.   In these Particulars of Claim, the following expressions have the following meanings:
    i.   "the Plan" means the plan annexed hereto, marked "A";
    ii.   "Blackacre" means the land and premises now known as and situated at [address], which is shown on Plan A as edged in red;
    iii. "Whiteacre" means the land and premises now known as and situated at [address], which is shown on Plan A as edged in blue;
    iv. "the Blackacre Conveyance" means a conveyance made on [date] between [name] as vendor and [name] as purchaser;
    v.   "the Conveyance Plan" means the plan attached to the Blackacre Conveyance;
    vi. "the Drive" means the gravel-surfaced drive shown edged and hatched in blue on the Plan and shown hatched on the Blackacre Conveyance;
    vii. "the Right of Way" means the right of way reserved over the Drive for the benefit of the owners of Blackacre by the Blackacre Conveyance.
2.   Annexed to these Particulars of Claim are true copies of the following:
    i.   as "Appendix A", the Plan;
    ii.   as "Appendix B", the Blackacre Conveyance, including the Conveyance Plan;
    iii. as "Appendix C", an Office Copy of the title to Blackacre, Title Number [. . . .];
    iv. as "Appendix D", an Office Copy of the title to Whiteacre, Title Number [. . . .]; and
    v.   as "Appendix E", a bundle of photographs.
Title:
3.   The Claimant is the registered proprietor, with freehold title absolute, of Blackacre, title to which is registered at HM Land Registry under Title Number [. . . .]. The Claimant purchased Blackacre on or about [date].
4.   The Defendant is the registered proprietor, with freehold title absolute,

198

of Whiteacre, title to which is registered at HM Land Registry under Title Number [. . . .]. The Defendant purchased "Whiteacre" on or about [date].

5. The land and premises now known as Blackacre and Whiteacre were in the common ownership of [name] until the Blackacre Conveyance, when [name] sold the land and premises now known as Blackacre (but then known as Whiteacre) away from his retained land and premises then and now known as Whiteacre.

6. By the Blackacre Conveyance, the Right of Way was granted over the Drive for the benefit of the owners from time-to-time of Blackacre, in the following terms:

> "TOGETHER WITH the right of way for all purposes of ingress and egress for the Purchasers and their successor in title the owners or occupiers for the time being of the property hereby conveyed or any part thereof their respective servants and licensees (in common with the Vendor and all other persons having like right) with or without vehicles to and from the property hereby conveyed or any part thereof over and along the drive shown on the said plan and thereon hatched black between the points marked 'A' and 'B'... "

The Claimant will refer to the Blackacre Conveyance and the Conveyance Plan at trial for their full terms and true legal effect.

7. The Right of Way remains recorded on the Registered Title to Blackacre.

The Obstruction of the Right of Way:

8. On or about [date] the Defendant erected a gate towards the north end of the Drive. This gate is represented by the line marked X–X on the Plan and is shown at photograph "E1" in Appendix E.

9. The said gate replaced a gate which was, at all times since [date] prior thereto, at the location marked Y–Y on the Plan.

10. The said gate wrongfully and materially interferes with and obstructs approximately the last 2 metres of the Right of Way.

11. Unless restrained by this Honourable Court, the Defendant threatens to continue to wrongfully interfere with the Right of Way by maintaining the said gate in its current position.

The Relocation of the Fence:

12. At all material times since [date] the western boundary between Blackacre and Whiteacre has been marked by a 2-metre high larchlap fence situated in a position consistent with the Conveyance Plan, which shows the western flank wall of the Blackacre being situated 5 metres from the boundary.

13. On the evening of [. . . .] while the Claimant was away on holiday, the Defendant, without the Claimant's prior knowledge or consent, proceeded to

take down the said fence and move it to the east of its former position so that it encroaches onto the Claimant's land by 2 metres.

14. Whilst they were digging out the fence, [name], a neighbour to the Defendant, approached the Defendant and asked him to stop digging up the fence. The Defendant refused to desist.

15. On his return from holiday on [date] the Claimant visited the Defendant at approximately [time]. The Claimant asked the Defendant if he had moved the fence. He said that he had. The Claimant asked him why and the Defendant said that the fence was in the wrong position and that he had moved it so that it no longer trespassed on the Defendant's land. The Claimant asked him to move the fence back but he refused. The fence has not, as at the date of these Particulars, been replaced by the Defendant.

16. Photograph "E2" shows the fence in its original position on the western boundary of Blackacre. Photograph "E3" shows the fence in its present position, as moved by the Defendant.

17. On [date] the Claimant sent a letter to the Defendant suggesting the joint appointment of a chartered surveyor to determine the line of the legal boundary between Blackacre and Whiteacre with reference to the Conveyance Plan and the physical features on the site. To date no response to that letter had been received.

18. The Defendant's conduct amounts to a trespass to Blackacre. Unless restrained by This Honourable Court, the Defendant will continue to trespass on Blackacre, as aforesaid.

Relief Sought:

19. By reason of all of the matters aforesaid, the Claimant is entitled to, and claims:

   i. An injunction requiring the Defendant to remove the gate on the Drive forthwith;

   ii. an injunction requiring the Defendant forthwith to reinstate the fence he moved on [date] to its original position and to make good all damage caused by its removal; and

   iii. a declaration that the western boundary between Blackacre and Whiteacre land forms a straight line with the western flank of Blackacre so that the western flank of Blackacre is no less than 5 metres from the fence at any point as shown on the Conveyance Plan.

20. Further, by reason of all of the matters aforesaid, the Defendant has caused the Claimant loss and damage.

21. Further, the Claimant is entitled to, and claims, interest pursuant to the County Courts Act 1984, section 69, on such damages as may be awarded, at such rate and for such period as this Honourable Court thinks fit.

AND THE CLAIMANT CLAIMS:

i.   An injunction requiring the Defendant to remove the gate from the Drive forthwith;

ii.   an injunction requiring the Defendant forthwith to reinstate the fence he moved on [date] to its original position and to make good all damage caused by its removal;

iii.   A declaration that the western boundary between Blackacre and Whiteacre land forms a straight line with the western flank of Blackacre so that the western flank of Blackacre is no less than 5 metres from the fence at any point as shown on the Conveyance Plan;

iv.   damages, as aforesaid;

v.   interest pursuant to the County Courts Act 1984, section 69, as aforesaid;

vi.   costs; and

vii.   further and other relief.

[Statement of Truth, etc.]

Specimen "Tomlin" Order
(See Chapters 2 and 12)

IN THE HIGH COURT OF JUSTICE   Claim No:
CHANCERY DIVISION
BETWEEN:

[name]	Claimant
– and –	
[name]	Defendant

MINUTE OF ORDER

UPON reading letters from the parties' solicitors

AND UPON the parties having agreed terms in full and final settlement of all claims arising between them in respect of [. . . .]

AND UPON the [Claimant] [Defendant] undertaking, by his solicitors, to [. . . .]

AND UPON IT BEING RECORDED that the parties have agreed that any claim for breach of contract arising from an alleged breach of the terms set out in the Schedule ("the Schedule") to this Order may, unless the court otherwise orders, be dealt with by way of an application to the Court without the need to start a new claim.

BY CONSENT IT IS ORDERED:

1.   All further proceedings in the claim be stayed upon the terms set out in the Schedule, signed by the solicitor for each party, except for the purpose of

enforcing those terms;

2.   That either party may be permitted to apply to the Court to enforce the terms upon which the claim has been stayed without the need to bring a new claim.

[Date]

THE SCHEDULE

THE PARTIES HEREBY AGREE THAT:

1.   The [Claimant] [Defendant] shall [. . . .]

2.   In consideration of the [Claimant] [Defendant] [. . . .] in accordance with paragraph 1 above and the undertaking given in the recitals of this Order, the [Claimant] [Defendant] agrees to pay to the [Claimant] [Defendant] the sum of [£. . . .] ("the payment") by [. . . .]

3.   The receipt of [. . . .] for the sum referred to in clause 2 shall be a sufficient discharge to the [Claimant] [Defendant].

4.   The payment is made in full and final settlement of all and any claims the [Claimant] [Defendant] may have against the [Claimant] [Defendant] arising out of [. . . .] and in relation to matters raised in these proceedings including (but not limited to) [. . . .]. [The payment also includes a contribution to payment of the [Claimant] [Defendant]'s costs.]

Signed [Solicitors for the Claimant] [Solicitors for the Defendant].

Party Walls

(See Chapter 3.)

Specimen Line of Junction Notice – Party Fence Wall

The Party Wall etc Act 1996 ("the 1996 Act")
To [name] of [address]
From: [name] of [address]

THIS is a notice under section 1(2) of the 1996 Act relating to the boundary between my property at [address] and your adjoining property at [address].

I HEREBY GIVE YOU NOTICE as follows:

(a) I wish to build a party fence wall on the line of junction between our said properties.

(b) If you agree to this work, I request that you serve on me a notice indicating your consent within 14 days of this notice being served upon you. This will lead to the consequences set out in section 1(3) of the 1996 Act.

(c) If you do not serve such a notice, I shall be entitled to carry out the work at my own expense, wholly on my own property (apart from the footings and foundations mentioned below).

(d) The work involved is described in the attached plans.

The work includes the placing of projecting footings and foundations below the level of your property, which I have a right to do under section 1(6) of the Act.

I propose to start work after the expiration of one month from the date this notice is served on you or earlier if you agree.

If a dispute arises between us over this work, it must be referred to one or more surveyors under section 10 of the 1996 Act. For the purposes of any dispute, I appoint [name and firm name] as my surveyor, and invite you to agree to his appointment as an Agreed Surveyor.

Signed ....   Dated ....

Specimen Three Metre Notice

Party Wall etc Act 1996 ("the 1996 Act")
To [name] of [address]
From: [name] of [address]

1.   THIS is a notice under section 6(5) of the 1996 Act relating to excavation works on my property at [address] which will be (or may be) within a prescribed distance from your adjoining property at [address].

I HEREBY GIVE YOU NOTICE as follows:

1.   I propose to carry out works on my property within 3 metres of the building on your property involving excavation below the level of the bottom of its foundations.

2.   (a) The proposed works, including the site and depth of the excavation and the site of the proposed building, are fully described in the attached plans and sections, ("the Plans").

(b) I [do not] propose to underpin or otherwise safeguard the foundations of the building on your property [and these works are also described in the Plans].

3.   I propose to start excavating after the expiration of one month from the date this notice is served upon you, or earlier if you agree.

4.   If you agree to the works, I request that you serve on me a notice indicating your consent within 14 days of this notice being served on you. If you do not, a dispute is deemed to arise between us, which has to be referred to one or more surveyors under section 10 of the 1996 Act.

5.   For the purposes of any dispute, I appoint [name and firm name] as my Surveyor and invite you to concur in appointing him as an agreed Surveyor.

Signed ....   Dated ....

Rights of Light
(See Chapter 6.)

Application for Certificate under Section 2 of the Rights of Light Act 1959
(Form 1, Lands Tribunal Rules 1996, SI 1996 No 1022)
To: The Registrar, Lands Tribunal
I/We .... of .... being [owner[s]] [tenant[s] for a term of years expiring in 20..] [mortgagee(s) in possession] of [*here describe the servient land*] apply to the Lands Tribunal for the issue of a certificate that adequate publicity has been given to my/our proposed application for the registration in the register of local land charges of the .... Council of a notice under section 2 of the Rights of Light Act 1959.

I/We attach two copies of the proposed application.

[I/We also apply for the issue of a certificate authorising the registration forthwith of the proposed notice as a temporary notice. The case is one of exceptional urgency because [*here insert reasons*]].

To the best of my/our knowledge persons likely to be affected by the registration of the notice are [*here insert names and addresses of all persons in occupation of the dominant building or having a proprietary interest in it*].

All communications regarding this application should be addressed to me/us at the address shown above [or to my/our solicitor agent .... of ....].
Strike out words not applicable.

Form A: Application for Registration of a Light Obstruction Notice
(Form A, Local Land Charges Rules 1977, SI 1977 No 985)
I .... of ...., being the freehold owner or the tenant for a term of years of which over 7 years remain unexpired or the mortgagee in possession [*delete inapplicable words*] of [*insert description of servient land*] which is shown on the plan attached hereto, hereby apply to the .... Council for registration of this notice under section 2 of the Rights of Light Act 1959 against the building known as [*insert description of dominant building (wherever practicable, a map or plan of the building should be attached)*].

Registration of this notice is intended to be equivalent to the obstruction of the access of light to the said building across my land which would be caused by the erection of an opaque structure on all the boundaries of my land or in the position on my land marked on the attached plan [*delete inappropriate words*] and of unlimited height or [. . . .] .
Signed ....   Dated ....

Specimen Particulars of Claim: Nuisance
(See Chapter 7.)

IN THE [. . . .] COUNTY COURT   Claim No:
BETWEEN:

[names]   Claimants

– and –

[names]   Defendants

PARTICULARS OF CLAIM

1.   The Claimants are the freehold owners of a property known as [. . . .] ("Property A") which is registered at HM Land Registry under title number [. . . .].

2.   The Defendants are the freehold owners of a property known as [. . . .] ("Property B") which is registered at HM Land Registry under title number [. . . .].

3.   The Claimants have lived at Property A since [. . . .]. The Defendants moved into Property B approximately two years ago, on or about [. . . .]. Since that date the Defendants have interfered with the Claimants' use and enjoyment of Property A as a family home.

PARTICULARS

1.   The Defendants' sixteen year old son plays his drum kit approximately three times a week between the hours of 10 pm and 1 am.

2.   The Defendants' fourteen year old daughter and her friends have carried out various acts of violence, criminal damage, harassment and intimidation as follows:

    i.   on [date] the Defendants' daughter and her friends climbed over the Claimants' garden wall, dug up various of the Claimants' shrubs and other plants and scattered them around the Claimants' garden,

    ii.   on various occasions the Defendants' daughter has waited for the First Claimant at the end of the Claimants' driveway and shouted abuse at her,

    iii.   on [date] the Defendants' daughter pushed a hosepipe through the Claimants' letter box and turned it on causing the Claimants' front hall to flood.

3.   The Defendants' three large dogs bark incessantly throughout the day and night.

4.   On [date] the First Defendant shot the First Claimant with his air rifle causing extensive bruising.

5.   Despite repeated requests from the Claimants the Defendants and their children have refused to discontinue the activities set out at paragraphs 2 i, ii and iii above.

6.   In the premises the Claimants are entitled to an injunction (a) preventing

the Defendants from intimidating, harassing or causing a nuisance to the Claimants or otherwise interfering with the Claimants' enjoyment of their property either by themselves or by permitting their children to do so (b) preventing the Defendants from entering any part of Property A at any time without the consent of the Claimants either by themselves or by allowing their children to do so (c) restricting the playing of drums or other musical instruments at Property B to the hours of 8 pm to 10 pm.

7.   Further, by reason of all of the matters aforesaid, the Defendants have caused the Claimant loss and damage and are entitled to damages representing the loss in value of Property A caused by the Defendants' activities.

8.   Further by the matters set out at paragraphs 2 i, ii and iii above the Claimants are entitled to and claim aggravated and/or exemplary damages.

9.   Further, the Claimants are entitled to, and claim, interest pursuant to the County Courts Act 1984, section 69, on such damages as may be awarded, at such rate and for such period as this Honourable Court thinks fit.

AND THE CLAIMANTS CLAIM:

  i.   an injunction (a) preventing the Defendants from intimidating, harassing or causing a nuisance to the Claimants or otherwise interfering with the Claimants' enjoyment of their property either by themselves or by permitting their children to do so (b) preventing the Defendants from entering any part of Property A at any time without the consent of the Claimants either by themselves or by allowing their children to do so (c) restricting the playing of drums or other musical instruments at Property B to the hours of 8 pm to 10 pm;

  ii.   damages, as aforesaid;

  iii. interest pursuant to the County Courts Act 1984, section 69, as aforesaid;

  iv.   costs; and

  v.   further and other relief.

[Statement of truth, etc].

Specimen Retainer Letter
(See Chapter 12.)

Dear ......

Dispute with owners of "Whiteacre"
Thank you for instructing us to act as your solicitors in connection with the above dispute. We shall be pleased to help.

This letter sets out the basis on which we shall act. I will carry out most of the day-to-day work on this matter. I am a [solicitor] [legal executive] [partner] [other] in the firm of [. . . .]. If I am unavailable when you telephone, please leave a message with my secretary, [. . . .]. Where appropriate the help of others within the firm, not always solicitors, may be enlisted.

We shall try to avoid changing the people who handle the work but, if this cannot be avoided, we will inform you promptly of who will be handling the matter (and why the change is necessary). We believe that we have the experience to co-ordinate the team in a way which is both efficient and cost effective, choosing the appropriate person for the actions identified.

What you want us to do
We are instructed that your neighbour, the owner of "Blackacre", has erected a gate across the drive to his property over which you have a right of way. Further, he has removed the boundary fence between your property, Whiteacre, and Blackacre and replaced it 6 feet closer to your property. You want us to take all necessary steps to rectify this.

In order to attain the outcome you would like us to achieve we shall prepare a detailed letter of claim, explaining to your neighbour that he must remove the gate within 14 days, in default of which you will be instructing us to issue legal proceedings against him. As the question of the boundary fence is not so straightforward we will invite him, with or without his legal representatives, to attend a meeting at these offices with his deeds and all relevant documents and other evidence so that we can try to resolve the apparent discrepancy between his deeds and yours. We will also need to interview the previous owner of Whiteacre (which originally incorporated Blackacre in one title) with whom we understand you are in contact, to see whether he can shed any light on what happened when the two titles were created.

If we receive no satisfactory response and no action is taken by your neighbour to rectify the situation, then we will review the situation with you further with a view to preparing to issue proceedings on your behalf claiming damages for nuisance. We will also seek an injunction compelling your neighbour to remove the gate. We will seek this on an interim basis since the gate makes it impossible for you to access the front door of your property. If, by then, we have satisfied ourselves that the fence is trespassing on your land, we will include a claim for trespass. We will also seek an interim injunction compelling the replacement of the fence since the removal of the fence means that you can no longer park your car.

Risk/cost benefit analysis

We have examined your deeds and compared them with the office copy entries that we have obtained for Blackacre. On the basis of our analysis of the deeds there is no question that the gate obstructs your right of way and we are confident that legal action to compel its removal will succeed. However, the position of the boundary is not so straightforward. You have produced a copy of an early conveyance of Blackacre containing measurements that appear to contradict the measurements on your deeds. We have not been able to ascertain any satisfactory explanation for this, so further evidence will need to be obtained before we can give you comprehensive advice upon your chances of success.

If, having analysed all the evidence, we take the view that you have a reasonable chance of success, we will consider with you including in your proceedings for the removal of the fence an additional claim for trespass. It would be sensible to include all the causes of action on one claim to save costs. I know that you are most anxious that the gate is removed because of difficulties with access. We will therefore investigate the boundary question as quickly as we are able to so that you do not have to suffer any undue delay.

When deciding whether or not to issue proceedings in respect of the boundary, we will give you an honest appraisal of the merits of your case. Boundary disputes can be expensive and you will need to bear in mind that if you lose, then you will have to pay your opponent's costs as well as your own. Once we have more information about the boundary, we will give you a full estimate of costs and an analysis of the likelihood of success, so that you are able to make an informed decision as to whether or not you wish to proceed.

What action you or third parties need to take

I should be grateful if you would please contact your predecessor in title and ask whether he would be prepared to talk to me. If so, I should be grateful if you would let me have his contact details.

Our fees

We will charge for time spent on an hourly basis. Time spent on your case will be recorded in units of 6 minutes. Accordingly, routine letters and emails that we send and receive and routine telephone calls will be charged at a minimum of 1/10th of the hourly rate. My current hourly rate is £ .... plus

VAT. It is our usual practice to bill monthly/quarterly/regularly.

Our charging rates for others in the Litigation and Dispute Resolution Department of the firm (excluding VAT) are:

- partners: £ .... an hour;
- solicitors with over four years' post-qualification experience: £ .... to £ .... an hour;
- solicitors and legal executives with up to four years' post-qualification experience: £ .... an hour;
- trainees: £ .... an hour.

If we provide advocacy services at a full trial of this case, the minimum daily fee will normally be £ .....

Our terms of business provide for our charging rates to be reviewed from time to time. This usually happens in [. . . .] of each year. We shall notify you of any variation in rates.

The total cost to you of our services is made up of our charge for time spent plus VAT and our disbursements (out of pocket expenses and money we pay on your behalf e.g. to barristers, experts, the court), most of which disbursements will be subject to VAT. We normally charge for photocopying.

Estimate of costs
It is very difficult to estimate at an early stage the probable cost of any litigation. Usually, it is not possible to give a reasonably accurate estimate until it becomes clear what steps are going to be necessary to take the matter through to a conclusion. It, therefore, may be necessary to wait until proceedings are issued before we are able to give an estimate (which will have to be provisional only) and which may have to be revised as circumstances change as your case proceeds. However, if proceedings are to be issued I estimate that the total costs excluding VAT are likely to be in the region of [. . . .] assuming the matter proceeds to a full trial. Of that total, the following are significant expenses with (where applicable) an estimate of when you will need to pay them:

- court issue fee;
- allocation fee (when claim is allocated to a track);
- listing fee (when claim is listed for trial);
- counsel's fees for representation at trial;
- expert's fees for producing report;
- expert's fee for attending trial.

I estimate that the costs for dealing with the first stage of your matter, up to and including [. . . .] will be [. . . .] on the basis that [. . . .] hours' work will be required.

This is a provisional estimate only which may have to be revised as circumstances change as your case proceeds. In the meantime you should reserve £ [. . . .] to get us to the stage of [. . . .].

You should note that there are two stages during the course of an action at which we will be under a duty to give the court an estimate of costs to date and the likely costs to be incurred in the future. These will be when the action is allocated (which happens after a defence has been filed) and shortly before trial (when a final listing questionnaire will normally have to be completed).

Payment on account of costs
It is our normal practice to request sums of money on account of anticipated fees and expenses both at the beginning and during a case. In order to commence work on this matter we will require the sum of £ .... plus VAT making a total payment of £ ..... You will understand that we may wish to ask you to pay further sums on account as each payment is used up.

Conflict
I have undertaken a conflict search against the name(s) of [. . . .] and can confirm that in this matter we have no apparent conflict of interest arising from other involvement with either/any of them/him/her.

Critical dates
[The critical dates applicable to your matter are . . . .] [There are no critical dates applicable to your matter at present]. We will advise you if and when any critical dates arise. Please advise us if you become aware of any critical dates.

Costs in litigation
If you are successful in the litigation, the court will usually order your opponent to pay a proportion of your legal fees and expenses. It must be realised that there may be a significant shortfall in such payments. These costs will be assessed by the court if they cannot be agreed between the parties. If you are unsuccessful in the litigation, you are likely to be ordered to pay a similar proportion of the opponent's costs as well as being liable for our fees in full (i.e. 100%) and disbursements.

Our clients are primarily responsible for our fees and expenses. An order against your opponent for payment of costs is only partial reimbursement if paid. You will be responsible for costs incurred on its behalf although, as explained, some of these may be recovered from your opponent. You should be aware that no costs are usually recoverable from a publicly funded party. You will also be responsible for paying the fees and expenses of seeking to recover costs awarded by the court.

Funding the litigation
You should check any insurance policies which you may hold to see whether they cover for legal fees and expenses.

Alternative dispute resolution

The Civil Procedure Rules require parties to explore every reasonable approach to negotiation or mediation of a dispute. This is known as alternative dispute resolution ("ADR"). This is particularly appropriate for neighbour disputes as it encourages the parties to reach a mutually acceptable solution. It can be considerably more cost-effective than a full-scale trial, but you should bear in mind that such settlements are usually agreed on the basis that both parties pay their own costs.

General

We value our relationship with our clients and we aim to carry out your instructions to your satisfaction in all respects. If there should be any queries or concerns about our work for you then please let me know immediately in order that the appropriate action can be taken. If that does not resolve the problem satisfactorily, or you would prefer not to speak to me, then please take it up with [name of person responsible for handling complaints].

If you are unclear about anything in this letter or if you have any queries, please let me know. If there are no other queries, please let me have your acceptance of the terms of this letter by returning the duplicate copy of this letter signed by you. Although your continuing instructions will amount to an acceptance of the terms of this letter, we ask that you do return the duplicate copy so that we can be confident you have understood the basis on which we are acting for you.

Yours sincerely

....

[I accept the terms of this letter
Signed (client) ....Date ....]

Index